T4-AQM-426

THE THEORY OF POSITIONAL GAMES

WITH APPLICATIONS IN ECONOMICS

This is a volume in
ECONOMIC THEORY, ECONOMETRICS, AND MATHEMATICAL ECONOMICS

A Series of Monographs and Textbooks

Consulting Editor: KARL SHELL

A complete list of titles in this series appears at the end of this volume.

THE THEORY OF POSITIONAL GAMES

WITH APPLICATIONS IN ECONOMICS

IOSIF A. KRASS
DEPARTMENT OF ECONOMICS
UNIVERSITY OF KANSAS
LAWRENCE, KANSAS

SHAWKAT M. HAMMOUDEH
TECHNO-ECONOMIC DIVISION
KUWAIT INSTITUTE FOR ECONOMIC RESEARCH
SAFAT, KUWAIT

1981

ACADEMIC PRESS
A Subsidiary of Harcourt Brace Jovanovich, Publishers
New York London Toronto Sydney San Francisco

ACADEMIC PRESS, INC.
111 Fifth Avenue, New York, New York 10003

United Kingdom Edition published by
ACADEMIC PRESS, INC. (LONDON) LTD.
24/28 Oval Road, London NW1 7DX

Library of Congress Cataloging in Publication Data

Krass, Iosif Aronovich.
The theory of positional games, with applications in economics.

(Economic theory, econometrics, and mathematical economics)
Bibliography: p.
Includes index.
1. Game theory. I. Hammoudeh, Shawkat M.
II. Title. III. Series.
HB144.K7 330'.01'5193 81-10922
ISBN 0-12-425920-0 AACR2

PRINTED IN THE UNITED STATES OF AMERICA

81 82 83 84 9 8 7 6 5 4 3 2 1

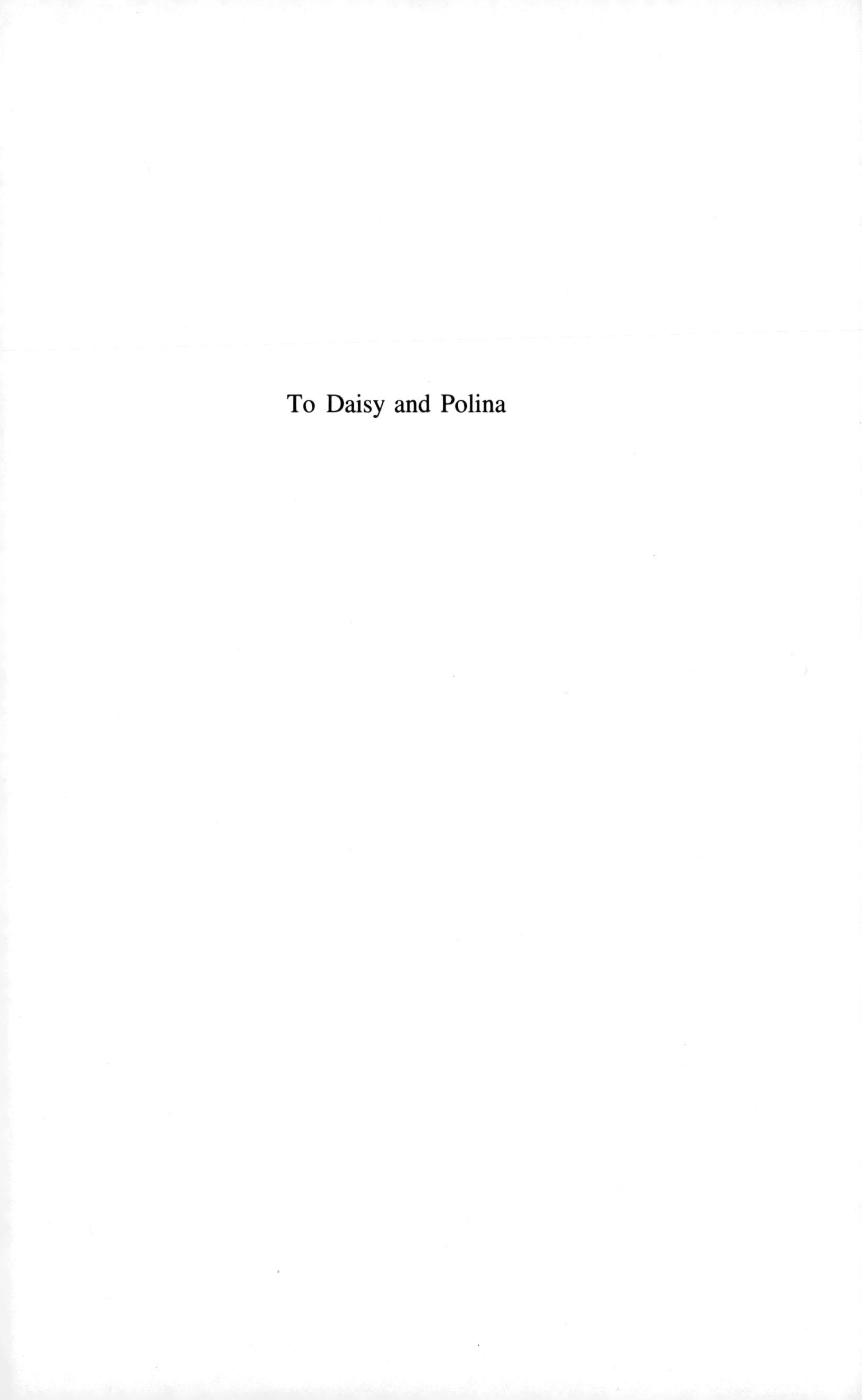

To Daisy and Polina

Contents

Preface

Game theory has developed rapidly over the past three decades and is now considered an important area of contemporary applied mathematics. The aim of this book is twofold: to present an account of some basic mathematical aspects of positional games and to provide economic applications of the theory.

To help achieve the above aim, the book starts with sections on games in extensive and normal forms. Information and probabilistic extensions of games in extensive form are then discussed. Two sections are devoted to the existence of solutions of infinite games and to the application of existence of a solution to a von Neumann model with conflict interaction. The final topics of the book are difference and differential games. The theory of differential games is based on Isaacs' equations, while all preceding theory is based on the definition of games in extensive form.

We believe that more than half of the topics treated here either appear in English for the first time or have never been published. The first category includes (a) Germeir's approach of information extension of games in extensive form; (b) examples of interaction or war between von Neumann's or Leontief's models (the existence of solutions is also considered); and (c) Krasovsky's theory of differential games. The second category includes (a) the theory of difference games from the viewpoint of extensive form, including a comparison of the difference game with its general form and proofs of the existence of a solution in mixed behavioral strategies and of the existence of a "full" solution for finite difference games; and (b) the theory of the existence of a solution in differential games, using Isaacs' equations and continuity and differentiability of Bellman's function in behavioral (synthetic) strategies.

The origins of the book lie in a series of lectures delivered by I. A. Krass at Novosibirsk University, USSR, during 1977 and 1978, and at the University of Kansas in 1979. The lecture notes were refined by S. M. Hammoudeh.

Iosif A. Krass
Stamford, Connecticut

Shawkat M. Hammoudeh
Safat, Kuwait

PART

I

General Games

CHAPTER

1

Games in Extensive and Normal Forms

There are many situations involving conflicts of interests in the real world. These conflicts occur with varying degrees of force, ranging from war to the interaction between spouses. While examples of a strong conflict, such as a war, are unnecessary here, an example of a mild conflict is that of competition in the soft drink industry between Coca-Cola and Pepsi-Cola. In a conflict situation, each participant designs his/her own strategy of behavior (i.e., expenditures on advertising and new technology, business spying, etc.), but the essential element is the conflict of interests, usually with incomplete information on which to base decisions.

In everyday life, a person is involved in large or small conflicts at almost every moment. For example, a person making a decision about what to buy is in a conflict situation because he/she must consider the likes and dislikes of family members, friends, etc., in addition to personal preferences.

The mathematical groundwork of the study of interest conflict, game theory, was laid by von Neumann and Morgenstern in the late 1920s and 1930s. They described the conflict situations axiomatically and defined solution concepts for these situations. While their articles were highly mathematical, their book *Theory of Games and Economic Behavior* achieved its aim of being of greater use to social scientists, through limited use of mathematics.

A convenient way of describing a conflict situation from a mathematical point of view, when the players have finite sets of options, is to use terminology from graph theory. The game then can be described by a tree with the junction of its branches representing points at which players make decisions. If the tree that describes a given game has a certain structure, then the game is called a game in extensive form. Describing games of this form makes it possible to define strategies of the players, as will be shown in Section 1.1. In Section 1.2 games will be redefined so that they can be represented by matrices. Games defined by matrices are known as games in normal form and will be discussed in Section 1.2.

The solutions of a two-person game are defined in Section 1.3. These solutions represent the optimal behaviors of the players participating in the game. In antagonistic games these solutions are called saddle points, and in nonantagonistic games these solutions are called Nash equilibria. In Section 1.4, we shall apply the definition of a Nash equilibrium to a game with complete information and show that this equilibrium always exists for such a game.

1.1 GAMES IN EXTENSIVE FORM

Situations of conflict can be described in several ways. The most general is through the use of a tree.

We define the notion of a *graph* as a finite set of points or vertices, some of which are connected by arcs. We assume that every arc has direction. If an arc goes from vertex a to vertex b, then b is called a *follower* of a, or a is a *predecessor* of b. If vertex a has no predecessors, then it is said to be *initial*, and if it has no followers, it is said to be *terminal*. If there is an arc from a_0 to a_1 [i.e., arc (a_0, a_1)] or from a_1 to a_0 [i.e., arc (a_1, a_0)], then it is said that vertices a_0 and a_1 are *connected*. Moreover, these vertices are connected if there is a sequence of vertices $b_0, \ldots, b_n$ such that $a_0 = b_0, a_1 = b_n$, and any two successive vertices (b_i and b_{i+1}), $i = 0, \ldots, n-1$, are connected.

The sequence of vertices $b_0, \ldots, b_n$ is also called a *chain*. If $b_0 = b_n$, then the chain is called a *cycle*. A graph that includes no cycles and that has any two of its vertices connected is called a *tree*.

Although it is always possible to describe a game through the use of a tree, it is sometimes hard to do so.

Example 1.1.1 (Elementary poker) Suppose for simplicity that the game is played by two players with three cards numbered 1, 2, and 3 to represent weak, medium, and strong cards, respectively. A dealer shuffles the cards and gives one to each player who, by looking at the card, can say "high" (H) or "low" (L). The third card is discarded. If both players say the same thing or if the first says H and the second says L, the game ends. If the first says L

TABLE 1.1.1

Payoff of the First Player

Moves of the first player	Moves of the second player	Second moves of the first player	Relative strength of card (first, with respect to second)	Payoff
H	L	none	not relevant	+1
H	H	none	stronger, weaker	+2, −2
L	L	none	stronger, weaker	+1, −1
L	H	L	not relevant	−1
L	H	H	stronger, weaker	+2, −2

but the second says H, the game will continue and the first can say either H or L to finish the game. Then each player wins or loses a number of dollars as his/her payoff. The payoff of the first player is shown in Table 1.1.1.

If, for example, both players say H and the first player holds the strong card, then the first player wins two dollars. If that player holds the weak card, he/she pays the second player two dollars.

Four branches of this game tree are shown in Figure 1.1.1.

The initial vertex is "0." There are six possible deals, namely, (1, 2), (1, 3), (2, 1), (2, 3), (3, 1), and (3, 2), occurring with the same probability, depicted in Figure 1.1.1 by six arcs going from the initial vertex "0." Then the first player has his/her move, followed by the second player's move. Both may say H or L, and these choices are written on the arcs which go from the appropriate vertices. The final node on any branch of the tree is the terminal vertex with the payoff of the first player attached to it.

The areas on the tree that are within the dotted lines contain vertices which give the same information about the game situation for a player.

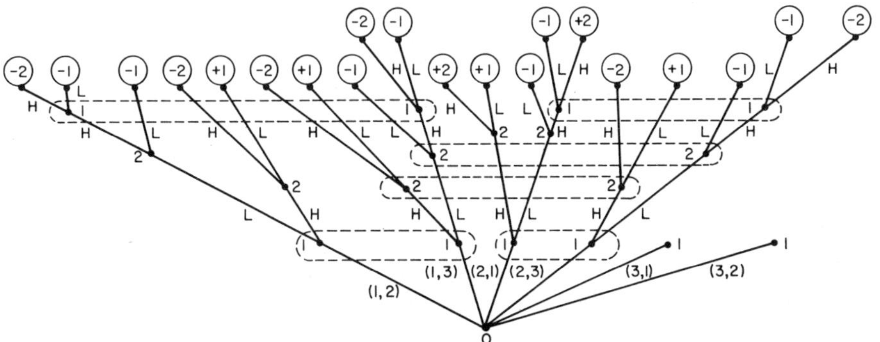

Figure 1.1.1

These sets are called the *information sets*. Each player knows which information set he/she is in but is not able to determine which vertex of the information set he/she is at. Each of the vertices of a given information set must belong to the same player and must have the same number of immediate followers.

The preceding discussion lays the groundwork for defining games in extensive form. An *n-person game in extensive form* means that there is a tree with the following structure:

1. A partition of the vertices of the tree into $(n + 1)$ sets $S_0, S_1, \ldots, S_n$. Set S_0 is called the *set of chance moves*, while the sets $S_1, S_2, \ldots, S_n$ are called the *player sets*.
2. A probability distribution, defined at every vertex of S_0, among the followers of that vertex.

In Figure 1.1.1, the chance vertex is "0" and the probability distribution is $(\frac{1}{6}, \frac{1}{6}, \frac{1}{6}, \frac{1}{6}, \frac{1}{6}, \frac{1}{6})$.

3. A function, called the *payoff n-vector function*, defined at every terminal vertex of the tree.

Formally, if a vertex x is a terminal vertex, then the payoff vector function is $f(x) = (f_1(x), \ldots, f_i(x), \ldots, f_n(x))$, where $f_i(x)$ is the payoff of the ith player. If $f_i(x) > 0$, then that player wins $f_i(x)$ dollars. The opposite is true if $f_i(x) < 0$.

In Figure 1.1.1 we have only written the payoff of the first player, having in mind that the second player has the opposite payoff. Therefore, we wrote (-2) instead of $(-2, 2)$ and $(+1)$ instead of $(+1, -1)$.

4. A subpartition of each set S_i, $i = 1, \ldots, n$, into subsets S_i^j, $j = 1, \ldots, m_i$, called *information sets* with the following properties:

(a) No vertex can follow another vertex in the same subset S_i^j.

(b) For each subset S_i^j there is a one-to-one mapping of an index set $I_i^j = \{1, 2, \ldots, n_i^j\}$ onto the set of followers of each vertex enclosed in the subset S_i^j. (This property means that at every vertex of set S_i^j, the ith player has the same information about the game situation; so his decision must be the same in any vertex of this set.)

If the initial vertex x_0 belongs to the set S_i, $i = 1, \ldots, n$, the first move will be a personal move and will be made by the ith player. In this case there is an information set $S_i^{j_0}$ which contains x_0 and an index set $I_i^{j_0}$ such that the ith player must choose a number from this index set according to the information set. (In the elementary poker example, for any vertex, the index set consists of two elements, H and L, and not numbers.) Thus the followers of

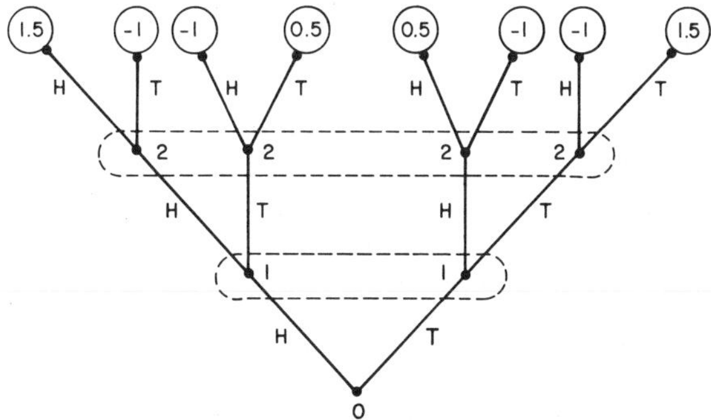

Figure 1.1.2

any vertex are exactly defined with the help of the one-to-one mapping associated with the definition of the game in extensive form.

If the initial vertex s_0 belongs to the set S_0, then the first move is done by chance. The followers will be defined by chance, as specified in the definition of probability distribution. The game continues in the same way until it reaches a termination point, that is, a terminal vertex x. The game finally assigns a payoff to the terminal vertex. Specifically, the ith player gets $f_i(x)$ dollars as a payoff.

Example 1.1.2 (Variant of matching pennies) In this game, a referee makes the chance move by tossing a coin with the results being either "heads" (H) or "tails" (T). Then the first player chooses H or T. The second player, not knowing the first player's choice, also chooses H or T. If both make the same choice, the first player wins 1.5 dollars from the second player if the matched choice of both players is the same as the chance move (e.g., the chance move is H and the matched move of both players is H also). The first player wins 0.5 dollars if the matched move of both players differs from the chance move (e.g., the chance move is H and both players choose T). If the players' answers do not match each other, the second player wins some dollars from the first. The tree of this game together with the information sets of both players and the payoff of the first player are shown in Figure 1.1.2.

1.2 PURE STRATEGIES AND THE NORMAL FORM

If the game is characterized by extensive form, the rules that describe the behaviors of the players are mathematically specified. In principle, the extensive form implies that every player would be able to state what he/she would do in each situation that might occur when the game is being played and would convey the decisions to his/her helper, who could play the game without the player's participation. Prior delineation of behavior that can be carried out on behalf of a player is impossible in complex games because the number of possible moves in such games is so great that no player can say in advance what he/she would do in every situation that might arise.

The intuitive meaning of a strategy is, thus, a prescription of what a player would do in every possible game situation that might arise (i.e., what decision to make in every information set). Therefore, a player must first describe his/her information sets exactly. In Example 1.1.1, the information sets of the first player may be described by a pair (α, β), where $\alpha \in \{1, 2, 3\}$ and $\beta \in \{1, 2\}$, i.e., α stands for the number of a card and β for the number of the first player's move. If the game continues to the second move of the first player, then $\beta = 2$. For example, (3, 2) describes the situation in which the first player gets card 3 and he/she is at the second move. This corresponds to the case in Table 1.1.1 in which the first move of the first player is L, while that of the second player is H. Similarly, for the second player, $\alpha \in \{1, 2, 3\}$ and $\beta \in \{1, 2\}$. β may also be written in terms of the first player's moves as $\beta \in \{H, L\}$.

In Example 1.1.2 the game has two information sets, one for each player; so it is rather simple. Now we present the exact mathematical definition of a pure strategy.

A *pure strategy* of the ith player in an n-person game in extensive form is a mapping $\tau_i\colon \{S_i^j\} \to \bigcup_{j=1}^{m_i} I_i^j$ such that $\tau_i(S_i^j) \in I_i^j$. Or it can be defined as a mapping $\tau_i\colon S_i \to \bigcup_{j=1}^{m_i} I_i^j$ which satisfies, for every j, the following conditions:

(a) $\tau_i(x) \in I_i^j$ if $x \in S_i^j$, and
(b) $\tau_i(x)$ is constant on S_i^j.

In the elementary poker example, the possible pure strategies for the first player are $(1, 1) \to$ H, $(1, 2) \to$ L, $(2, 2) \to$ H, $(2, 1) \to$ L, $(3, 1) \to$ H, and $(3, 2) \to$ H. A pure strategy $(1, 1) \to$ H means that if the first player has card 1 and he/she is at the first move, then that player will say H (which is a pure bluff because he/she holds a weak card). A pure strategy $(1, 2) \to$ L means that if that player holds the same card but he/she is at the second move, the player will say L. Other strategies can be explained in the same fashion.

For the second player, the possible strategies are (1, H) $\to$ L, (1, L) $\to$ H, (2, H) $\to$ L, (2, L) $\to$ H, (3, H) $\to$ H, and (3, L) $\to$ H. A pure strategy (1, H) $\to$ L means that if the second player has card number 1 and the first player says H, then the second player will say L. A strategy (1, L) $\to$ H is a pure bluff on the part of the second player.

If all the players' strategies are chosen and all chance moves are specified with the probability distribution defined over the followers of every occasional (chance) vertex in the set S_0, then every player's share of the payoff can be determined. The payoff associated with a given chance move and a given realization of the game (i.e., sequence of choices, one following another until a game is terminated with a payoff) does not qualify as a serious criterion for choosing or rejecting strategies. In general, no one knows what the payoffs are, except probabilistically, if the chance moves are not specified. Thus it makes sense to compute the average of some realizations of the game as the selection of a strategy vector does not uniquely determine a realization but determines a probability distribution over all possible realizations. If pure strategies are chosen and the terminal vertex x is determined, the probability of going to that terminal vertex from an initial vertex can be computed. Given the chosen strategies, this probability will be denoted by $p_\tau(x)$, where $\tau = (\tau_1, \tau_2, \ldots, \tau_n)$ is an n-tuple of pure strategies of all players. In the elementary poker example, the probabilities of going into the terminal vertexes, given the above pure strategies, counted from left to right in Figure 1.1.1 are $\frac{1}{6}, 0, 0, 0, 0; \frac{1}{6}, 0, 0, 0, 0; 0, 0, 0, 0, \frac{1}{6}$.

Given that the players are using strategy vector τ, the expected value of the ith player's payoff may be written as $H^i_\tau = \sum_{x \in E} p_\tau(x) f_i(x)$, where E is the set of terminal vertexes. In our example of elementary poker, the expected value of the first player, which is the negative of that of the second player, is

$$H^1_\tau = 1 \times \tfrac{1}{6} - 2 \times \tfrac{1}{6} + 2 \times \tfrac{1}{6} - 2 \times \tfrac{1}{6} + 1 \times \tfrac{1}{6} + 1 \times \tfrac{1}{6} = \tfrac{1}{6} = -H^2_\tau.$$

A serious problem would arise if such a value is used to evaluate the quality of the strategies of players. This question has been tackled by many studies and will not be discussed here. However, we can say that if the game is played very many times, there is a good reason for taking the average of the payoff function in order to evaluate strategies (e.g., consider the average as a utility function). But if the game is played only once, as, for example, when a surgeon performs a serious operation on which the patient's life depends, then an average is not a good base for strategy evaluation. However, from now on we shall use the average as a good base for choosing among strategies of every player.

In a finite game tree, the quantity of all pure strategies of every player is finite and strategies can be enumerated. For example, in elementary poker a pure strategy can be described by a subset of triples (α, β, γ), where the pair (α, β) describes an information set and $\gamma \in \{H, L\}$ and stands for a chosen move mapped from the information set $\{(\alpha, \beta)\}$. Thus the elements of the set of all strategies of the first player, i.e., subsets $\{(\alpha, \beta, \gamma)\}$, can be enumerated and the player can say, for example, "This time I choose number 13." This is adequate.

The enumeration can be generalized to an n-person game. Suppose J_i is an index set for the ith player such that $J_i = \{1, 2, \ldots, |J_i|\}$, where $|J_i|$

is the number of that player's strategies.[1] Then if every player chooses $j_i \in J_i$, $i = 1, 2, \ldots, n$, as the number of his/her strategy, the ith player will have his/her expected payoff written as $H^i_{j_1,\ldots,j_n}$ instead of $H^i_{\tau_1,\ldots,\tau_n}$.

Therefore, using the notion of a strategy, every game in extensive form can be redefined in the following form: each player chooses one number from the index set, i.e., $j_1 \in J_i$ $(i = 1, 2, \ldots, n)$, and the payoff to the players is determined from $H^i_{j_1,\ldots,j_n}$ $(i = 1, \ldots, n)$. From this the game can be reduced to n massives defined by $\|H^i_{j_1,\ldots,j_n}\|$ $(i = 1, 2, \ldots, n;\ j_i = 1, \ldots, |J_i|)$ and each one is a $|J_1| \times |J_2| \times \cdots \times |J_n|$-dimensional massive.[2] This reduction of a game to a matrix is called the *normal form* of the game.

If in a two-person game the sets of strategies of the first and second players are denoted by J_1 and J_2, respectively, the game can be defined by two $m \times n$ matrices, namely, A and B, where $m = J_1$ and $n = J_2$. If the first player chooses strategy $i \in J_1$ and the second player chooses strategy $j \in J_2$, then the payoffs for both players are, respectively, a_{ij} (which is an element of matrix A) and b_{ij} (which is an element of matrix B). This case is referred to in the literature as a *bimatrix game*.

Finally, in the case of a two-person game with opposing interests, the payoffs are $a_{ij} = -b_{ij}$. In this case it suffices to have one payoff matrix for the first player, namely an $m \times n$ matrix A. This kind of game is called an *antagonistic*, or *two-person zero-sum game*, or just a *matrix game*.

The elementary poker and the variant of matching pennies games are both examples of matrix games. The number of strategies of the first player in the first example is $|J_1| = 32$ strategies (i.e., $2^{3 \times 2}$), while that of the second player is $|J_2| = 64$ strategies. Thus the payoff matrix has a dimension of (32×64).

In the variant of matching pennies, each player has two strategies: "heads" (H) and "tails" (T). Thus the number of strategies for each player is two. The normal form of the game in Figure 1.1.2 is the matrix[3]

	H	T
H	+1	−1
T	−1	+1

.

[1] $|J_i|$ is the cardinality of the set J_i.

[2] A $|J_1| \times \cdots \times |J_n|$-dimensional massive is a function $A: J_1 \times \cdots \times J_n \to R$. For example, if $n = 3$, then $A = \|a_{ijk}\| i = 1, \ldots, |J_1|, j = 1, \ldots, |J_2|$, and $k = 1, \ldots, |J_2|$.

[3] The entries of this matrix are the expected values of the payoffs in Figure 1.1.2. For example, $1 = \frac{1}{2}(1.5) + \frac{1}{2}(0.5)$.

with each row representing a strategy of the first player, each column representing a strategy of the second player, and the matrix representing the payoffs of the first player.

If the strategies of both players are alike, the first player wins one dollar; otherwise he/she loses this amount to the second player.

1.3 SOLUTION OF A GAME

What does the solution(s) of a game mean? In other words, what are the best behaviors of the players of a game? In practice, this is a difficult question because the answers might hinge on human psychology. However, there are some aspects of human behavior that all people perceive similarly.

Suppose we have a two-person game in normal form. Then this game is defined by the sets of strategies T_1 and T_2 and by payoff functions $A\colon T_1 \times T_2 \to R$ and $B\colon T_1 \times T_2 \to R$ for the first and second players, respectively. Let us suppose that the first player is pessimistic because he/she thinks that the second player is, say, omniscient or vicious. Then the first player will use a strategy that will guarantee him/her a certain level of payoff. This level will be defined by[4]

$$V_1 = \max_{\tau_1 \in T_1} \min_{\tau_2 \in T_2} A(\tau_1, \tau_2). \tag{1.3.1}$$

This is so because if the first player chooses strategy τ_1, then the second player will choose strategy $\tau_2(\tau_1)$ to make sure that the former's payoff is

$$A(\tau_1, \tau_2(\tau_1)) = \min_{\tau_2 \in T_2} A(\tau_1, \tau_2). \tag{1.3.2}$$

Therefore, in order to guarantee the level V_1, the first player should choose strategy τ_1^* such that

$$V_1 = A(\tau_1^*, \tau_2(\tau_1^*)) = \max_{\tau_1 \in T_1} A(\tau_1, \tau_2(\tau_1)).$$

Here V_1 is called the *ensurance level* of the first player, and τ_1^* is the *ensurance strategy* of that player.[5]

[4] This study assumes that maximum and minimum exist. This can be shown if T_1 and T_2 are compact in metric space and function A is continuous.

[5] This level is also referred to in the literature as "gain floor," or "security level."

Similarly, the second player can secure at least

$$M = \max_{\tau_2 \in T_2} \min_{\tau_1 \in T_1} B(\tau_1, \tau_2), \tag{1.3.3}$$

and his/her ensurance strategy τ_2^* is such that

$$M = \min_{\tau_1 \in T_1} B(\tau_1, \tau_2^*).$$

In the case of an antagonistic game [i.e., $A(\tau_1, \tau_2) = -B(\tau_1, \tau_2) = H(\tau_1, \tau_2)$], it can be shown that[6]

$$M = -\min_{\tau_2 \in T_2} \max_{\tau_1 \in T_1} H(\tau_1, \tau_2).$$

(Once the maximin value for the second player is known, its negative is the minimax value for the first player.)

Define $V_2 = -M$. Then we can say that the first player guarantees himself/herself a payoff level no less than V_1 and the second player can lose no more than V_2, where

$$V_1 = \max_{\tau_1 \in T_1} \min_{\tau_2 \in T_2} H(\tau_1, \tau_2), \qquad V_2 = \min_{\tau_1 \in T_1} \max_{\tau_2 \in T_2} H(\tau_1, \tau_2).^7$$

The ensurance strategy of the first player is also called the *maximin strategy*, and that of the second player is the *minimax strategy*.

Lemma 1.3.1 $V_2 \geq V_1$.

Proof $\min_{\tau_2 \in T_2} H(\tau_1, \tau_2) \leq \max_{\tau_1 \in T_1} H(\tau_1, \tau_2)$. Also, since the left-hand side of this inequality does not depend on τ_2, then

$$\min_{\tau_2 \in T_2} H(\tau_1, \tau_2) \leq \min_{\tau_2 \in T_2} \max_{\tau_1 \in T_1} H(\tau_1, \tau_2).$$

[6] The proof is rather simple.

$$M = \max_{\tau_2 \in T_2} \left[-\max_{\tau_1 \in T_1} - B(\tau_1, \tau_2) \right] = \max_{\tau_2 \in T_2} \left[-\max_{\tau_1 \in T_1} A(\tau_1, \tau_2) \right]$$

$$= -\min_{\tau_2 \in T_2} - \left[-\max_{\tau_1 \in T_1} A(\tau_1, \tau_2) \right] = -\min_{\tau_2 \in T_2} \max_{\tau_1 \in T_1} A(\tau_1, \tau_2).$$

[7] V_2 is a "loss ceiling" for the second player.

Now the left-hand side depends on τ_1 only, while the right-hand side depends neither on τ_1 nor on τ_2.

Hence

$$\max_{\tau_1 \in T_1} \min_{\tau_2 \in T_2} H(\tau_1, \tau_2) \le \min_{\tau_2 \in T_2} \max_{\tau_1 \in T_1} H(\tau_1, \tau_2) \quad \text{Q.E.D.}$$

Therefore, $V_1 \le V_2$ always holds. If $V_1 = V_2$, the ensurance strategies of both players, τ_1^* and τ_2^*, are called *optimal strategies.*

The function H is said to have a *saddle point* at (τ_1^*, τ_2^*) if

$$\min_{\tau_2 \in T_2} H(\tau_1^*, \tau_2) \ge H(\tau_1^*, \tau_2^*) \ge \max_{\tau_1 \in T_1} H(\tau_1, \tau_2^*). \tag{1.3.4}$$

Inequality (1.3.4) is called a *saddle inequality*, and the number $H(\tau_1^*, \tau_2^*)$ is called the *saddle value*, or just the value of the game. If $H(\tau_1^*, \tau_2^*) = V_1 = V_2 = V$, it is said that the game has a *solution.*

If the game has a solution, then the game has optimal strategies for all players. τ_1^* is the optimal strategy for the first player because he/she can secure a payoff at least $H(\tau_1^*, \tau_2^*) = V$ and more than V if the second player deviates from his/her optimal strategy τ_2^* [this can be seen from the left-hand side of (1.3.4)]. Any attempt on the part of the first player to increase his/her payoff above $V = H(\tau_1^*, \tau_2^*)$ can be blocked by the second player by choosing τ_2^* as the optimal strategy. [The blocking can be seen from the right-hand side of Eq. (1.3.4).]

The definition of a saddle point is essentially the same as that of a solution of an antagonistic game. Nash tried to apply this notion to a more general case. For a two-person game the definition is as follows: We say that $(\bar{\tau}_1, \bar{\tau}_2)$ is a *Nash equilibrium* of the game if

$$A(\bar{\tau}_1, \bar{\tau}_2) = \max_{\tau_1 \in T_1} A(\tau_1, \bar{\tau}_2),$$

$$B(\bar{\tau}_1, \bar{\tau}_2) = \max_{\tau_2 \in T_2} B(\bar{\tau}_1, \tau_2).$$

In other words, $(\bar{\tau}_1, \bar{\tau}_2)$ is a Nash equilibrium if no player benefits from changing his/her strategy, assuming that the other player is not going to change his/her strategy. At this stage, it is worth mentioning that (1) a Nash equilibrium is the same as a saddle point in the case of an antagonistic game and (2) ensurance strategies are equivalent to optimal strategies only if the game is antagonistic.

Example 1.3.1 Suppose the antagonistic game matrix is

	I	II
I	3	4
II	5	6

where I and II are strategies of both players. Then the ensurance level is

$$V_1 = H(\tau_1^*, \tau_2(\tau_1^*)) = H(\text{II}, \tau_2(\text{II})) = A(\text{II}, \text{I}) = 5.$$

The value 5 is also the saddle value of the game. The strategies (II, I) are the maximum strategies, the saddle point, and the Nash equilibrium of the game.

An example of a game that has neither a saddle point nor a Nash equilibrium is Example 1.1.2, the variant of matching pennies.

1.4 GAMES WITH COMPLETE INFORMATION

Let Γ denote a game. Γ with complete information requires that every participant know all information about the state of the game. In other words, every player knows which vertex he/she is now at and which moves other players have already made. An example of the game Γ with complete information is chess.

We say that the game Γ in extensive form is a *game with complete information* if all information sets S_i^j, $j = 1, 2, \ldots, m_i$, are one-element subsets of the player sets S_i for each $i = 1, 2, \ldots, n$.

Players in Γ with no Nash equilibrium are usually secretive, and they try to outguess each other. It turns out that a Nash equilibrium always exists in Γ with complete information, leading to the following theorem.

Theorem 1.4.1 Every game with complete information has a Nash equilibrium.

Before presenting the proof of this theorem for the case of two players, we shall introduce three definitions. Let Γ be a game in extensive form. We say that Γ is *decomposed* at a vertex x if the information set of this vertex contains only one element (in other words, if information sets do not contain vertices from both vertex x plus all its followers and the remaining vertices of the game tree). In this case we can define new games, the game consisting of the vertex x and all its followers, as a *truncated game* or *subgame* Γ_x, and the *quotient game* Γ/x, which consists of x and the remaining vertices.

It should now be obvious from the definition of game decomposition that the game Γ with complete information is decomposed at any vertex.

Proof of Theorem 1.4.1 (The proof is by induction on the length of a game.[8]) Since the game is finite, it has finite length. Suppose the theorem is true for all games with length $(n-1)$. If Γ has length 1, then at most one player makes a move and the equilibrium will be his/her best choice. Thus for $n = 1$ the theorem is correct. Let Γ have length n and let the initial vertex have r followers $a_1, a_2, \ldots, a_r$. Consider the truncated games Γ_{a_i} ($i = 1, 2, \ldots, r$). Any of these games is a game with complete information and has length $(n-1)$. We must consider two cases.

First, the initial vertex of the game Γ belongs to the initial (occasional) set S_0. Then by the induction hypothesis, any truncated game Γ_{α_i}, $i = 1, \ldots, r$, has a Nash equilibrium $(\bar{p}_i, \bar{q}_i)$ for both players

$$\begin{aligned} A(\bar{p}_i, \bar{q}_i) &\geq A(p_i, \bar{q}_i), \\ B(\bar{p}_i, \bar{q}_i) &\geq B(\bar{p}_i, q_i), \end{aligned} \tag{1.4.1}$$

where p_i, q_i are arbitrary strategies for the first and second players, respectively, in the game Γ_{a_i} ($i = 1, \ldots, r$). Then we shall construct the strategies of the total game Γ (i.e., $\bar{\tau}_1, \bar{\tau}_2$) of both players as a combination of the separate strategies $(\bar{p}_i, \bar{q}_i)$ in any truncated game Γ_{a_i} ($i = 1, 2, \ldots, r$). Suppose $(\lambda_1, \lambda_2, \ldots, \lambda_n)$ is the probability distribution over the followers $a_1, a_2, \ldots, a_r$ of the initial vertex. Then the payoffs of the first and second players are, respectively,

$$\begin{aligned} A(\tau_1, \tau_2) &= \sum_{j=1}^{r} \lambda_j A(p_j, q_j), \\ B(\tau_1, \tau_2) &= \sum_{j=1}^{r} \lambda_j B(p_j, q_j). \end{aligned} \tag{1.4.2}$$

Then from (1.4.1) and (1.4.2) we get

$$\begin{aligned} A(\bar{\tau}_1, \bar{\tau}_2) &\geq A(\tau_1, \bar{\tau}_2), \\ B(\bar{\tau}_1, \bar{\tau}_2) &\geq B(\bar{\tau}_1, \tau_2), \end{aligned}$$

[8] The length of a game is the largest possible number of vertices before reaching a terminal vertex.

where (τ_1, τ_2) are any arbitrary strategies. Hence $(\bar{\tau}_1, \bar{\tau}_2)$ is a Nash equilibrium.

Second, the initial vertex belongs to the first player's set S_1. Then if $(\bar{p}_i, \bar{q}_i)$ is a Nash equilibrium in the truncated game Γ_{a_i} $(i = 1, 2, \ldots, n)$, the first player in the total game Γ should choose his/her move $j_0 \in \{1, 2, \ldots, r\}$ according to

$$\max_{j \in \{1, \ldots, r\}} A(\bar{p}_j, \bar{q}_j) = A(\bar{p}_{j_0}, \bar{q}_{j_0}) = A(\bar{\tau}_1, \bar{\tau}_2). \tag{1.4.3}$$

Thus we have strategies $(\bar{\tau}_1, \bar{\tau}_2)$ in the total game Γ. To prove that the strategies $(\bar{\tau}_1, \bar{\tau}_2)$ are a Nash equilibrium for the total game Γ (obviously we only need to check the equilibrium conditions for the first player), we take an arbitrary strategy τ_1, which can be decomposed on the strategy p_i in the truncated game Γ_{a_i} $(i = 1, \ldots, r)$ and with the first move of the player taken as j_1. Then we have from (1.4.3)

$$A(\bar{\tau}_1, \bar{\tau}_2) = A(\bar{p}_{j_0}, \bar{q}_{j_0}) \geq A(\bar{p}_{j_1}, \bar{q}_{j_1}) \geq A(p_{j_1}, \bar{q}_{j_1}) = A(\tau_1, \bar{\tau}_2).$$

Therefore, $(\bar{\tau}_1, \bar{\tau}_2)$ is a Nash equilibrium for the total game Γ.[9] Q.E.D.

[9] This method of constructing optimal strategies is very useful for a game with a manageable number of vertices and is similar to Bellman's dynamic programming method (i.e., going from the end).

CHAPTER

2

Information Extension of Games

In nonantagonistic games the definition of Nash equilibrium may give rise to a multitude of incomparable solutions. This incomparability stems from the fact that each solution is advantageous to one of the two players. In Section 2.1 we shall show that this problem of incomparability does not exist in the case of antagonistic games because all solutions have an equal payoff.

Incomparability follows from two assumptions: absolute equality between the players and complete ignorance on the part of each player about the decisions of the other player. These assumptions seldom conform to reality. Thus attempts have been made to overcome this problem by replacing these assumptions with assumptions on the rules of the game or on the rules of transmitting information. *Y*. Germeir, a Russian mathematician, worked out an information extension of games that uses different assumptions concerning the information advantage that one player has over the other players. He describes different information extensions of the given game (i.e., metagames). The extensions, together with economic examples, will be described in Section 2.2.

2.1 SOME PROPERTIES OF NASH EQUILIBRIUM

In nonantagonistic games Nash equilibria may be nonexistent or incomparable as different payoffs are assigned to them. The meaningfulness of this can be seen from the following example.

Example 2.1.1 (Battle of the sexes) Suppose, for convenience, the payoff matrices of both players are arranged in one matrix as

	I	II
I	(2, 1)	(−1, −1)
II	(−1, −1)	(1, 2)

This game may be interpreted as follows. A husband, the first player, and a wife, the second player, each have two choices for a holiday's entertainment, and both think it is very important to go out together. Each can either go to a boxing match or to a ballet. However, the husband prefers the first, while the wife prefers the second. If both choose to go to the boxing match, the husband will get two utils as an estimate of his utility, while the wife will get one util. If both decide to go to the ballet, the husband will get one util, while the wife will get two utils. If they cannot make a common choice, then they stay at home and each gets −1 util since it is very important that they go out together.

This game has two Nash equilibria, namely, (I, I) and (II, II) with payoffs (2, 1) and (1, 2), respectively. Then the question is: Can these equilibria be compared? Obviously, the first equilibrium makes the first player better off and the second player worse off. The opposite is true of the second equilibrium. Moreover, suppose the wife wants to please her husband and decides to go to the boxing match, while at the same time the husband decides to go to the ballet to please his wife. Then both players will be worse off, i.e., their payoff will be (−1, −1).

This disadvantage is nonexistent in the case of an antagonistic game. All Nash equilibria have the same value, and hence all players rank them equal. This will formally be seen from the following theorem.

Theorem 2.1.1 In the antagonistic game $\Gamma = (T_1, T_2, H)$, let $(\bar{\tau}_1, \bar{\tau}_2)$ and $(\tilde{\tau}_1, \tilde{\tau}_2)$ be two Nash equilibria. Then

(i) $(\bar{\tau}_1, \tilde{\tau}_2)$ and $(\tilde{\tau}_1, \bar{\tau}_2)$ are also Nash equilibria, and
(ii) $H(\bar{\tau}_1, \bar{\tau}_2) = H(\tilde{\tau}_1, \tilde{\tau}_2) = H(\bar{\tau}_1, \tilde{\tau}_2) = H(\tilde{\tau}_1, \bar{\tau}_2)$.

Proof Let $(\bar{\tau}_1, \bar{\tau}_2)$ and $(\tilde{\tau}_1, \tilde{\tau}_2)$ be Nash equilibria. Then

$$H(\bar{\tau}_1, \bar{\tau}_2) \geq H(\tilde{\tau}_1, \bar{\tau}_2) \qquad \text{and} \qquad H(\tilde{\tau}_1, \tilde{\tau}_2) \leq H(\tilde{\tau}_1, \bar{\tau}_2).$$

Therefore,

$$H(\tilde{\tau}_1, \tilde{\tau}_2) \leq H(\tilde{\tau}_1, \bar{\tau}_2) \leq H(\bar{\tau}_1, \bar{\tau}_2).$$

Similarly,

$$H(\bar{\tau}_1, \bar{\tau}_2) \leq H(\tilde{\tau}_1, \bar{\tau}_2) \leq H(\tilde{\tau}_1, \bar{\tau}_2),$$

and these two sets of inequalities prove part (ii) of the theorem.

Now, for any τ_1,

$$H(\tilde{\tau}_1, \bar{\tau}_2) = H(\bar{\tau}_1, \bar{\tau}_2) \geq H(\tau_1, \bar{\tau}_2).$$

Similarly, for any τ_2,

$$H(\tilde{\tau}_1, \bar{\tau}_2) = H(\tilde{\tau}_1, \tilde{\tau}_2) \leq H(\tilde{\tau}_1, \tau_2).$$

Thus from the above inequalities, $(\tilde{\tau}_1, \bar{\tau}_2)$ is a Nash equilibrium. Also, it can similarly be proved that $(\bar{\tau}_1, \tilde{\tau}_2)$ is a Nash equilibrium. Q.E.D.

The theorem that follows is equivalent to Theorem 2.1.1.

Theorem 2.1.2 Let the antagonistic game $\Gamma = (T_1, T_2, H)$ have two saddle points $(\bar{\tau}_1, \bar{\tau}_2)$ and $(\tilde{\tau}_1, \tilde{\tau}_2)$. Then $(\bar{\tau}_1, \tilde{\tau}_2)$ and $(\tilde{\tau}_1, \bar{\tau}_2)$ are also saddle points, and $H(\bar{\tau}_1, \bar{\tau}_2) = H(\tilde{\tau}_1, \tilde{\tau}_2) = H(\bar{\tau}_1, \tilde{\tau}_2) = H(\tilde{\tau}_1, \bar{\tau}_2)$.

As seen from Example 2.1.1, the above theorems do not apply for non-antagonistic games. The payoffs are different, the strategies (I, I) and (II, II) are the only Nash equilibria, and neither (I, II) nor (II, I) is a Nash equilibrium.

2.2 INFORMATION EXTENSION OF GAMES: THE GERMEIR APPROACH

It is now obvious from Example 2.1.1 that Nash equilibria in the non-antagonistic games may not exist if players are stubborn or fastidious, and even if the equilibria do exist, they are not comparable. If, however, there is an exchange of information, there will be no such problems, but the theory of bimatrix games does not usually make this assumption. Thus without information exchange the concept of Nash equilibrium leads to incomparability and indeterminacy of the optimal strategies. These drawbacks led to a search for other approaches to solutions of games. One approach, which will be discussed below, was developed by the Russian scientist Germeir (1976). This approach may be dubbed an information extension of games. It describes a method of exchanging information in games more accurately than other approaches.

Let the game be denoted by the game $\Gamma = (T_1, T_2, A, B)$. There are different methods of extending Γ by exchanging information.

1. Extension Γ_1 of the game Γ (i.e., the dictator solution). In this game the first player is entitled to the first move and he/she conveys the decision to the second player. The first player does not know the response of the second player, but does know that the second player needs the decision that was conveyed in order to maximize the payoff. The payoff of the first player in the game Γ_1 is the ensurance level

$$V_1(\Gamma_1) = \max_{\tau_1 \in T_1} \min_{\tau_2 \in C_1(\tau_1)} A(\tau_1, \tau_2), \tag{2.2.1}$$

where

$$C_1(\tau_1) = \left\{\tau_2 : \max_{\tilde{\tau}_2 \in T_2} B(\tau_1, \tilde{\tau}_2) = B(\tau_1, \tau_2)\right\}$$

and is called the *maximizing set* of the second player in the game Γ_1. In other words, the first informs the second of his/her decision, knowing only that the latter needs the decision to maximize his/her payoff function. Therefore, if $\bar{\tau}_1$ is the solution of Eq. (2.2.1), then the second player's maximum payoff is

$$L_2(\Gamma_1) = \max_{\tau_2 \in C_1(\bar{\tau}_1)} B(\bar{\tau}_1, \tau_2).$$

2. Extension Γ_2 of the game Γ. This approach is more flexible than the first one. The first player, who also has the first move, conveys to the second not his/her move but his/her behavior. He/she informs the second player what move he/she will make if the second player makes a specific move τ_2. In other words, the first player conveys to the second a whole function $\xi_1 : T_2 \to T_1$. Then the set $\{\xi_1\}$ is the set of all functions $\xi_1 : T_2 \to T_1$, and the ensurance level of the game Γ_2 is defined as

$$V_1(\Gamma_2) = \max_{\{\xi_1\}} \min_{\tau_2 \in C_2(\xi_1)} A(\xi_1(\tau_2), \tau_2),$$

where

$$C_2(\xi_1) = \left\{\tau_2 : \max_{\tilde{\tau}_2 \in T_2} B(\xi_1(\tilde{\tau}_2), \tilde{\tau}_2) = B(\xi_1(\tau_2), \tau_2)\right\}$$

and is called the maximizing set of the second player in the game Γ_2. As a rule, the set $\{\xi_1\}$ is denoted as $T_1^{T_2}$; hence the ensurance level is defined as

$$V_1(\Gamma_2) = \max_{\xi_1 \in T_1^{T_2}} \min_{\tau_2 \in C_2(\xi_1)} A(\xi_1(\tau_2), \tau_2).$$

It should now be clear that the definitions of optimal strategies and the values of the payoff functions of both players are more complex in this game than in the previous game. Therefore, we need to introduce additional definitions.

A function $\xi_1^p: T_2 \to T_1$ is called a *punishment strategy* if

$$B(\xi_1^p(\tau_2), \tau_2) = \min_{\tau_1 \in T_1} B(\tau_1, \tau_2).$$

Then the ensurance level of the second player is

$$L_2(\Gamma_2) = \max_{\tau_2 \in T_2} B(\xi_1^p(\tau_2), \tau_2) = \max_{\tau_2 \in T_2} \min_{\tau_1 \in T_1} B(\tau_1, \tau_2)$$

and his/her *set of ensuring strategies* is

$$E = \{\tau_2 : B(\xi_1^p(\tau_2), \tau_2) = L_2(\Gamma_2)\}.$$

Furthermore, we introduce the value K such that

$$K = \begin{cases} \sup\limits_{(\tau_1, \tau_2) \in D} A(\tau_1, \tau_2) & \text{if} \quad D \neq \varnothing, \\ -\infty & \text{if} \quad D = \varnothing, \end{cases}$$

where

$$D = \{(\tau_1, \tau_2) : B(\tau_1, \tau_2) > L_2(\Gamma_2)\}$$

and is called the *set of compromises* of the second player. Since the set D is not closed, we write sup instead of max and define the *optimal strategies* $(\bar{\tau}_1^\varepsilon, \bar{\tau}_2^\varepsilon)$ as follows: for any $\varepsilon > 0$, $A(\bar{\tau}_1^\varepsilon, \bar{\tau}_2^\varepsilon) \geq K - \varepsilon$, where $(\bar{\tau}_1^\varepsilon, \bar{\tau}_2^\varepsilon) \in D \neq \varnothing$.

Moreover, we define the *ensurance value*

$$M = \min_{\tau_2 \in E} \max_{\tau_1 \in T_1} A(\tau_1, \tau_2)$$

as the payoff that the first player can ensure for himself/herself when the second player chooses strategies from the set E. Then, given $\tau_2 \in E$, the first player ensures himself/herself the payoff M by taking the *ensurance strategy*

$$\xi_1^{c\varepsilon}: T_2 \to T_1$$

such that $\varepsilon > 0$ and

$$A(\xi_1^{c\varepsilon}(\tau_2), \tau_2) \geq M - \varepsilon.$$

This definition can be written without having $\varepsilon > 0$. But we choose to do so because we define the optimal strategies $(\bar{\tau}_1^{\varepsilon}, \bar{\tau}_2^{\varepsilon})$ such that the value of their payoff holds within $\varepsilon > 0$ of the value K.

To provide better insight into the optimal strategies of the game Γ_2, the following remarks will be presented prior to their utilization in the proof of the theorem concerning these optimal strategies.

If $K > M$, then the compromise set D contains pairs of strategies that are of interest to both players. The first player will be better off if the pairs of strategies are chosen from D because they will furnish him/her with a payoff greater than the value M. Moreover, these strategies will provide the second player with payoffs greater than those associated with the strategies of the ensuring set E. For D to accommodate the interests of both players, however, the first player must convince the second player that the latter should choose his/her strategies from the set D. Thus the condition $K > M$ implies that the interests of both players are not contradictory and that an optimal pair of strategies may be an element of the set D.

Now let us suppose that $K \leq M$. If $K = M$, the interests of both players may be compatible. If $K < M$, these interests diverge because what is advantageous for one player is not advantageous for the other. For example, if the game Γ is antagonistic, it is obvious that $K \leq M$ because the first player's gains cannot exceed the second player's losses, i.e.,

$$M = \min_{\tau_2 \in E} \max_{\tau_1 \in T_1} A(\tau_1, \tau_2) = \min_{\tau_2 \in T_2} \max_{\tau_1 \in T_1} A(\tau_1, \tau_2) = -L_2.$$

Note that these equalities hold because the ensurance level L_2 is such that

$$-L_2 = -\max_{\tau_2 \in T_2} \min_{\tau_1 \in T_1} B(\tau_1, \tau_2) = \min_{\tau_2 \in T_2} \max_{\tau_1 \in T_1} A(\tau_1, \tau_2),$$

and by the definitions of set E and level L_2, the strategies $\tau_2 \in T_2$ have to be elements of E and any $\tau_2 \in E$ is a minimax strategy of the second player. Hence

$$\min_{\tau_2 \in T_2} \max_{\tau_1 \in T_1} A(\tau_1, \tau_2) = \min_{\tau_2 \in E} \max_{\tau_1 \in T_1} A(\tau_1, \tau_2).$$

If $K = M$, the first player gains the amount M and the second player ensures himself/herself the level L_2. Therefore, if the game Γ is antagonistic and $K = M$, the interests of the first and second players are compatible and their optimal pairs of strategies are $\xi_1^{c\varepsilon}$ and $\tau_2 \in E$, respectively. Moreover, if $K \leq M$, $A(\tau_1, \tau_2)$ is continuous and the game Γ is antagonistic, then $K = M$. This is so because the compromise set D becomes

$$D = \{(\tau_1, \tau_2) : A(\tau_1, \tau_2) < M\}.$$

Therefore, the optimal pairs of strategies $(\xi_1^p(\tau_2), \tau_2)$ lie on the boundary of the set D.[1] Now if the game is Γ_2 and $K \leq M$, then the ensurance level of the first player $V_1(\Gamma_2) = M$ (whereas in the antagonistic game Γ the ensurance level is $V_1 \leq M$). This result is due to the specifications of the game Γ_2 in which the first player has the right to the first move, and hence the punishment strategy is always available to him/her. Therefore, the first player will choose $\xi_1^{c\varepsilon}$ as his/her minimax strategy, considering it to be the optimal strategy. A conflict of interest in this case will take place if the second player attempts to choose his/her strategy outside of the set E, which may make the payoff of the first player less than the amount M and would compel him/her to threaten to use the punishment strategy.

Finally, the third part of the optimal strategy is very controversial because the first player applies it occasionally and may get the worst results, $\min_{\tau_1 \in T_1} \min_{\tau_2 \in T_2} A(\tau_1, \tau_2)$. This result can happen if the second player violates the rules of the game. Therefore, the first player will not find it necessary to use the punishment strategy if the rules of the game are clear and the second player does not violate them. He/she only needs to use it to "frighten" the second player. In other words, the first player will use the punishment strategy when the second player violates the rules of the game and his/her behavior becomes unexplainable.

[1] The boundary of set D is the set $\partial D = \bar{D} - \mathring{D}$, where $\bar{D}$ is the closure and $\mathring{D}$ is the interior of the set D.

Theorem 2.2.1 In the game Γ_2 the strategy

$$\bar{\xi}_1^{\varepsilon} = \begin{cases} \bar{\tau}_1^{\varepsilon} & \text{if } \tau_2 = \bar{\tau}_2^{\varepsilon} \text{ and } K > M, \\ \xi_1^{c\varepsilon} & \text{if } \tau_2 \in E \text{ and } K \leq M, \\ \xi_1^{p} & \text{in other cases} \end{cases} \tag{2.2.2}$$

ensures the payoff $\max[K, M] - \varepsilon$ to the first player and, in general, his/her ensurance level is equal to or less than $\max[K, M]$ for any $\varepsilon > 0$.

Proof Let $K > M$. Then for $(\bar{\tau}_1^{\varepsilon}, \bar{\tau}_2^{\varepsilon})$ we have

$$B(\xi_1^p(\tau_2), \tau_2) \leq L_2(\Gamma_2) < B(\bar{\tau}_1^{\varepsilon}, \bar{\tau}_2^{\varepsilon}).$$

Thus the second player chooses strategy $\bar{\tau}_2^{\varepsilon}$, which makes him better off. This ensures the first player the payoff $K - \varepsilon$ as required.

Now let $K \leq M$. Then for $\tau_2 \notin E$ we have

$$B(\xi_1^p(\tau_2), \tau_2) < L_2(\Gamma_2),$$

and the second player must choose his/her move from the set E. Then the first player's ensurance level is

$$\min_{\tau_2 \in E} A(\bar{\tau}_1^{\varepsilon}, \tau_2) = \min_{\tau_2 \in E} A(\xi_1^{c\varepsilon}(\tau_2), \tau_2)$$

$$\geq \min_{\tau_2 \in E} \max_{\tau_1 \in T_1} A(\tau_1, \tau_2) - \varepsilon = M - \varepsilon,$$

as required.

Now, to complete proving the theorem, we must show that the first player cannot get more than $\max[K, M]$. Let $\xi_1(\tau_2)$ be the optimal strategy of the first player. Then the second player will choose a strategy from the set D if

$$\sup_{\tau_2 \in T_2} B(\xi_1(\tau_2), \tau_2) > L_2(\Gamma_2).$$

But then $(\xi_1(\tau_2), \tau_2) \in D$ and the first player can get no more than $K \leq \max[K, M]$. In another case

$$\sup_{\tau_2 \in T_2} B(\xi_1(\tau_2), \tau_2) = L_2.$$

[The case in which $\sup_{\tau_2 \in T_2} B(\xi_1(\tau_2), \tau_2) < L_2(\Gamma_2)$ is impossible by the definition of $L_2(\Gamma_2)$.]

Thus the second player will choose his/her moves from the set E in which the ensurance level is guaranteed. Then the first player will use ensurance strategies and his/her payoff is such that

$$\inf_{\tau_2 \in E} A(\xi_1(\tau_2), \tau_2) \le \inf_{\tau_2 \in E} \max_{\tau_1 \in T_1} A(\tau_1, \tau_2)$$
$$= M \le \max(K, M). \qquad \text{Q.E.D.}$$

Now let $V_1(\Gamma_1)$ and $V_1(\Gamma_2)$ stand for the ensurance levels of the first player in the games Γ_1 and Γ_2, respectively. Then

$$V_1(\Gamma_2) \ge V_1(\Gamma_1).$$

This is so because the constant strategy of the first player in the game Γ_1 is included in his/her admissible set of strategies in the game Γ_2.

In Example 2.1.1, the battle of the sexes, the first player (i.e., the husband) keeps his strategy constant I, and the optimal solution will be in the form: "If you (wife) take strategy I, I shall do the same [i.e., $\xi_1^{\bar{\xi}\varepsilon} = \bar{\tau}_1^{\varepsilon}$ in (2.2.2)]. But if you take strategy II, I shall take strategy I again [i.e., $\xi_1^{\bar{\xi}\varepsilon} = \xi_1^{\xi p}$ in (2.2.2)]." Moreover, $V_1(\Gamma_1) = V_1(\Gamma_2)$ because the constant strategy $\xi_1(\tau_2) = \text{I}$ ensures better payoffs to the first player (i.e., husband). This case is not true in the following example.

Example 2.2.1 Consider the game with the payoff matrices

$A =$

	I	II	III	
	3	4	3	I
$A =$	−1	2	5	II
	4	−5	−4	III

and

	−1	2	−4	I
$B =$	2	−3	2	II,
	1	10	3	III

where A is the payoff matrix of the first player and B is the payoff matrix of the second player.

The ensurance level of the second player is $L_2(\Gamma_2) = -1$. The punishment strategy is

$$\xi_1^p(\tau_2) = \begin{cases} \text{I} & \text{if} \quad \tau_2 = \text{I}, \\ \text{II} & \text{if} \quad \tau_2 = \text{II}, \\ \text{I} & \text{if} \quad \tau_2 = \text{III}. \end{cases}$$

The sets of ensuring strategies and of compromises of the second player are $E = \{\text{I}\}$ and $D = \{(\text{II}, \text{I}), (\text{III}, \text{I}), (\text{I}, \text{II}), (\text{III}, \text{II}), (\text{II}, \text{III}), (\text{III}, \text{III})\}$, respectively. The value $K = 5$. Then $(\bar{\tau}_1^\varepsilon, \bar{\tau}_2^\varepsilon) = (\text{II}, \text{III})$. Moreover, $M = 4$.

Hence $K > D$ and $D \neq \varnothing$. The optimal strategy of the first player is

$$\bar{\xi}_1^\varepsilon(\tau_2) = \begin{cases} \text{I} & \text{if} \quad \tau_2 = \text{I}, \\ \text{II} & \text{if} \quad \tau_2 = \text{II}, \\ \text{II} & \text{if} \quad \tau_2 = \text{III}. \end{cases}$$

3. In modern books, the information extensions described above are often called metagames. So instead of being called game Γ_1 and Γ_2, they are often called metagames Γ_1 and Γ_2 of the game Γ.

It is possible to consider metagames more complex than Γ_1 and Γ_2. In the metagame Γ_3, the second player must first produce answers and make them available to the first player who plans his/her behavior accordingly. Therefore, the behavior of the first player is determined by the function $\xi_1\colon T_2 \to T_1$. Then the second player must produce new responses to the first's behavior, i.e., the map $\Xi_2\colon T_1^{T_2} \to T_2$. This is the second player's reaction to the first's behavior—what that player will do if he/she knows the behavior of the first player, which is determined by the function ξ_1. Finally, knowing the map of the second player Ξ_2, the first player chooses the strategy

$$\Xi_1\colon T_2^{(T_1^{T_2})} \to T_2^{T_1}.$$

By the same reasoning as in metagames Γ_1 and Γ_2, we define the ensurance level of the first player in the metagame Γ_3 as

$$V_1(\Gamma_3) = \max_{\{\Xi_1\}} \min_{\Xi_2 \in \bar{C}_2(\Xi_1)} \max_{\{\xi_1\}} \min_{\tau_2 \in C_2(\xi_1)} A(\Xi_1(\Xi_2)(\tau_2), \Xi_2(\xi_1)(\tau_2)),$$

where the set $C_2(\xi_1) \subset T_2$ and has the same definition as it does in $V_1(\Gamma_2)$, the set $\{\xi_1\}$ is the set of all functions from T_2 to T_1 (that is, the set $T_1^{T_2}$), and the set $\bar{C}_2(\Xi_1)$ is the subset of all maps defined in the same way as in the set $C_2(\xi_1)$ but at a more complex "informationally hierarchic" level, i.e.,

$$\bar{C}_2(\Xi_1) = \left\{ \Xi_2 : \max_{\{\tilde{\Xi}_2\}} \min_{\xi_1 \in C_1(\tilde{\Xi}_2)} \max_{\tilde{\tau}_2 \in T_2} B(\Xi_1(\tilde{\Xi}_2)(\tilde{\tau}_2), \Xi_2(\xi_1)(\tilde{\tau}_2)) \right.$$
$$\left. = \min_{\xi_1 \in C_1(\Xi_2)} \max_{\tau_2 \in T_2} B(\Xi_1(\Xi_2)(\tau_2), \Xi_2(\xi_1)(\tau_2)) \right\},$$

where $\{\Xi_2\}$ is the set of all maps of $T_1^{T_2}$ into T_2, i.e., all answers of the second player on any strategy behavior of the first player. The set $\{\tilde{\Xi}_2\}$ may be denoted as $T_2^{(T_1^{T_2})}$. Moreover, the set $C_1(\Xi_2)$, more correctly written as $C_1(\Xi_1, \Xi_2)$, is defined as

$$C_1(\Xi_1, \Xi_2) = \left\{ \xi_1 : \max_{\{\tilde{\xi}_1\}} \min_{\tau_2 \in C_2(\xi_1)} A(\Xi_1(\Xi_2)(\tau_2), \Xi_2(\tilde{\xi}_1)(\tau_2)) \right.$$
$$\left. = \min_{\tau_2 \in C_2(\xi_1)} A(\Xi_1(\Xi_2)(\tau_2), \Xi_2(\xi_1)(\tau_2)) \right\},$$

which is the set of optimal responses of the first player. In this definition, as in the definition of $V_1(\Gamma_3)$, the set $C_2(\xi_1)$, which is the set ε of optimal answers of the second player, may more precisely be written as $C_2(\Xi_1, \Xi_2, \xi_1)$ and is defined as

$$C_2(\Xi_1, \Xi_2, \xi_1) = \left\{ \tau_2 : \max_{\tilde{\tau}_2 \in T_2} B(\Xi_1(\Xi_2)(\tilde{\tau}_2), \Xi_2(\xi_1)(\tilde{\tau}_2)) \right.$$
$$\left. = B(\Xi_1(\Xi_2)(\tau_2), \Xi_2(\xi_1)(\tau_2)) \right\}.$$

Finally, the set $\{\Xi_1\}$, in the definition of $V_1(\Gamma_3)$, is the set of all maps of the set of all behavior strategies of the second player, $T_2^{(T_1^{T_2})}$ into the set of all behavior strategies of the first player, $T_1^{T_2}$. $\{\Xi_1\}$ is the set of metaoperators and is denoted by $(T_1^{T_2})^{T_2^{(T_1^{T_2})}}$.

Theorem 2.2.2 In the metagames Γ_2 and Γ_3 of the game $\Gamma = (T_1, T_2, A, B)$, $V_1(\Gamma_2) = V_1(\Gamma_3)$.

Proof In the metagame Γ_3, among the strategies of the first player, there is a metaoperator Ξ_1 that defines the "constant" strategy $\bar{\xi}_1^\varepsilon$ (as in Theorem 2.2.1) independent of any responses from the set of all optimal behavior strategies of the second player, $\bar{C}_2(\Xi_1)$, and then we have $V_1(\Gamma_3) \geq V_1(\Gamma_2)$, i.e., $V_1(\Gamma_3) \geq \max(K, M) - \varepsilon$, where $\varepsilon > 0$. On the other hand, the second player, as shown in Theorem 2.2.1, can always take his/her optimal response from the set T_2 and can force the first player to have no more than $\max(K, M)$, i.e., $V_1(\Gamma_3) \le \max(K, M)$. Then by the arbitrariness of $\varepsilon > 0$ we have $V_1(\Gamma_3) = V_1(\Gamma_2)$. Q.E.D.

Corollary In the game Γ_3 the first player can always consider his/her strategy as a function of T_2 into T_1 (i.e., a behavior).

By the same token, we can construct more complex metagames $\Gamma_4, \Gamma_5, \Gamma_6, \ldots$, and by the same reasoning it can be shown that $V_1(\Gamma_2) = V_1(\Gamma_3) = V_1(\Gamma_4) = \cdots$. (It is not sufficient that the first player consider constant strategies from the set $\{\xi_1\}$. This can be seen from Example 2.2.1.)

The following are examples that apply Germeir's approach to economics.

Example 2.2.2 Consider a game situation with two players, the center and one producer. The latter produces commodity x at the cost of $\Psi(x)$ dollars and gets awarded bonus y from the center for his/her production.

The center's utility function is defined as $W_0(y, x) = cx - y$, where $x \ge 0$, $y \ge 0$, and $c \ge 0$ is the center's retail price of commodity x in the domestic market.

The net bonus function of the producer is

$$W_1(y, x) = y - \Psi(x)$$

such that $\Psi(x)$ is monotone increasing, $\Psi(0) = 0$, $x \le a$, and $y \le Y_0$, where a is the production possibility frontier and Y_0 is the bonus stock. Moreover, suppose the production cost is defined by the function $\Psi(x) = b \ln[a/(a - x)]$, $a > 0, b > 0$.

Written in the notation used in the metagame Γ_2, we have $\tau_1 = y$; $\tau_2 = x$; $A(\tau_1, \tau_2) = c\tau_2 - \tau_1$; $B(\tau_1, \tau_2) = \tau_1 - \Psi(\tau_2)$, where $\Psi(\tau_2) = b \ln[a/(a - \tau_2)]$ and $\tau_2 \le a$. Then the punishment strategy is such that $\xi_1^p(\tau_2) = 0$ (i.e., no bonus) the ensurance level is

$$L_2(\Gamma_2) = \max_{0 \le \tau_2 \le a} B(\xi_1^p(\tau_2), \tau_2) = \max_{0 \le \tau_2 \le a} b \ln[a/(a - \tau_2)] = 0$$

and the set of compromises is

$$D = \{(\tau_1, \tau_2) \colon \tau_1 - \Psi(\tau_2) > 0\}.$$

In Figure 2.2.1, set D is the shaded area and the payoff function of the first player is $A(\tau_1, \tau_2) = c\tau_2 - \tau_1$ and attains its maximum at the boundary of D.

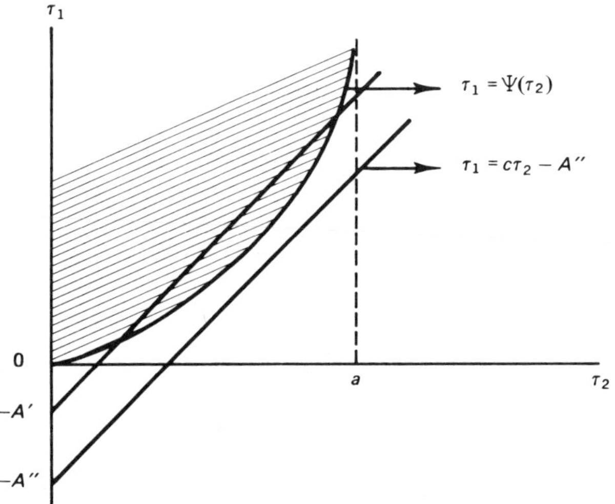

Figure 2.2.1

To find the value $K = \sup_{(\tau_1, \tau_2) \in D} A(\tau_1, \tau_2)$, we first take the limit case in which the pairs (τ_1, τ_2) lie on the boundary of the set D [i.e., $\tau_1 = \Psi(\tau_2)$]. Then the optimal strategy that maximizes the first player's payoff $A(\tau_1, \tau_2) = c\tau_2 - \Psi(\tau_2)$ is $\bar{\tau}_2 = a - (b/c)$ assuming that $\bar{\tau}_2 > 0$ (i.e., $a > b/c$). In the case $a < b/c$, the cost of production is very high, and hence it is profitable for the producer to produce zero output, i.e., $\tau_2 = 0$. This case is not interesting, and, therefore, we assume that $a > b/c$. Then $K = b \ln(ac/b) > 0$.

Moreover, the ensurance set of the second player is

$$E = \{\tau_2 : B(\xi_1^p(\tau_2), \tau_2) = -\Psi(\tau_2) = 0\} = \{0\}$$

and the ensurance value is

$$M = \min_{\tau_2 \in E} \max_{0 \leq \tau_1 \leq Y_0} A(\tau_1, \tau_2) = 0.$$

Hence $K > M$ and $D \neq 0$. Then the pair of strategies $(\bar{\tau}_1^\varepsilon, \bar{\tau}_2^\varepsilon)$ that satisfies $A(\bar{\tau}_1^\varepsilon, \bar{\tau}_2^\varepsilon) \geq K - \varepsilon$ is

$$\bar{\tau}_1^\varepsilon = b \ln \frac{ac}{b} + \varepsilon \qquad \text{and} \qquad \bar{\tau}_2^\varepsilon = a - \frac{b}{c}.$$

The payoffs of both players assigned to these strategies are

$$A(\bar{\tau}_1^{\varepsilon}, \bar{\tau}_2^{\varepsilon}) = ac - b - b \ln \frac{ac}{b} - \varepsilon \qquad \text{and} \qquad B(\bar{\tau}_1^{\varepsilon}, \bar{\tau}_2^{\varepsilon}) = \varepsilon.$$

The optimal strategy of the first player is

$$\bar{\xi}_1^{\varepsilon} = \begin{cases} \bar{\tau}_1^{\varepsilon} & \text{if} \quad \tau_2 = \bar{\tau}_2^{\varepsilon}, \\ 0 & \text{if} \quad \tau_2 \neq \bar{\tau}_2^{\varepsilon}. \end{cases}$$

It is interesting to note that if the center decides to set the price and buy the output from the producer, then the center will gain less than when it gives a bonus commensurate with output. In the case in which the price is set, the payoffs become

$$A(K, \tau_2) = c\tau_2 - K\tau_2 \qquad \text{and} \qquad B(K, \tau_2) = K\tau_2 - \Psi(\tau_2),$$

where K is the price charged by the center (i.e., the strategy). Therefore, the producer takes the price as given and derives his/her optimal output, which is $\bar{\bar{\tau}} = a - (b/K)$, and then the center calculates the optimal price to be $\bar{K} = \sqrt{cb/a}$. The center's payoff assigned to these optimal strategies is

$$A(\bar{K}, \bar{\bar{\tau}}_2) = (\sqrt{ca} - \sqrt{b})^2.$$

It can be verified that

$$A(\bar{K}, \bar{\bar{\tau}}_2) < A(\bar{\tau}_1, \bar{\tau}_2).$$

In other words, the center gains more by choosing Germeir's optimal strategy $\bar{\xi}_1^{\varepsilon}$ than by setting the price of output.

It can also be shown that Germeir's optimal strategy provides more for the center in comparison with a price strategy even in the presence of more than one producer (Vatel, 1975).

Example 2.2.3 This is an example of trade involving barter between countries in which one has an information advantage, i.e., when one of the countries evaluates its information first and then conveys it to the other country, which acts accordingly.

The countries are denoted by Y and X. Country Y, which has the information advantage, has the stock y^* of good Y and country X has the stock x^*

of good x. The objective function of each of these countries depends on both goods. The objective function of country Y is represented by

$$W_1 = a_1 x_1 + b_1 y_1,$$

where x_1 and y_1 are the amounts of goods x and y that this country has after trading with country X. The objective function of country X is represented by

$$W_2 = a_2 x_2 + b_2 y_2,$$

where x_2 and y_2 are the amounts of goods x and y that country X has after trading with country Y.

It should be clear that the initial stock of country X is

$$x^* = x_1 + x_2$$

and the initial stock of country Y is

$$y^* = y_1 + y_2,$$

where x_1 is the amount of good x that country X trades with country Y for the amount y_2. Therefore, the strategy of country Y amounts to choosing the amount of good y that it will use domestically. Then the set of strategies of country Y can be defined as

$$T_1 = \{y_1 : 0 \leq y_1 \leq y^*\}.$$

Therefore, $y_2 = y^* - y_1$ is the amount of good y that country Y intends to trade with country X.

Similarly, the set of strategies of country X is defined as

$$T_2 = \{x_2 : 0 \leq x_2 \leq x^*\}.$$

Thus $x_1 = x^* - x_2$ is the amount of good x that country X intends to trade with country Y. Then the objective functions and the strategies of these countries totally describe the game Γ in this example.

The extension Γ_1 of Γ is not interesting because the dictator solution for country Y in this case is

$$\bar{y}_1^d = y^*.$$

The best strategy for country X is

$$\bar{x}_1^d = x^*.$$

Then the objective function of country Y is given by

$$W_1^d = b_2 y^*$$

and that of country X is

$$W_2^d = a_2 x^*.$$

Note that the dictator solution $(\bar{y}_1^d, \bar{x}_1^d)$ of game Γ_1 coincides with the Nash equilibrium of game Γ.

Before discussing the extension Γ_2 of this game, the following restrictions will be imposed on the parameters of the game. First, the ensurance level of country Y is greater than that of country X. Specifically,

$$L_1(\Gamma_2) = b_2 y^* > L_2(\Gamma_2) = a_2 x^*.$$

Second, the marginal rate of substitution between goods x and y is greater in country Y than in country X. That is,

$$\frac{a_1}{b_2} > \frac{a_2}{b_2}.$$

The set of compromises D is defined as

$$D = \{(y_1, x_2) : a_2 x_2 + b_2(y^* - y_1) > a_2 x^*,$$
$$0 \le x_2 \le x^*, \quad \text{and} \quad 0 \le y_1 \le y^*\},$$

and then

$$K = \sup_{(y_1, x_2) \in D} W_1(y_1, x_2)$$
$$= \sup_{(y_1, x_2) \in D} [a_1(x^* - x_2) + b_1 y_1] = a_1 x^* + b_1\left(y^* - \frac{a_2}{b_2} x^*\right).$$

The set D and four indifference curves of the function $W_1(y_1, x_2)$ are shown in Figure 2.2.2.

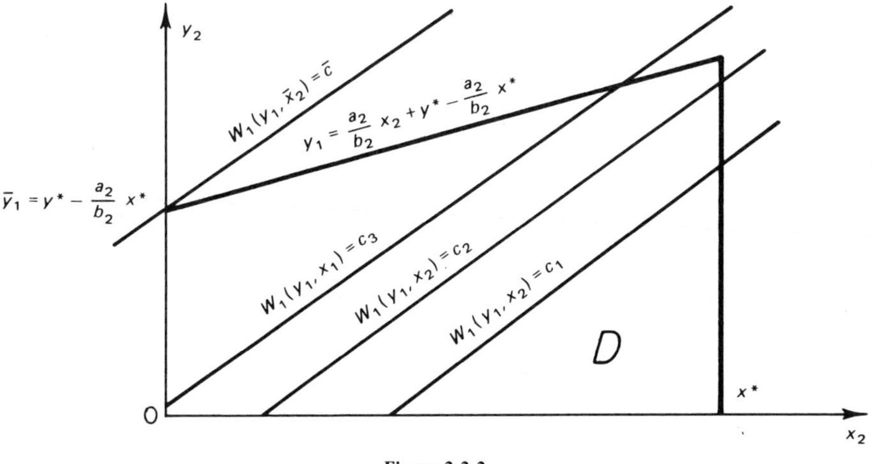

Figure 2.2.2

Set D is defined by the area $0\bar{y}_1\bar{z}x^*$. The optimal solution of Γ_2 is $\bar{x}_2 = 0$ and $\bar{y}_1 = y^* - (a_2/b_2)x^*$. This is the point at which the supremum of function $W_1(y_1, x_2)$ on the set D occurs.

Set E, the set in which country X guarantees itself the ensurance value $L_1(\Gamma_2)$, is $E = \{x^*\}$. Then, due to the restrictions on the parameters of the game,

$$K = a_1x^* + b_1\left(y^* - \frac{a_2}{b_2}x^*\right) > a_1x^* + b_1\left(y^* - \frac{a_1}{b_1}x^*\right) = b_1y^* = M$$
$$= L_1(\Gamma_2).$$

Then from Theorem 2.2.1 it follows that the ε-optimal strategy of

$$\bar{y}_1^\varepsilon = \begin{cases} y^* - \dfrac{a_2}{b_2}x^* - \dfrac{\varepsilon}{b_1} & \text{if } \; x_2 = x^*, \\ y^* & \text{if } \; x_2 < x^*. \end{cases}$$

In other words, if country X agrees to cooperate with country Y by offering to trade all its stock of goods x, then the latter will exchange

$$\frac{a_2}{b_2}x^* + \frac{\varepsilon}{b_1}$$

with country X. In the other case, if country X offers country Y an amount of x less than x^*, country Y will decline to trade any amount of its goods y, i.e., country Y applies its punishment strategy. The values of the objective functions of both countries are

$$\overline{W}_1^{\varepsilon} = a_1 x^* + b_1\left(y^* - \frac{a_2}{b_2}x^*\right) - \varepsilon,$$

$$\overline{W}_2^{\varepsilon} = a_2 x^* + \varepsilon\frac{b_1}{b_2}.$$

If $\varepsilon < K - M$, both countries will gain in game Γ_2, as compared to game Γ_1. Therefore, a preliminary information advantage concerning its decisions on the part of country Y benefits both countries.

CHAPTER

3

Probabilistic Extension of Games

As discussed in the preceding chapter, the definition of a Nash equilibrium in a nonantagonistic game may give rise to incomparable solutions. This problem does not exist in antagonistic games. These games, however, may have no Nash equilibrium or no saddled point. Therefore, the definition of a Nash equilibrium is useless in such situations. Von Neumann and Morgenstern worked out a way to surmount this difficulty. They assumed that every player can consider a probabilistic mixture of his/her pure strategies. This method of choosing pure strategies at random is called a probabilistic extension of games. It will be discussed in Section 3.1. In Section 3.2 we shall show that the solution of this kind of game can be reduced to a linear programming problem. This solution always exists if the game is antagonistic.

3.1 DEFINITIONS AND BASIC PROPERTIES

As stated in Section 2.2, the analysis of antagonistic games tells us how to play matrix games with saddle points. Most games, however, do not have saddle points. Therefore, such analysis is of limited use in helping players find their best choices.

Let us consider a game that has no saddle points and is defined by the matrix

	I	II
I	1	3
II	5	0

Obviously,

$$\max_{\{I, II\}} \min_{\{I, II\}} A(\tau_1, \tau_2) = 1$$

and

$$\min_{\{I, II\}} \max_{\{I, II\}} A(\tau_1, \tau_2) = 3.$$

Hence the game has no saddle point. Note that the first player is better off using strategy II with which he wins five units if that player predicts with certainty that the second player will take strategy I. However, let us suppose that the second player is very unpredictable and smart and, so, will correctly guess the first player's move. In this case the second player will choose strategy II and the first player will end winning zero units. Therefore, the first player has to be wary and is better off using strategy I. But the second player will certainly guess that decision and will use strategy I, giving the first player one unit. Then the first player thinks he/she will be better off choosing strategy II, hoping that the second player will use strategy I. Hence the game goes around in circles. But how can this circle be broken? Von Neumann and Morgenstern were confronted with this dilemma and saw one answer—strategies should be chosen at random and according to a randomization scheme. In this case the player aims to make it hard for the opponent to ascertain the former's strategies as he/she attempts to raise his/her ensurance level.

This argument can be reinforced by noting that in the first column of the above matrix the first player can, by choosing his moves at random, hedge against the 1-unit payoff with the 5-unit payoff, just as a player may increase the ensurance level when betting on the horses by not putting all of his/her money on a single horse.

As mentioned before, if the game is played many times the desirability of strategies can be assessed with the use of mathematical expectations (i.e., probabilistic averages). Therefore, von Neumann and Morgenstern argue that it is possible that games have saddle points when the players use a probabilistic mixture of pure strategies.

One reason for advocating mixed strategies is that in certain situations it is desirable to keep secret the choice of pure strategies and, therefore, the mixed strategy will be used. Another reason is that in certain strategic situations they provide a more flexible and profitable hedge than do any of the pure strategies. This convention of using mixed strategies is termed, as defined before, a probabilistic extension of games.

In this section we first introduce the definition of mixed strategies in finite games, i.e., games with a finite set of strategies for every player. A more general definition will then be presented. Before we do that we will introduce some definitions.

Recalling that if the set $S = \{s_1, s_2, \ldots, s_n\}$ is finite, then any *probability distribution* on it is defined by the vector $x \in R^n_+$ such that

$$\sum_{i=1}^{n} x_i = 1 \qquad \text{and} \quad 0 \leq x_i \leq 1, \qquad i = 1, 2, \ldots, n,$$

where x_i is the ith component of the vector x and is defined as the probability of choosing the element s_i of the set S.

Let $f: S \to R$ and x be a probability distribution on S. Then the average of f given x is $\sum_{i=1}^{n} f_i(s_i)x_i$. Finally, if the vector $x = (x_1, \ldots, x_n)$ is a probability distribution on the set $S_1 = \{s_1^1, s_2^1, \ldots, s_n^1\}$ and the vector $y = (y_1, \ldots, y_m)$ is a probability distribution on the set $S_2 = \{s_1^2, s_2^2, \ldots, s_m^2\}$, then the vector $x \otimes y$ is a probability distribution on the set $S_1 \times S_2$ such that the vector $x \otimes y \in R_+^{n \cdot m}$ and its components are $x_i \cdot y_i$, $i = 1, \ldots, n$ and $j = 1, \ldots, m$. Therefore, $x_i \cdot y_i$ is the probability of choosing the element (s_i^1, s_j^2) of the set $S_1 \times S_2$. If $f: S_1 \times S_2 \to R$, then its average is $\sum_{i,j} x_i \times y_j f(s_i^1, s_j^2)$. It is easy to verify that the vector $x \otimes y$ is a probability distribution on the set $S_1 \times S_2$.

Let $\Gamma = \{T_1, T_2, A, B\}$ be a game, where $T_1 = \{\tau_1^1, \tau_2^1, \ldots, \tau_n^1\}$ and $T_2 = \{\tau_1^2, \tau_2^2, \ldots, \tau_m^2\}$. Then the *mixed strategy* of the first player (second player) is a probability distribution x (y) on T_1 (T_2), where $x = (x_1, x_2, \ldots, x_n)$ and $y = (y_1, y_2, \ldots, y_m)$. If the first player chooses strategy x and the second player chooses strategy y, then the former's expected payoff is

$$\sum_{j=1}^{m} \sum_{i=1}^{n} x_i A(\tau_i^1, \tau_j^2) y_j$$

and that of the second player is

$$\sum_{j=1}^{m} \sum_{i=1}^{n} x_i B(\tau_i^1, \tau_j^2) y_i.$$

Let us now consider a generalization to infinite games in which each player has a continuum of strategies. We again first recall some definitions.

Let Ω be a set. The class $\mathfrak{A}$ of subsets of Ω is called an *algebra* if $\mathfrak{A}$ contains the sets Ω and $\varnothing$ and is closed under the operations of complementation, finite union, and finite intersection.

Let $(\Omega, \mathfrak{A})$ stand for the algebra $\mathfrak{A}$ on the set Ω. $(\Omega, \mathfrak{A})$ is called a *σ-algebra* if the class $\mathfrak{A}$ is closed under the operations of complementation, countable union, and countable intersection.

If M is a class of subsets of the set Ω, then an algebra (or a σ-algebra) can be generated from M by considering all finite (countable) unions and intersections of subsets from M. Such algebra (or σ-algebra) is called the algebra (or the σ-algebra) generated by M. For example, if we begin from class M of all open sets in R^n, we get the σ-algebra generated by M that is called a *Borel σ-algebra* on R^n, i.e., $B(R^n)$, which can be generated first by considering closed subsets, open rectangles, etc., of R_n, then by taking their countable unions and intersections.

Let $(\Omega, \mathfrak{A})$ be a σ-algebra. The function v is called a *(probability) measure* on $(\Omega, \mathfrak{A})$ if it maps the class $\mathfrak{A}$ into $[0, 1]$ such that $v(\Omega) = 1$ and for every sequence $\{E_i\}$ with $E_i \in \mathfrak{A}$ and $E_i \bigcap_{i \neq j} E_j = \varnothing$; then

$$v\left(\bigcup_{i=1} E_i\right) = \sum_{i=1} v(E_i), \qquad \text{i.e.} \quad v \text{ is } \sigma\text{-additive.}$$

(Note that the sequence $\{E_i\}$ can be finite or countable.)

Let us suppose that $(\Omega, \tilde{\mathfrak{A}})$ is a σ-algebra and $\tilde{v}$ is a (probability) measure defined on it. Then one can consider a σ-algebra $(\Omega, \mathfrak{A})$ generated by the algebra $(\Omega, \tilde{\mathfrak{A}})$. It turns out that there is a unique extension v of the measure $\tilde{v}$ on the σ-algebra $(\Omega, \mathfrak{A})$ such that $v(A) = \tilde{v}(A)$ for any $A \in \tilde{\mathfrak{A}}$. A σ-algebra $(\Omega, \mathfrak{A})$ and a (probability) measure v defined on it defines a *measure space* and is denoted by $(\Omega, \mathfrak{A}, v)$. Let $(\Omega_1, \mathfrak{A}_1, v_1)$ and $(\Omega_2, \mathfrak{A}_2, v_2)$ be two measure spaces. One can also consider the algebra $\mathfrak{A}$ generated by the algebra of all sets $A_1 \times A_2$, where $A_1 \in \mathfrak{A}_1$, $A_2 \in \mathfrak{A}_2$ and a measure $v = v_1 \times v_2$ defined on $A_1 \times A_2$ such that

$$v(A_1 \times A_2) = v(A_1) \times v(A_2).$$

Then it is easy to see that the triple $(\Omega_1 \times \Omega_2, \mathfrak{A}_1 \times \mathfrak{A}_2, v_1 \times v_2)$ is a new measure space and $\mathfrak{A}_1 \times \mathfrak{A}_2$ is the new algebra. Then if the measure v_1 is defined on R^L and the measure ν_2 is defined on R^K, one can consider the product measure $\nu = \nu_1 \times \nu_2$ to be defined on R^{L+K}. Moreover, if $S \subset R^L$ and $T \subset R^K$, then the measure $\nu_1(S)$ may be interpreted as the probability of being in S, the measure $\nu_2(T)$ as the probability of being in T, and the product measure $\nu_1(S) \cdot \nu_2(T)$ as the probability of being in $S \times T$.

Given a σ-algebra $(\Omega, \mathfrak{A})$, a mapping $f: \Omega \to R$ is said to be *measurable* if

$$F_L = \{x : f(x) \leq L\} \in \mathfrak{A} \qquad \text{for every} \quad L \in R.$$

The set F_L is often called the *Lebesgue set.*

Let $(\Omega, \mathfrak{A}, \nu)$ be a measure space and f be a step function of Ω into R, i.e., there is a partition $\{A_i\}$, $i = 1, 2, \ldots, n$ such that $\Omega = \bigcup A_i$, $A_i \in \mathfrak{A}$, $A_i \bigcap_{i \neq j} A_j = \varnothing$, and f is constant on every A_i. If the step function f is measurable, then we associate with it the real number $\sum_i f(A_j)\nu(A_i)$. This number is called the *integral* of f, i.e.,

$$\sum_{i=1}^{n} f(A_i)\nu(A_i) = \int_{\Omega} f \, d\nu.$$

Let f be a nonnegative measurable function of Ω into R. Then there exists an increasing sequence of measurable step functions $\{f_n\}$, which converges to f from below for any point of Ω, excluding points of a set A_f such that $\nu(A_f) = 0$; and for any such sequence the $\lim_{n\to\infty} \int_\Omega f_n \, d\nu$ exists (which may be infinite). This limit is independent of the particular sequence $\{f_n\}$. Hence f is said to be *integrable* if $\lim_{n\to\infty} \int_\Omega f_n \, d\nu < \infty$, and in this case the integral of f is defined by

$$\int_\Omega f \, d\nu = \lim_{n\to\infty} \int_\Omega f_n \, d\nu.$$

In general, a function f is said to be *integrable* if there are two nonnegative integrable functions f_1 and f_2 such that

$$f = f_1 - f_2 \qquad \text{and} \qquad \int_\Omega f = \int_\Omega f_1 - \int_\Omega f_2.$$

Theorem 3.1.1. Let $(\Omega_1, \mathfrak{A}_1, \nu_1)$ and $(\Omega_2, \mathfrak{A}_2, \nu_2)$ be two measure spaces and f be an integrable function on the measure space $(\Omega_1 \times \Omega_2, \mathfrak{A}_1 \times \mathfrak{A}_2, \nu_1 \times \nu_2)$. Then there exists a unique measure ν such that

$$\int_\Omega f(x_1, x_2) \, d\nu = \int_{\Omega_1} \left(\int_{\Omega_2} f(x_1, x_2) \, d\nu_2 \right) d\nu_1 = \int_{\Omega_2} \left(\int_{\Omega_1} f(x_1, x_2) \, d\nu_1 \right) d\nu_2,$$

where $\nu = \nu_1 \times \nu_2$ and $\Omega = \Omega_1 \times \Omega_2$. This theorem is known as Fubini's theorem and is often referred to as the rule of repeated integrals.

If $\Omega = R^1$ (a σ-algebra in this case is a Borel σ-algebra) and ν is a probability measure on R^1, then for any $x \in R^1$, the probability distribution function $F(x) = \nu((-\infty, x])$. If $F(x)$ is differential, its derivative $f(x)$ is called a density of measure ν at point x. A measure ν with density $f(x) = 1$ is called a *Lebesgue measure* and is denoted by ν_L. For this case the integral of $\phi(x)$ defined by ν_L is denoted by[1]

$$\int_R \phi(x)\, d\nu_L = \int_{-\infty}^{\infty} \phi(x)\, dx.$$

Moreover, if ν_L is a Lebesgue measure, then $\nu_L([a, b]) = b - a$. Analogously, by considering a parallelepiped A in R^n, i.e., $A = \prod_{i=1}^n [a_i, b_i]$, one may define the Lebesgue measure ν_L on R^n as $\nu_L(A) = \prod_{i=1}^n (b_i - a_i)$. The measure $\nu_L(A)$ is usually called the volume of A, and the integral of ν_L is denoted as

$$\int_{R^n} \phi(x_1, x_2, \ldots, x_n)\, d\nu_L = \int_{-\infty}^{\infty} \cdots \int_{-\infty}^{\infty} \phi(x_1, x_2, \ldots, x_n)\, dx_1, \ldots, dx_n.$$

Now let us go back to the game (T_1, T_2, A, B) with a continuum of strategies. We shall assume here that $T_1 \subset R^L$, $T_2 \subset R^K$, and the σ-algebras on R^L and R^K are Borel σ-algebras. We shall also denote the set of all probability measures ν_i on T_i by $\pi(T_i)$.

If the first player chooses the mixed strategy ν_1 and the second player chooses ν_2, the expected payoffs will be

$$A(\nu_1, \nu_2) = \int_{T_1 \times T_2} A(\tau_1, \tau_2)\, d\nu_1\, d\nu_2$$

and

$$B(\nu_1, \nu_2) = \int_{T_1 \times T_2} B(\tau_1, \tau_2)\, d\nu_1\, d\nu_2,$$

respectively.

If the first player chooses the pure strategy $\tau_1 \in T_1$, then we define the measure associated with τ_1 by ν_{τ_1} such that $\nu_{\tau_1}(\{\tau_1\}) = 1$ (where $\{\tau_1\}$ is a set consisting of one element, $\tau_1 \in T_1$, the set obviously belonging to a Borel

[1] Because $dF(x) = f(x)\, dx$ and $f(x) = 1$ since ν_L is a Lebesgue measure.

σ-algebra)[2] and $\nu_{\tau_1}(E) = 0$ (where E is an arbitrary Borel subset of T_1 such that $\tau_1 \notin E$). The measure ν_{τ_2} can be defined similarly if the second player chooses $\tau_2 \in T_2$. Then the payoffs of the first and second players, respectively, may be written

$$\int_{T_1 \times T_2} A(\xi_1, \xi_2)\, d\nu_{\tau_1}\, d\nu_{\tau_2} = A(\tau_1, \tau_2),$$

$$\int_{T_1 \times T_2} B(\xi_1, \xi_2)\, d\nu_{\tau_1}\, d\nu_{\tau_2} = B(\tau_1, \tau_2),$$

where $\xi_1 \in T_1$ and $\xi_2 \in T_2$, i.e., the set of pure strategies is included in the set of mixed strategies.

Let $T_1 = \{\tau_1^1, \tau_2^1, \ldots, \tau_n^1\}$ be a finite set and ν_1 any probability measure on T_1. Then as before, ν_1 is a vector that defines a probabilty distribution $x = (x_1, x_2, \ldots, x_n)$ on the set T_1 with the use of equalities $\nu_1(\{\tau_i^1\}) = x_i$, $i = 1, 2, \ldots, n$, and vice versa. That is, if $x = (x_1, x_2, \ldots, x_n)$ is a probability distribution on T_1, then this vector defines a probability measure ν on T_1. Therefore, if the existence of a solution is proven for the case of a continuous payoff function associated with infinite sets of strategies, then the existence of a solution in the case of finite sets of strategies follows. (Recall that, by definition, any function defined on a finite set is continuous.) We shall, however, consider the game with a continua of strategies because this is the case in economic applications.

3.2 FINITE ANTAGONISTIC GAMES VIA LINEAR PROGRAMMING

We shall show in this section that the solution of a finite game can be reduced to a special linear programming problem. In general, the linear programming problem is to find $(x_1, x_2, \ldots, x_n)$ in order to

$$\text{maximize} \quad \sum_{i=1}^{n} c_i x_i$$

subject to

$$\sum_{i=1}^{n} a_{ij} x_i \leq bj, \qquad j = 1, 2, \ldots, m, \qquad \text{and} \quad x_i \geq 0. \tag{3.2.1}$$

[2] $\{\tau_1\}$ is a Borel subset because it is closed and all closed subsets belong to a Borel σ-algebra of R^L.

The dual of problem (3.2.1) is to find $(y_1, y_2, \ldots, y_m)$ so as to

$$\text{minimize} \quad \sum_{j=1}^{m} b_j y_j$$

subject to

$$\sum_{j=1}^{m} a_{ij} y_j \geq c_i, \qquad i = 1, 2, \ldots, n, \qquad \text{and} \quad y_j \geq 0. \tag{3.2.2}$$

If $\bar{x} = (\bar{x}_1, \bar{x}_2, \ldots, \bar{x}_n)$ is the solution of problem (3.2.1), the number $\sum_{i=1}^{n} c_i \bar{x}_i$ is called the *value* of the problem. We define the value of the dual similarly.

Theorem 3.2.1. The linear programming problem has a solution $\bar{x} = (\bar{x}_1, \bar{x}_2, \ldots, \bar{x}_n)$ if and only if the dual problem has a solution $\bar{y} = (\bar{y}_1, \bar{y}_2, \ldots, \bar{y}_m)$ and

$$\sum_{i=1}^{n} c_i \bar{x}_i = \sum_{j=1}^{n} b_j \bar{y}_j$$

(i.e., the values coincide).

Let the game Γ be defined by the payoff matrix $H = [h_{ij}]$, $i = 1, 2, \ldots, n$, $j = 1, 2, \ldots, m$.[3] Moreover, let $\bar{x} = (\bar{x}_1, \bar{x}_2, \ldots, \bar{x}_n)$ be a mixed strategy of the first player such that

$$\sum_{i=1}^{n} h_{ij} \bar{x}_i \geq V_0, \qquad j = 1, 2, \ldots, m,$$

where V_0 is an arbitrary fixed number (e.g., the value of the game). Then the mixed strategy $\bar{x}$ ensures the payoff V_0 for the first player in the sense that there is no strategy of the second player by which he/she can force the first player to get less than V_0, i.e., if $y = (y_1, y_2, \ldots, y_m)$ is an arbitrary mixed strategy of the second player, then

$$\sum_{j=1}^{m} \sum_{i=1}^{n} h_{ij} \bar{x}_i y_j \geq V_0.$$

[3] As usual, we use the game $\Gamma = (T_1, T_2, A, B)$ to represent the game $\Gamma = (\Pi(T_1), \Pi(T_2), A, B)$, where $\Pi(T_i)$ is the set of mixed strategies of the ith player, $i = 1, 2$.

In other words, we have

$$\min_{y \in \Pi(T_2)} \sum_{j,i=1}^{m,n} h_{ij}\bar{x}_i y_j \geq V_0,$$

which leads to the following theorem, even if the game is nonantagonistic.

Theorem 3.2.2 If the game $\Gamma = (T_1, T_2, A, B)$ is finite, the ensurance mixed strategy of the first player $\bar{x} = (\bar{x}_1, \bar{x}_2, \ldots, \bar{x}_n)$ is a solution of the linear programming problem of finding $(x_1, x_2, \ldots, x_n)$ in order to

$$\text{maximize} \quad V_1$$

$$\text{subject to} \quad \sum_{i=1}^{n} A_{ij}x_i \geq V_1, \qquad j = 1, 2, \ldots, m, \tag{3.2.1'}$$

$$\sum_{i=1}^{n} x_i = 1 \qquad \text{and} \qquad x_i \geq 0.$$

The solution of problem (3.2.1′) is the ensurance mixed strategy of the first player and the value $\bar{V}_1$ of the problem is the ensurance level of the player. If the game is antagonistic, the solution of (3.2.1′), i.e., $\bar{x}$, is called the maximin mixed strategy of the first player.

Similarly for the second player, the problem will be to find $y_1, y_2, \ldots, y_m$ so as to

$$\text{maximize} \quad V_2$$

$$\text{subject to} \quad \sum_{j=1}^{m} B_{ij}y_j \geq V_2, \qquad i = 1, 2, \ldots, n, \tag{3.2.2'}$$

$$\sum_{j=1}^{m} y_j = 1 \qquad \text{and} \qquad y_j \geq 0.$$

The solution of problem (3.2.2′) is the ensurance mixed strategy of the second player and the value is his/her ensurance level.

If the game is antagonistic (i.e., $A = H$ and $B = -H$), then the problem of finding the ensurance mixed strategy of the second player becomes finding $(y_1, y_2, \ldots, y_m)$ so as to

$$\begin{aligned}
&\text{minimize} \quad V_2 \\
&\text{subject to} \quad \sum_{j=1}^{m} h_{ij} y_j \le V_2,^4 \qquad i = 1, 2, \ldots, n, \\
&\qquad \sum_{j=1}^{m} y_j = 1 \qquad \text{and} \quad y_j \ge 0.
\end{aligned} \tag{3.2.2''}$$

The solution of (3.2.2″) is the maximin mixed strategy of the second player.

Theorem 3.2.3 A finite antagonistic game always has a solution in mixed strategies.

Proof We shall prove this theorem when the payoff matrix has nonnegative elements only. There is, however, no loss of generality in this case. If the payoff matrix $H = [h_{ij}]$, $i = 1, 2, \ldots, n$, $j = 1, 2, \ldots, m$, of the antagonistic game Γ has negative entries, then a new antagonistic game can be defined such that the new payoff matrix is $H_a = [h_{ij} + a]$, $i = 1, 2, \ldots, n$, $j = 1, 2, \ldots, m$, where a is a nonnegative arbitrary number and this game has the same solution (i.e., ensurance strategies) as Γ. If the original game has the value V, the new game will have the value $V + a$ and vice versa. Note that by choosing a number a that is somewhat large (i.e., $a \ge \max_{(i,j)} |h_{ij}|$), we have the inequalities $h_{ij} + a \ge 0$ for all i and j.

To this end, let us write problem (3.2.1′) for the antagonistic game $\Gamma = (T_1, T_2, H)$. Then the problem becomes to find $(x_1, x_2, \ldots, x_n)$ in order to

$$\begin{aligned}
&\text{maximize} \quad V_1 \\
&\text{subject to} \quad \sum_{i=1}^{n} h_{ij} x_i \ge V_1, \qquad j = 1, 2, \ldots, m, \\
&\qquad \sum_{i=1}^{n} x_i = 1 \qquad \text{and} \quad x_i \ge 0.
\end{aligned}$$

Since the constraint set is bounded (because $\sum_{i=1}^{n} x_i = 1$, $x_i \ge 0$, and the maximand is bounded above by the constraint $\sum_{i=1}^{n} h_{ij} x_i \ge V_1$), it follows

[4] Note that $h_{ij} = -B_{ij}$, and to maximize $-V_2$ is equivalent to minimize V_2.

that the problem has a solution $\bar{x} = (\bar{x}_1, \bar{x}_2, \ldots, \bar{x}_n)$.[5] Then by Theorem 3.2.1, the dual problem has a solution too.

Rewriting the problem in a standard form, we have

$$\text{maximize} \quad V_1$$

$$\text{subject to} \quad -\sum_{i=1}^{n} h_{ij}x_i + V_1 \leq 0, \qquad j = 1, 2, \ldots, m,$$

$$\sum_{i=1}^{n} x_i \leq 1, \qquad -\sum_{i=1}^{n} x_i \leq -1^{6} \qquad \text{and} \quad x_i \geq 0.$$

If the variables of the dual problem are denoted by $y_1, y_2, \ldots, y_m, \xi$, and η, the dual will be

$$\text{minimize} \quad \xi - \eta$$

$$\text{subject to} \quad -\sum_{j=1}^{m} h_{ij}y_j + \xi - \eta \geq 0, \qquad i = 1, 2, \ldots, n,$$

$$\sum_{j=1}^{m} y_j \geq 1 \qquad \text{and} \quad y_j \geq 0.$$

Note that without loss of generality, we can change the inequality $\sum_{j=1}^{m} y_j \geq 1$ to an equality. If $\bar{y} = (\bar{y}_1, \bar{y}_2, \ldots, \bar{y}_m)$ is the solution of the dual problem such that $\sum_{j=1}^{m} \bar{y}_j > 1$, then all elements of $\bar{y}$ can be reduced, and, consequently, the value $\sum_{j=1}^{m} h_{ij}\bar{y}_j$ is reduced also. Hence $\overline{V}_2$ will be reduced, which contradicts the optimality of $\bar{y}$. Therefore, $\sum_{j=1}^{m} \bar{y}_j = 1$.

Now let $\xi - \eta = V_2$. Then the dual problem will become problem (3.2.2″). From Theorem 3.2.1 it follows that the dual has a solution $\bar{y} = (\bar{y}_1, \bar{y}_2, \ldots, \bar{y}_m)$ and the value of the minimand of the dual problem coincides with the value of the maximand of the primal problem, i.e.,

$$V = \min_{y \in \Pi(T_2)} \max_{x \in \Pi(T_1)} \sum_{i,j=1}^{n,m} h_{ij}x_i y_j = \max_{y \in \Pi(T_2)} \min_{x \in \Pi(T_1)} \sum_{j,i=1}^{m,n} h_{ij}x_i y_j.$$

Hence the game $\Gamma = (T_1, T_2, H)$ has a solution. Q.E.D.

[5] If the standard linear programming problem has no solution, then one of two things went wrong: the constraint set is empty or the value of the optimand is arbitrarily large or small.

[6] The inequalities $\sum_{i=1}^{n} x_i \leq 1$ and $-\sum_{i=1}^{n} x_i \leq -1$ are equivalent to the equality $\sum_{i=1}^{n} x_i = 1$. We choose to write the inequalities in this form to conform to the standard linear programming problem (3.2.1).

The solution of the primal is the optimal (maximin) mixed strategy of the first player, and the solution of the dual is the optimal mixed strategy of the second player.

Corollary If $\bar{x} = (\bar{x}_1, \bar{x}_2, \ldots, \bar{x}_n)$ is an optimal mixed strategy of the first player, then

$$\sum_{i=1}^{n} h_{ij}x_i \geq V, \qquad j = 1, 2, \ldots, m.$$

If $\bar{y} = (\bar{y}_1, \bar{y}_2, \ldots, \bar{y}_m)$ is an optimal mixed strategy of the second player such that for $j_0 \in \{1, 2, \ldots, m\}$ the corresponding inequality above is greater than V, then $y_{j_0} = 0$.

This corollary holds because if $\sum_{i=1}^{n} h_{ij_0}\bar{x}_i > V$ for any y_{j_0}, then $\sum_{i,j=1}^{n,m} h_{ij}\bar{x}_i\bar{y}_j > V$ since $\sum_{j=1}^{m} y_j = 1$, $\bar{y}_j \geq 0$, and $h_{ij} \geq 0$. In other words, the first player gets more than the level V, which contradicts the optimality of the strategy $\bar{y}$.

Next we shall demonstrate the relevance of Theorem 3.2.2 in computing the optimal solutions of some games.

Let us first consider the case of a 2×2 game that is defined by the matrix $[h_{ij}]$, $i = 1, 2$, $j = 1, 2$. Suppose that this game has no saddle point in pure strategies. Then from the corollary of Theorem 3.2.2, the optimal strategy of the first player, for example, is such that

$$h_{11}\bar{x}_1 + h_{21}\bar{x}_2 \geq V,$$
$$h_{12}\bar{x}_1 + h_{22}\bar{x}_2 \geq V.$$

These inequalities must hold as equalities because if, for example, $h_{11}\bar{x}_1 + h_{21}\bar{x}_2 > V$, then by the corollary $\bar{y}_1 = 0$. This means that the second player cannot use his/her first mixed strategy. In this case the game has a saddle point, and hence we have a contradiction. The same thing holds for the second equation. It follows that both equations must equal V. Therefore

$$h_{11}\bar{x}_1 + h_{21}\bar{x}_2 = V,$$
$$h_{12}\bar{x}_1 + h_{22}\bar{x}_2 = V,$$
$$\bar{x}_1 + \bar{x}_2 = 1,$$
$$\bar{x}_i \geq 0, \qquad i = 1, 2,$$

or in matrix notation

$$\bar{x}H = (V, V),$$
$$\bar{x}I^t = 1,$$

where I is the row vector (1, 1) and I^t is its transpose.

Similarly, for the second we have

$$\begin{aligned} h_{11}\bar{y}_1 + h_{12}\bar{y}_2 &= V, \\ h_{21}\bar{y}_1 + h_{22}\bar{y}_2 &= V, \\ \bar{y}_1 + \bar{y}_2 &= 1, \\ \bar{y}_j \geq 0, &\qquad j = 1, 2, \end{aligned}$$

or in matrix form

$$H\bar{y}^t = \begin{pmatrix} V \\ V \end{pmatrix},$$
$$\bar{y}I^t = 1.$$

These equations can be used to solve for $\bar{x} = (\bar{x}_1, \bar{x}_2)$, $\bar{y} = (\bar{y}_1, \bar{y}_2)$, and V. If the matrix H is nonsingular (i.e., det $H \neq 0$), the solution of the above system of equations will be[7]

$$\bar{x} = \frac{IH^{-1}}{IH^{-1}I^t}, \qquad \bar{y} = \frac{H^{-1}I^t}{IH^{-1}I^t}, \tag{3.2.3}$$

and

$$V = \frac{1}{IH^{-1}I^t}.$$

[7] This expression is derived by writing $x = VIH^{-1}$, and V is eliminated by noting that $\bar{x}I^t = 1 = VIH^{-1}I^t$; similarly for $\bar{y}$.

In the case of Example 1.1.2 (i.e., a variant of matching pennies, the game is defined by the matrix

$$H = \begin{array}{|c|c|} \hline 1 & -1 \\ \hline -1 & 1 \\ \hline \end{array}.$$

Note that det $H = 0$. But in order to use the results in (3.2.3), we define the game by the matrix

$$H_e = \begin{array}{|c|c|} \hline 1 + \varepsilon & -1 + \varepsilon \\ \hline -1 & 1 \\ \hline \end{array},$$

where $\varepsilon > 0$. In this case det $H_e \neq 0$, and by applying the results in (3.2.3), we have

$$\bar{x} = \left(\frac{1}{2}, \frac{1}{2}\right), \qquad \bar{y} = \left(\frac{1}{2} - \frac{\varepsilon}{4}, \frac{1}{2} + \frac{\varepsilon}{4}\right) \qquad \text{and} \quad V = \frac{1}{2\varepsilon}.$$

By taking $\varepsilon \to 0$, we get $\bar{x} = \bar{y} = (\frac{1}{2}, \frac{1}{2})$ and $V = 0$.

Another case of interest is the case of a $(2 \times m)$ game in which the first player has only two strategies. Similar analysis can be used for a $(n \times 2)$ game.

If the first player takes a strategy (x_1, x_2), then the second player's job is to minimize over $j = 1, 2, \ldots, m$ the terms $h_{1j}x_1 + h_{2j}x_2$, giving the function

$$V(x_1) = \min_j \{h_{1j}x_1 + h_{2j}x_2\} \qquad x_2 = 1 - x_1.$$

Therefore, the first player's problem becomes finding x so as to

$$\text{maximize } V(x_1) = \min_j \{(h_{1j} - h_{2j})x_1 + h_{2j}\}.$$

The optimal mixed strategy of the first player, $\bar{x}_1$, which maximizes this expression is shown in Figure 3.2.1.

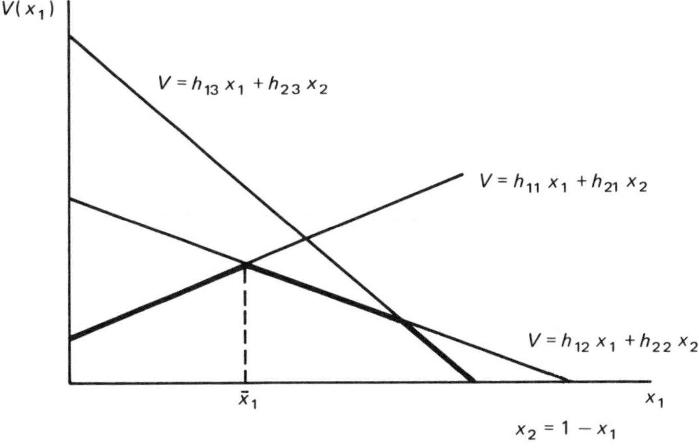

Figure 3.2.1

The graph is drawn by plotting the constraints as functions of x_1, determining the function $V_1(x_1) = V_1$ (the heavy, angular line). The highest intersection on this line is chosen to define $\bar{x}_1$ and $V_1(\bar{x}_1) = \bar{V}_1$.

Example 3.2.1 Consider the antagonistic game defined by the matrix

9	1	2
1	5	4

Then the problem of finding optimal (ensurance) mixed strategies of the first player is to find $(\bar{x}_1, \bar{x}_2)$ so as to

$$\begin{aligned} \text{maximize} \quad & V_1 \\ \text{subject to} \quad & 9x_1 + x_2 \geq V_1 \\ & x_1 + 5x_2 \geq V_1 \\ & 2x_1 + 4x_2 \geq V_1 \\ & x_1 + x_2 = 1 \\ & x_i \geq 0, \qquad i = 1, 2. \end{aligned}$$

In order to solve this problem, we write the constraints as functions of x_1, as in Figure 3.2.2. Then the derived optimal (ensurance) mixed strategy and the

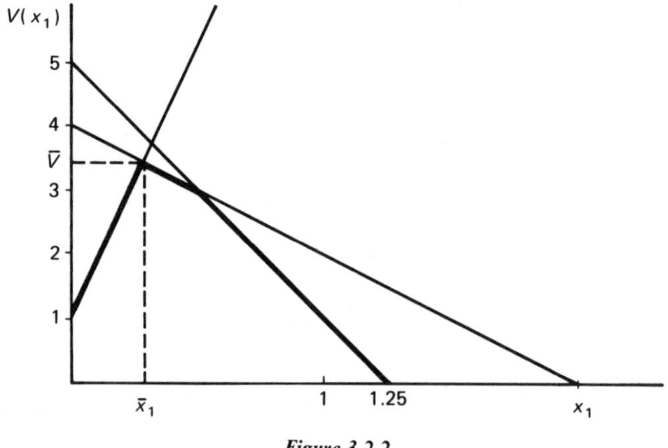

Figure 3.2.2

ensurance level of the first player are $\overline{x} = (0.3, 0.7)$ and $\overline{V}_1 = 3.4$, respectively.[8]

The dual problem which amounts to finding the optimal (ensurance) mixed strategy of the second player is finding $(\overline{y}_1, \overline{y}_2, \overline{y}_3)$ in order to

$$\begin{aligned}
&\text{minimize} \quad V_2 \\
&\text{subject to} \quad 9y_1 + y_2 + 2y_3 \leq V_2, \\
&\qquad y_1 + 5y_2 + 4y_3 \leq V_2, \\
&\qquad y_1 + y_2 + y_3 = 1, \\
&\qquad y_j \geq 0, \qquad j = 1, 2, 3.
\end{aligned}$$

Then the optimal mixed strategy and the ensurance level of the second player are $\overline{y} = (0.2, 0.8, 0.0)$ and $\overline{V}_2 = V = 3.4$. Note that, by the corollary of Theorem 3.2.3, $\overline{y}_3 = 0$ because of the unbinding constraint $\overline{x}_1 + 5\overline{x}_2 > V_1$, which can be seen in Figure 3.2.2.

Although this section deals with antagonistic games, the formulas in (3.2.3) are also applicable to nonantagonistic games. This can be seen from the following example.

[8] $\overline{V}_1 = V = \overline{V}_2$ because the game is antagonistic.

Example 3.2.2 Consider the nonantagonistic game defined by the bimatrix

(3, −5)	(1, 10)
(2, 7)	(4, 1)

.

The primal problem becomes to find $(\bar{x}_1, \bar{x}_2)$ in order to

$$\begin{aligned} &\text{maximize} \quad V_1 \\ &\text{subject to} \quad 3x_1 + 2x_2 \geq V_1 \\ &\qquad x_1 + 4x_2 \geq V_1 \\ &\qquad x_1 + x_2 \geq 1 \\ &\qquad x_i \geq 0, \qquad i = 1, 2. \end{aligned}$$

The optimal results for the first player are $x_1 = x_2 = \frac{1}{2}$ and $\overline{V}_1 = 2.5$. The dual problem is to find $(\bar{y}_1, \bar{y}_2)$ so as to

$$\begin{aligned} &\text{minimize} \quad V_2 \\ &\text{subject to} \quad -5y_1 + 10y_2 \geq V_2, \\ &\qquad 7y_1 + y_2 \geq V_2, \\ &\qquad y_1 + y_2 = 1, \\ &\qquad y_j \geq 0, \qquad j = 1, 2. \end{aligned}$$

Therefore, the optimal mixed strategy and the ensurance level of the second player are $\bar{y} = (0.43, 0.57)$ and $\overline{V}_2 = 3.5$.

Note that the optimal results can also be computed by the application of the formulas (3.2.3) of (2×3) matrix games.

It is easy to show that the pair of optimal mixed strategies $\bar{x} = (\frac{1}{2}, \frac{1}{2})$ and $\bar{y} = (0.43, 0.57)$ is not a Nash equilibrium in the probabilistic extension of this game. If the strategy $(\frac{1}{2}, \frac{1}{2})$ is a Nash equilibrium for the first player, the second player will be better off taking the strategy (0.1) and not (0.43, 0.57). Moreover, the proof of existence of a solution via linear programming, demonstrated in Theorem 3.2.3, is not reliable in the case of nonantagonistic games. However, we shall show the existence of a solution and a Nash equilibrium in the case of infinite games in Chapter 4. The existence of Nash equilibrium in finite games follows from such solutions.

It is somewhat difficult to find a real economic example that is an application of a pure antagonistic situation in which the payoff functions of both players are such that $A = -B$. The following example, however, may be helpful.

Example 3.2.3 Consider a duopolistic situation in which the same customers lost by one seller are gained by the other.

Let us suppose the two sellers are denoted by D_1 and D_2 and the former has the technology advantage over D_2. Moreover, suppose that each seller spends part of his/her profit on increasing advertising (i.e., strategy I) or on improving technology (i.e., strategy II). Finally, the game is defined by the payoff matrix

0	$\frac{1}{2}$
1	$\frac{1}{4}$

If both sellers decide to spend their money to finance more advertisements (i.e., each takes strategy I), then neither will gain new customers and, therefore, $h_{11} = 0$. The advertising campaign will just air "additional noise" in the market. If seller D_1 decides to invest his/her money in advancing the technology (i.e., takes II), while seller D_2 chooses to speed up his/her advertising campaign, then D_1 can reduce production cost at the end of the production period, reduce prices of products, and attract new customers from D_2. So the payoff $h_{21} = 1$. If D_1 takes the advertising strategy whereas D_2 takes the technology strategy, D_1 can win a few customers from D_2 because D_2 improves his/her technology and can shave prices. Hence $h_{12} = \frac{1}{2}$ since D_1 has the technology advantage. Finally, if both decide to improve their technology, then $h_{12} = \frac{1}{4}$. D_1 manages to get more than zero because of his/her technological advantage, but the payoff is not larger because both sellers shave prices.

Note that this game has no saddle point in pure strategies. Therefore, we can apply the formulas in (3.2.3) or employ the technique used in Figure 3.2.1 to solve for $\bar{x}_1$, $\bar{x}_2$, and V. Specifically, the optimal strategy of the first player is $\bar{x} = (\frac{3}{5}, \frac{2}{5})$, that of the second player is $y = (\frac{1}{5}, \frac{4}{5})$, and the value of the game is $V = \frac{2}{5}$. That is, both sellers must change their strategies from period to period as they choose their pure strategies according to the given randomization scheme. This would indicate that the game would be repeated as the realization of the game changes. D_1 must apply the advertising strategy more often, while D_2 must take the technology strategy more often. In this case each seller's aim is to make it hard for the opponent to ascertain the other's strategies as each attempts to raise his/her ensurance level. Therefore, the specific decision of a specific period is a top secret of each player.

CHAPTER

4

Infinite Games

It has been shown in Chapter 3 that finite antagonistic games always have solutions in mixed strategies. These solutions can be calculated using linear programming techniques. In real-life situations, however, there are numerous cases in which each player has a continuum of options. Such instances are often encountered in economics. The state of the economy that an economic agent (or, more accurately, a group of economic agents) can change is usually described as a continuum of variables. Therefore, it is necessary to consider infinite games and to work out their probabilistic extensions.

In Section 4.1 we shall introduce the definitions that are necessary for analyzing these games and we shall prove that these games have saddle points if the payoff functions are continuous. In Section 4.2 an example of a game of survival between economies, which are represented by von Neumann models, is provided. Because of the specially defined payoff function, this game converges to the class of games considered in Section 4.1 and, therefore, has a solution.

4.1 EXISTENCE THEOREM

So far we have primarily discussed finite games, i.e., games in which each player has a finite number of strategies. In Section 3.1 we introduced a definition of mixed strategy where each player has a continuum of pure strategies, usually represented as points in the interval (0, 1) if the set of strategies of the player is a subset of R^1. In this section we shall introduce a proof of a theorem of existence of solutions in infinite games. This theorem can also be used to show the existence of solutions in finite games. It is an important theorem because in applying game theory to economics, cases in which each player has an infinite number of strategies are often encountered. Before introducing the proof, some relevant definitions will be presented.

Let ϕ be a multivalued mapping of R^n into 2^{R^n}. This mapping is called *upper hemicontinuous* (u.h.c.) at the point x_0 if given any $x_n \to x_0$, then any $y_n \to y_0$, where $y_n \in \phi(x_n)$ implies $y_0 \in \phi(x_0)$. The mapping ϕ is called u.h.c. if it is u.h.c. at every $x \in R^n$. However, differences in definitions of upper hemicontinuity have been a source of confusion.[1]

Kakutani made use of such mappings to generalize Brower's fixed point theorem,[2] proving the following theorem.

Theorem 4.1.1 If S is a nonempty compact and convex subset of R^n and for every $x \in S$, the image set $\phi(x)$ is closed- and convex-valued and ϕ is an u.h.c. mapping of S into 2^S, then there exists at least one point $x^* \in S$ such that $x^* \in \phi(x^*)$ (i.e., a fixed point).

Before presenting Fan's generalization of this theorem, we introduce additional definitions.

Let S be a nonempty compact subset of R^n and $\Pi(S)$ be a set of probability measures on S such that $v_n \in \Pi(S)$, $n = 1, 2, \ldots$. The sequence $\{v_n\}$ is said to *weakly converge* to a measure v on S if

$$\int_S f\, dv_n \to \int_S f\, dv$$

for any bounded and continuous function $f: S \to R$. It is easy to show that if the function f is continuous, then f is Borel measurable and f is integrable on S for any probability measure.

[1] See, for example Hildenbrand (1974). "Core and Equilibrium of a Large Economy," p. 21. Princeton University Press, Princeton, New Jersey.

If, however, the range Y of the mapping ϕ of R^n into 2^Y (the class of all subsets of Y) is compact in R^n, then our definition is equivalent to that of Hildenbrand. This fact is proved in Nikaido (1966). "Convex Structures and Economic Theory", pp. 66–67. Academic Press, New York. Moreover, Nikaido uses Hildenbrand's definition of u.h.c. to define u.s.c. and calls our definition a *closed* mapping.

[2] This theorem says if $S \in R^n$ is nonempty, compact, and convex and $f(x)$ is a continuous function of S into itself, then there exists at least one point $x^* \in S$ such that $f(x^*) = x^*$ and x^* is a fixed point of the function $f(x)$.

By defining the notion of weak convergence in $\Pi(S)$, we define Ψ as an u.h.c. of $\Pi(S)$ into $2^{\Pi(S)}$ as before.

Theorem 4.1.2 Let S be a nonempty compact subset of R^n. If for every $v \in \Pi(S)$ the image set $\Psi(v)$ is closed- and convex-valued and Ψ is an u.h.c. mapping of $\Pi(S)$ into $2^{\Pi(S)}$, then there exists at least one point $v^* \in \Pi(S)$ such that $v^* \in \Psi(v^*)$ (i.e., fixed point).[3]

The following facts of measure space will also be used in proving the existence theorem.

(i) If $v \in \Pi(S)$, then $|\int_S f\, dv| \leq \|f\| \cdot v(S) = \sup_{x \in S} |f(x)| \cdot v(S)$.

(ii) If $H(x, y)$ is a continuous function of the product space $S_1 \times S_2$ into R, where $x \in S_1$, $y \in S_2$, and $v_1 \in \Pi(S_1)$, then the function

$$F(y) = \int_{S_1} H(x, y)\, dv_1$$

is continuous, where $F: S_2 \to R$.

This fact is straightforward from (i) because

$$\begin{aligned} |F(y_1) - F(y_2)| &= \left| \int_{S_1} [H(x, y_1) - H(x, y_2)]\, dv_1 \right| \\ &\leq \max_{x \in S_1} |H(x, y_1) - H(x, y_2)| \to 0 \qquad \text{if} \quad y_1 \to y_2. \end{aligned}$$

(iii) If $v_1^n \xrightarrow{w} v_1$ and $v_2^n \xrightarrow{w} v_2$, where $v_i^n \in \Pi(S_i)$ and $i = 1, 2$, then $v_1^n \times v_2^n \xrightarrow{w} v_1 \times v_2$.

To see (iii), recall that if H is a continuous function on $S_1 \times S_2$, then

$$\begin{aligned} &\left| \int_{S_1 \times S_2} H\, dv_1^n\, dv_2^n - \int_{S_1 \times S_2} H\, dv_1\, dv_2 \right| \\ &\quad \leq \left| \int_{S_1 \times S_2} H\, dv_1^n\, dv_2^n - \int_{S_1 \times S_2} H\, dv_1^n\, dv_2 \right| \\ &\qquad + \left| \int_{S_1 \times S_2} H\, dv_1^n\, dv_2 - \int_{S_1 \times S_2} H\, dv_1\, dv_2 \right| \\ &\quad \leq \max_{x \in S_1} \left| \int_{S_2} H(x, y)\, dv_2^n - \int_{S_2} H(x, y)\, dv_2 \right| \\ &\qquad + \left| \int_{S_2} \left(\int_{S_1} H\, dv_1^n - \int_{S_1} H\, dv_1 \right) dv_2 \right|. \end{aligned}$$

[3] Closedness is here defined in terms of weak convergence, i.e., the set $Q \subset \Pi(S)$ is *closed* if given $v_n \xrightarrow{w} v$, where $v_n \in Q$, then $v \in Q$.

Applying (i) and (ii), it follows that

$$\left|\int_{S_1 \times S_2} H\, dv_1^n\, dv_2^n - \int_{S_1 \times S_2} H\, dv_1\, dv_2\right| \to 0 \qquad \text{as} \quad v_1^n \xrightarrow{w} v_1 \quad \text{and} \quad v_2^n \xrightarrow{w} v_2.$$

(iv) If $v_n \in \Pi(S)$, $n = 1, 2, \ldots$, where S is a compact set in R^n, then there exists a subsequent $\{v_{n_k}\}$, $k = 1, 2, \ldots$, and $v_0 \in \Pi(S)$ such that $v_{n_k} \xrightarrow{w} v_0$ as $k \to \infty$. (This fact is called weak compactness.)

The following existence theorem will be proved in the case of the probabilistic extension of the game $\Gamma = (T_1, T_2, H)$, i.e., the game $\tilde{\Gamma} = (\Pi(T_1), \Pi(T_2), H)$. But as usual we shall adopt the notation $\Gamma = (T_1, T_2, H)$. The method of the proof will be the method of the optimal answer mappings of the players.

Theorem 4.1.3 Let T_1 and T_2 be convex compact sets in R^n and R^k, respectively. If H is a continuous function of $T_1 \times T_2$ into R, the game (T_1, T_2, H) has a solution (i.e., a solution in mixed strategies).

Proof Let us consider for any given $v_2 \in \Pi(T_2)$, the first player's set of optimal answers

$$A_1(v_2) = \left\{\bar{v}_1\colon \max_{v_1 \in \Pi(T_1)} \int_{T_1 \times T_2} H(\tau_1, \tau_2)\, dv_1\, dv_2 = \int_{T_1 \times T_2} H(\tau_1, \tau_2)\, d\bar{v}_1\, dv_2\right\},$$

where $A_1\colon \Pi(T_2) \to 2^{\Pi(T_1)}$. Similarly, given $v_1 \in \Pi(T_1)$, the second

$$A_2(v_1) = \left\{\bar{v}_2\colon \min_{v_2 \in \Pi(T_2)} \int_{T_1 \times T_2} H(\tau_1, \tau_2)\, dv_1\, dv_2 = \int_{T_1 \times T_2} H(\tau_1, \tau_2)\, dv_1\, d\bar{v}_2\right\},$$

where $A_2\colon \Pi(T_1) \to 2^{\Pi(T_2)}$.

We shall first show that $A_1(v_2) \neq \varnothing$. Let $v_2 \in \Pi(T_2)$ and $v_1^n \in \Pi(T_1)$ such that

$$\int_{T_1 \times T_2} H(\tau_1, \tau_2)\, dv_1^n\, dv_2 \to \sup_{v_1 \in \Pi(T_1)} \int_{T_1 \times T_2} H(\tau_1, \tau_2)\, dv_1\, dv_2.$$

From (i) it follows that

$$\left|\sup_{v_1 \in \Pi(T_1)} \int_{T_1 \times T_2} H(\tau_1, \tau_2)\, dv_1\, dv_2\right| < +\infty.$$

Let $\nu_0 \in \Pi(T_1)$. Then by (iv) we can assume that $\nu_n \xrightarrow{w} \nu_0$, where $\nu_0 \in \Pi(T_1)$. Hence by (ii) and the continuity of H we have

$$\int_{T_1 \times T_2} H(\tau_1, \tau_2)\, d\nu_1^n\, d\nu_2 \to \int_{T_1 \times T_2} H(\tau_1, \tau_2)\, d\nu_1^0\, d\nu_2.$$

Therefore, $\nu_1^0 \in A_1(\nu_2)$ and maximum replaces supremum in the above equations.

To show closedness of $A_1(\nu_2)$, let $\nu_1^n \in A_1(\nu_2)$ and $\nu_1^n \xrightarrow{w} \nu_1^0$. Hence by definition of $A_1(\nu_2)$,

$$\int_{T_1 \times T_2} H(\tau_1, \tau_2)\, d\nu_1^n\, d\nu_2 \geq \int_{T_1 \times T_2} H(\tau_1, \tau_2)\, d\nu_1\, d\nu_2$$

for any $\nu_1 \in \Pi(T_1)$.

Therefore, by (ii) and the continuity of H, as above, we have $\nu_1^0 \in A_1(\nu_2)$.

Convexity of $A_1(\nu_2)$ follows from the fact that if $\nu_1^1, \nu_1^2 \in \Pi(T_1)$ and $\lambda \in [0, 1]$, then

$$\nu = \lambda \nu_1^1 + (1 - \lambda)\nu_1^2 \in \Pi(T_1)$$

and

$$\int_{T_1 \times T_2} H\, d\nu\, d\nu_2 = \lambda \int_{T_1 \times T_2} H\, d\nu_1^1\, d\nu_2 + (1 - \lambda) \int_{T_1 \times T_2} H\, d\nu_1^2\, d\nu_2$$

by the definition of a measure. Thus if $\nu_1^i \in A_1(\nu_2)$, $i = 1, 2$, then

$$\int_{T_1 \times T_2} H\, d\nu_1^i\, d\nu_2 = \max_{\tilde{\nu}_1 \in \Pi(T_1)} \int_{T_1 \times T_2} H(\tau_1, \tau_2)\, d\tilde{\nu}_1\, d\nu_2 \equiv c(\nu_2), \qquad i = 1, 2.$$

Therefore,

$$\int_{T_1 \times T_2} H\, d\nu\, d\nu_2 = \lambda c(\nu_2) + (1 - \lambda)c(\nu_2) = c(\nu_2).$$

That is, $\nu \in A_1(\nu_2)$.

We now show that mapping A_1 is u.h.s. (i.e., closed). If $\nu_2^n \xrightarrow{w} \nu_2^0$, $\nu_1^n \to \nu_1^0$, and $\nu_1^n \in A_1(\nu_2^n)$, then

$$\int_{T_1 \times T_2} H\, d\nu_1^n\, d\nu_2^n \geq \int_{T_1 \times T_2} H\, d\nu_1\, d\nu_2^n$$

for all $\nu_1 \in \Pi(T_1)$.

Therefore, by (ii) and (iii) as before, we have $v_1^0 \in A_1(v_2^0)$, i.e., the mapping A_1 is closed or u.h.c.

Similarly, $A_2(v_1)$ can be shown to satisfy the same properties.

Therefore, the product $A_1(v_2^0) \times A_2(v_1^0)$ is closed- and convex-valued and $A_1 \times A_2$ is an u.h.c. mapping of the nonempty compact and convex product set $\Pi(T_1) \times \Pi(T_2)$ into $2^{\Pi(T_1) \times \Pi(T_2)} \subset 2^{\Pi(T_1 \times T_2)}$. Applying Theorem 4.1.2 (i.e., Fan's theorem), there exists at least one point $(v_1^*, v_2^*) \in A_1(v_2^*) \times A_2(v_2^*)$.

Finally, we can conclude that (v_1^*, v_2^*) is a saddle point (i.e., solution) of the game, i.e.,

$$\int_{T_1 \times T_2} H\, dv_1^*\, dv_2^* \geq \int_{T_1 \times T_2} H\, dv_1\, dv_2^* \qquad \text{for all} \quad v_1 \in \Pi(T_1)$$

and

$$\int_{T_1 \times T_2} H\, dv_1^*\, dv_2^* \leq \int_{T_1 \times T_2} H\, dv_1^*\, dv_2 \qquad \text{for all} \quad v_2 \in \Pi(T_2)$$

since $v_1^* \in A(v_2^*)$ and $v_2^* \in A_2(v_1^*)$. Q.E.D.

A discussion similar to that of Theorem 4.1.3 can be used to show existence of a Nash equilibrium in the probabilistic extension of the game $\Gamma = (T_1, T_2, A, B)$ when A and B are continuous functions of T_1 and T_2, respectively, into R.

Corollary 4.1.1 If in the game $\Gamma = (T_1, T_2, H)$ the sets of optimal answers of both players are nonempty, closed- and convex-valued, and their answers mappings are u.h.c., then Γ has a solution.

This corollary enables us to explore nonlinear cases of payoff functions in the search of solutions.

The following definitions will be used in Corollary 4.1.2, which follows.

Let $f(x)$ be a function of R^n into R. Then f is called *quasiconvex* in x if, for any $L \in R$, the set $F^-(L) = \{x: f(x) \leq L\}$ is convex. The function $f(x)$ is quasiconcave if $F^+(L) = \{x: f(x) \geq L\}$ is convex.

If $f(x)$ is convex, then it is quasiconvex. However, the converse is not true. In Figure 4.1.1 the function is a quasiconvex function of R^1, but it is not convex.

Corollary 4.1.2 Let $H(\tau_1, \tau_2)$ be a continuous function of $T_1 \times T_2$ into R, where $\tau_i \in T_i$ which is a nonempty compact subset of R^{n_i}, $i = 1, 2$, If

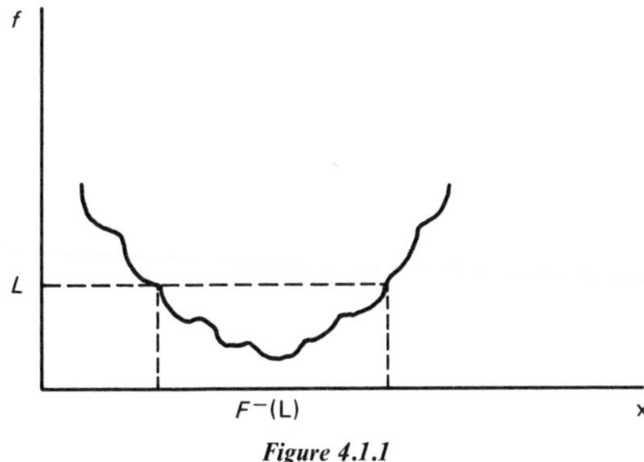

Figure 4.1.1

H is quasiconcave in τ_1 and quasiconvex in τ_2, then the game $\Gamma = (T_1, T_2, H)$ has a solution in pure strategies.

4.2 INFINITE ANTAGONISTIC GAMES IN THE VON NEUMANN MODELS: AN EXAMPLE

The following example is an application of the theory of infinite antagonistic games to a conflict situation between two economic systems.

We shall consider two input–output models. The first and main model will be a von Neumann model, which describes an expanding economy whose outputs and inputs vary with time. The model involves n commodity inputs, $x \in R^n_+$ (the nonnegative orthant of R^n), n commodity outputs, $y \in R^n_+$, and m activities or processes. All inputs are produced.

The technological process or activity of this model transforms the n commodity inputs into n commodity outputs. Accordingly, the activity can be described as two nonnegative vectors $(x, y) \in R^{2n}_+$, where x are outputs of one period that will become inputs to be consumed in the next period. Thus the planning horizon is discrete. The jth basic activity, or process, is represented by a nonnegative input vector $a_j = (a_{1j}, a_{2j}, \ldots, a_{nj})$ and a nonnegative output vector $b_j = (b_{1j}, b_{2j}, \ldots, b_{nj})$, where a_{ij} is the amount of commodity i consumed in activity j and b_{ij} is the amount of commodity i produced by activity j when it operates at a unit level. The corresponding $n \times m$ nonnegative matrices $A = [a_{ij}]$ and $B = [b_{ij}]$ are called the basic input and output matrices, respectively. The basic processes are operating at different intensities (i.e., levels), $u_j \geq 0$ $j = 1, 2, \ldots, m$, and the corresponding input and output vectors are $u_j a_j$ and $u_j b_j$, i.e., $u_j(a_j, b_j) = (u_j a_j, u_j b_j)$. In such a model it is permissible to use any process with any intensity, and even the process can be represented as the sum of the products of basic activities and intensities. Therefore, the technology set Z of model M can be described by

$$Z = \left\{(x, y) : (x, y) = \sum_{j=1}^{m} (a_j, b_j)u_j;\ u_j \geq 0\right\}$$

or in matrix form

$$Z = \{(x, y) : (x, y) = (Au, Bu);\ u \in R_+^m\}. \tag{4.2.1}$$

The technology mapping of this model is the mapping a of R_+^n into $2^{R_+^n}$ (the class of all subsets of R_+^n) such that for any $x \in R_+^n$,

$$a(x) = \{y : (x, y) \in Z\} = \{y : y = Bu;\ x = Au;\ u \in R_+^m\}.$$

The economic interpretations are that given an initial bundle of commodities $x \in R_+^n$ at the beginning of the planning period, one can obtain the set $a(x) \subset R_+^n$ at the end of that period. Moreover, the vector u is sometimes called a control for attaining output y.

The second model is a simple Leontief model. This model has no intrinsic products (i.e., produced and consumed in the same period) and hence is the simplest model of the class of the von Neumann models.

This simple Leontief model is defined by a nonnegative $n \times n$ input matrix Q, and its technology set is

$$Z_{\mathrm{L}} = \{(x, y) : Qy \leq x;\ x \geq 0;\ y \geq 0\}. \tag{4.2.2}$$

The economic interpretation is that Z consists of bundles (x, y) such that x is an input needed in producing output y. Moreover, it is permissible to use x to produce not only y but also any $y_1 \leq y$, i.e., the model assumes free disposability.

In order to construct a von Neumann model from the simple Leontief model, i.e., to make formula (4.2.2) resemble formula (4.2.1), we first introduce two kinds of processes, namely, (q_j, e_j) and $(e_j, 0)$, $j = 1, 2, \ldots, n$, where q_j is the jth column of matrix Q and e_j is the jth unit vector (i.e., $[0, \ldots, 0, 1, 0, \ldots, 0]$ with 1 in the place of the jth component). The process (q_j, e_j) represents the transformation of the input vector q_j into a unit output of commodity j. The process $(e_j, 0)$ represents the free disposability of a unit of commodity j. Then we form from these processes two $n \times 2n$ nonnegative matrices, i.e., an input matrix $A_{\mathrm{L}} = (Q, I)$ and an output matrix $B_{\mathrm{L}} = (I, 0)$, where I is the $n \times n$ identity matrix and 0 is the $n \times n$ zero matrix. The intensity vector is $u \in R_+^{2n}$. Thus we have a von Neumann model in which any process produces one commodity, as is the case in the simple Leontief model, i.e.,

$$Z_L = \{(x, y):(x, y) = (A_L u, B_L u); u \in R_+^{2n}\},$$

which resembles formula (4.2.1).

In a one-dimension case, the Leontief model is defined by a nonnegative number α (i.e., a growth factor) such that

$$Z'_L = \{(x, y): y \leq \alpha x; \alpha \geq 0; x \geq 0; y \geq 0\}.$$

In applying game theory to the von Neumann models, we must have two models M_1 and M_2 defined by $n \times m$ nonnegative matrices A_i, B_i, $i = 1, 2$. The technology mappings are a_i, $i = 1, 2$. The first player controls the processes of M_1. For the description of the conflict situation, we introduce two nonnegative matrices $S^i = [s_{kj}^i]$ (interaction matrices), where $i = 1, 2$, and $k, j = 1, 2, \ldots, n$, and s_{kj}^1 is the damage to the quantity of the kth commodity produced by M_2 caused by the transfer of a unit of the jth input to M_1s military industry during a given time period of the game. If the first player chooses to inflict damages worth $S_1 f_1$ commodities to the second player's output, then that player has to transfer the $n \times 1$ input vector f_1 to its military industry. The $n \times n$ nonnegative matrix S_2 is defined similarly, i.e., if the second player transfers f_2 to its military industry, then that player can destroy $S_2 f_2$ worth of commodities of the first player's outputs. This conflict description is valid not only for "hot" conflict or war, but also for a "cold war" when countries invest part of their wealth in military hardware as a preventive measure. Therefore, if x_i is the initial state of M_i, $i = 1, 2$, then after damage exchange takes place, the states of M_1 belong to the set

$$(a_1(x_1 - f_1) - S_2 f_2) \cap R_+^n$$

and the states of the second player (i.e., M_2) belong to the set

$$(a_2(x_2 - f_2) - S_1 f_1) \cap R_+^n,$$

where $0 \leq f_i \leq x_i$ and $i = 1, 2$. Then the first player's output bundle is $y_1 = (\tilde{y}_1 - S_\perp f_1)^+$,[4] where $\tilde{y}_1 = B_1 u_1$, $u_1 \geq 0$, and $x_1 - f_1 = A_1 u_1$.

[4] We denote the nonnegative parts of the components of the vector v by (v^+), i.e., if $v = (v_1, v_2, \ldots, v_n)$, then $(v)^+ = (v_1^+, v_2^+, \ldots, v_n^+)$ where $v_i^+ = \max(v_i, 0)$, $i = 1, 2, \ldots, n$.

We shall say that the first player is the winner if

$$(a_1(x_1 - f_1) - S_2 f_2) \cap \mathring{R}^n_+ \neq \varnothing$$

and

$$(a_2(x_2 - f_2) - S_1 f_1) \cap \mathring{R}^n_+ = \varnothing,$$

where $\mathring{R}^n_+$ is the interior of R^n_+. In other words, there exists in model M_1 a feasible state $y_1 \in (a_1(x_1 - f_1) - S_2 f_2) \cap R^n_+$ such that all the components of y_1 are positive (i.e., $y_1 > 0$), and at the same time, for any feasible state $y_2 \in (a_2(x_2 - f_2) - S_1 f_1) \cap R^n_+$ of the model M_2, there exists at least $i_0 \in \{1, 2, \ldots, n\}$ such that $y^2_{j_0} = 0$. Similarly, the second player is the winner if

$$(a_2(x_2 - f_2) - S_1 f_1) \cap \mathring{R}^n_+ \neq \varnothing$$

and

$$(a_1(x_1 - f_1) - S_2 f_2) \cap \mathring{R}^n_+ = \varnothing.$$

In other cases we shall say the game ends in a draw.

Such a game, as described above, is called a *game of survival* or a *qualitative game*,[5] Games in extensive or normal form are called *games of degree.* It is possible, however, to associate a payoff function with a game of survival and to define the function so as to make that game equivalent to a game of degree. In the example, the payoff function of the first player can be defined in terms of the states of the models as

$$H(y_1, y_2) = \begin{cases} +1 & \text{if } \ y_1 \in \mathring{R}^n_+ \quad \text{and} \quad y_2 \in R^n_+ \backslash \mathring{R}^n_+, \\ -1 & \text{if } \ y_1 \in R^n_+ \backslash \mathring{R}^n_+ \quad \text{and} \quad y_2 \in \mathring{R}^n_+, \\ \ \ 0, & \text{otherwise,} \end{cases}$$

where y_i is a state of the model M_i, $i = 1, 2$, after damage exchange and the set $R^n_+ \backslash \mathring{R}^n_+$ is the relative complement of $\mathring{R}^n_+$ in R^n_+. Therefore, $R^n_+ \backslash \mathring{R}^n_+$ is the set of all nonnegative vectors which have at least one zero component. This game is a game of degree. Obviously, with such a payoff function, it is equivalent to the game of survival (kind) previously defined. These games

[5] A game of kind in Isaacs' terminology.

can also be reduced to their normal forms by defining the players' sets of pure strategies, T_i, $i = 1, 2$. Let the set of pure strategies of the first player be

$$T_1 = \{(u_1, f_1): x_1 - f_1 = A_1 u_1; 0 \leq f_1 \leq A_1 u_1; u_1 \in R_+^m\},$$

i.e., each strategy of the first player is a pair of moves: f_1, the tactical move, and u_1, the economic (control) move. Similarly, for the second player

$$T_2 = \{(u_2, f_2): x_2 - f_2 = A_2 u_2; 0 \leq f_2 \leq A_2 u_2; u_2 \in R_+^n\}.$$

Having (u_1, f_1) and (u_2, f_2) defined in sets T_1 and T_2, respectively, $y_1 = (B_1 u_1 - S_2 f_2)^+$ and $y_2 = (B_2 u_2 - S_1 f_1)^+$. Moreover, the payoff function, which is defined above, can be used to define a new payoff function in terms of the pure strategies of both players, namely,

$$H((B_1 u_1 - S_2 f_2)^+, (B_2 u_2 - S_1 f_1)^+) = \tilde{H}((u_1, f_1), (u_2, f_2)),$$

where $\tilde{H}: T_1 \times T_2 \to R$. Therefore, the game acquires the normal form.

In the one-dimensional case, we know that the technology mappings are

$$a_i(x) = \{y_i: 0 \leq y_i \leq \alpha_i x_i; \alpha_i \geq 0; x_i \geq 0\}, \qquad i = 1, 2,$$

where α_i is the growth factor of model M_i. Then

$$y_1 = \max(\alpha_1(x_1 - f_1) - S_2 f_2, 0),$$
$$y_2 = \max(\alpha_2(x_2 - f_2) - S_1 f_1, 0),$$

where $0 \leq f_i \leq x_i$, $i = 1, 2$. The payoff function $H(y_1, y_2)$ is depicted in Figure 4.2.1. The function $H(y_1, y_2) = 0$ in the positive orthant $\mathring{R}_{\text{I}}^2$ and at the origin. $H(y_1, y_2) = 1$ on the y_1 axis and $H(y_1, y_2)\lambda = -1$ on the y_2 axis. Theorem 4.1.3 does not apply to this case since $H((u_1, f_1), (u_2, f_2))$ is not continuous and even the sets of optimal answers are not closed and the answer mappings are not u.h.c. So in order for this case to satisfy the assumptions of Theorem 4.1.3, the function H, while its properties are preserved, should be replaced by a continuous function $\tilde{H}$. Therefore, in the one-dimensional case, $\tilde{H}$ may take the form

$$H(y_1, y_2) = \frac{(2\varepsilon - \min(y_1, \varepsilon) - \min(y_2, \varepsilon))}{\varepsilon} f(y_1 - y_2),$$

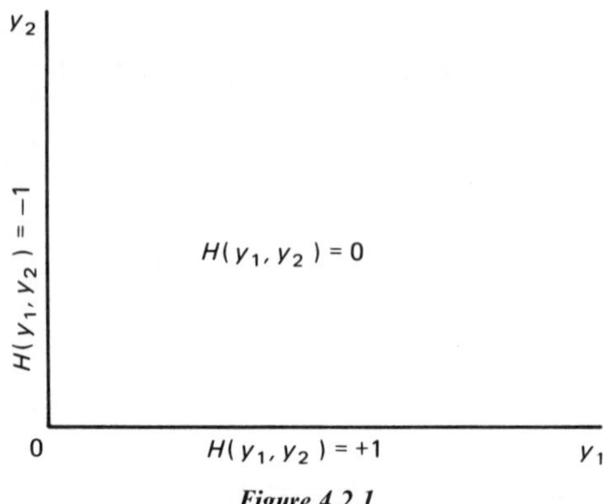

Figure 4.2.1

where $f(\cdot)$ is a continuous function of R^1 to R^1. The function $f(\cdot)$ may be defined as

$$f(x) = \begin{cases} +1 & \text{if } x > +\varepsilon, \\ \dfrac{1}{\varepsilon}x & \text{if } -\varepsilon \leq x \leq \varepsilon, \\ -1 & \text{if } x < -\varepsilon, \end{cases}$$

and x is substituted for $y_1 - y_2$.

A graph of $f(x)$ is depicted in Figure 4.2.2.

If $y_1 \geq \varepsilon$ and $y_2 = 0$, then $f(y_1) = 1$, and hence $\tilde{H}(y_1, y_2) = 1$. Similarly, if $y_1 = 0$ and $y_2 \geq \varepsilon$, then $f(-y_2) = -1$ and $\tilde{H}(y_1, y_2) = -1$. If $y_1 \geq \varepsilon$ and $y_2 \geq \varepsilon$, then $\tilde{H}(y_1, y_2) = 0$. In other cases (i.e., the transition states of

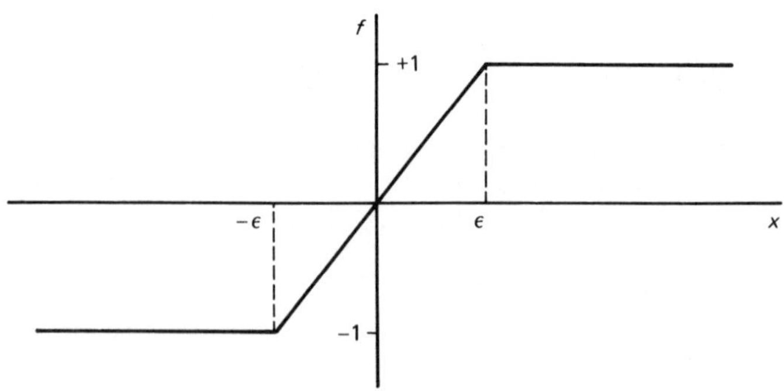

Figure 4.2.2

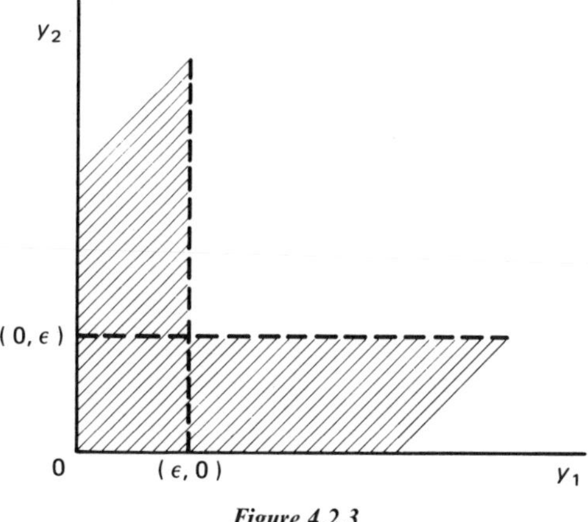

Figure 4.2.3

(y_1, y_2) in the shaded area in Figure 4.2.3), the function $\tilde{H}(y_1, y_2)$ takes on values in the interval $[1, -1]$ and is continuous whereas $H(y_1, y_2)$ is not.

Therefore, since $\tilde{H}$ is continuous, all the assumptions of Theorem 4.1.3. (i.e., existence theorem) are now satisfied. Hence the game $(T_1, T_2, \tilde{H})$ has a solution in mixed strategies.

Note that Theorem 4.1.3 provides only sufficient conditions for the existence of a solution. However, a solution of the game $(T_1, T_2, \tilde{H})$ exists even if the payoff function $H(y_1, y_2)$ is not continuous (Krass, 1978).

PART

II

Difference Games

CHAPTER

5

Difference Games with Constant Control Sets

Among all games that generally describe conflict situations, it is convenient to consider a special class known as difference games. These games describe dynamic conflicts, i.e., conflicts that develop from stage to stage. These stages are usually considered as moments of time at which players make decisions.

This chapter begins with definitions of a difference game, the control sets of players, and behavioral and general strategies. These definitions will be discussed in Section 5.1. The existence of optimal behavioral strategies in finite difference games will also be established in that section.

Finite difference games are not ideal for describing conflict in economics. Infinite difference games, however, are very difficult to employ. Therefore, in Section 5.2 we shall describe a special class of difference games, continuous difference games with constant control sets. These games are suitable for describing conflicts between two economies that have constant supply during the game. For these games, we shall prove that optimal behavioral and general strategies exist and that the values of the game evaluated at these strategies coincide.

5.1 STRATEGIES AND CONTROL SETS

In a two-person game in extensive form, as discussed in Sections 1.1 and 1.2, the moves, or vertices, of that game are divided into the players' sets

S_i, $i = 1, 2$, and $j = 1, 2, \ldots, m_i$. Let us suppose that Γ is a game of two players in extensive form and the chance set $S_0 = \varnothing$ (i.e., no chance moves). If all followers of any vertex $s \in S_i$ belong to the set S_j, where $i \neq j$ and $i, j = 1, 2$, then Γ is called a *two-person general difference game*.

In addition, for every information set S_i^j, $i = 1, 2$, and $j = 1, 2, \ldots, m_i$, of a game in extensive form, there is an index set I_i^j and a one-to-one mapping of I_i^j onto the followers of every $s \in S_i^j$. In this chapter we shall assume that any information set S_i^j in a difference game will be represented by a number j_i, which will be termed the jth *state* of the ith player. In the two-person difference game Γ, the set I_i^j is denoted as $U_i(j_i)$, $i = 1, 2$, or just $U(j_1)$ for the first player and $V(j_2)$ for the second player, $j_i = 1, 2, \ldots, m_i$. The set $U_i(j_i)$ is called a *control set* of the ith player in the jth state. If $I_i^j = I_i$ (i.e., the number of moves is the same at any vertex of any information set of the ith player), or in a difference game notation $U_i(j_i) = U_i$ (i.e., the control set of the ith player does not depend on the jth state of that player), the game is called *a game with a constant control set.*

Example 5.1.1 Consider the game tree of an antagonistic difference game, as depicted in Figure 5.1.1. In this game, the first player has two information sets S_1^1 and S_1^2, or, in difference game notation 1_1 and 2_1, respectively. S_1^1 contains only one element, the initial vertex of the tree. The second player has only one information set S_2^1 (i.e., 1_2). Then Figure 5.1.1 depicts a game with a constant control set because $U_i = \{\text{H, L}\} = \{1, 2\}$, $i = 1, 2$.

A pure strategy in the difference game Γ is defined in a way similar to the definition of a pure strategy in a game in extensive form (see Section 1.2) and is called a *behavioral strategy* by convention. Then, adopting the notation of control sets, a behavioral strategy of the ith player in the difference game Γ is a mapping u_i of $\{S_i^j\}$ into $\{U_i(j_i)\}$ such that $u_i(S_i^j) \in U_i(j_i)$ or $u_i(j_i) \in U_i(j_i)$.

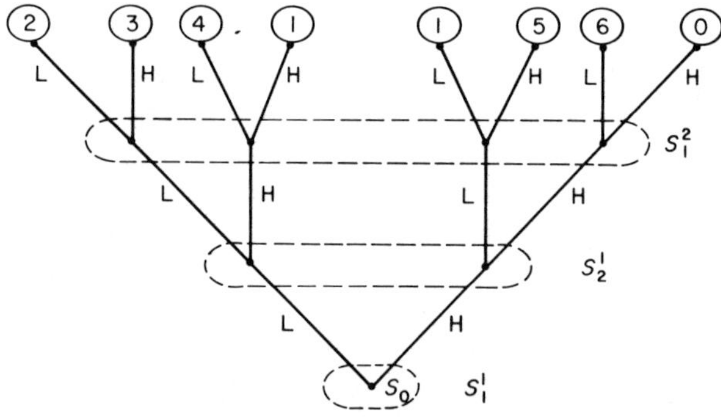

Figure 5.1.1

Accordingly, a *mixed behavioral strategy* of the ith player in the difference game Γ is a mapping v_i of $\{S_i^j\}$ into $\{\Pi_i(U_i(j_i))\}$ such that $v_i(S_i^j) \in \Pi_i(U_i(j_i))$ or $v_i(j_i) \in \Pi_i(U_i(j_i))$. In other words, the ith player makes his/her choice on every information set S_i^j with the probability distribution $v_i(j_i)$. As in Section 1.2, given a vector of mixed behavioral strategies of the first and second players, $v = (v_1, v_2)$, the probability of going to the terminal vertex x is $p_v(x)$. Then the expected payoff of the ith player in mixed behavioral strategies is defined as

$$H_i(v) = \sum_{x \in E} p_v(x) f_i(x),$$

where E is the set of terminal vertices and $f_i(x)$ is the payoff of the ith player at the vertex x.

However, in games in extensive form, it is assumed at least implicitly that each player considers all stages of moves from the first to the last (i.e., all possible pure strategies). In this case the number of pure strategies may be astronomical and any attempt to enumerate them will be discouraging. In the difference game Γ, this issue is simplified because Γ evolves stage by stage beginning from the initial positions (i.e., states) of the players. If, for example, at the initial stage the initial state belongs to the first player's set S_1, then by the definition of difference games, the game Γ evolves on the game tree to a vertex belonging to the second player's set S_2. After the second player makes a choice, the game again evolves on the tree to the second stage to a vertex in S_1. Therefore, instead of considering all possible strategies, the ith player considers all possible choices of one information set at one stage.

It is now convenient to introduce sets that contain the vertices of the game Γ as it evolves stage by stage. Let Q_i^t be the set of the moves, or vertices, of the ith player at the tth stage, where $t = 1, 2\ \ldots, T_i$ and $i = 1, 2$. So if the initial vertex belongs to the set S_1 and forms the information set S_1^1, then $S_1^1 = Q_1^1$, where Q_1^1 is the set of the first player at the initial stage. All immediate followers of the initial vertex form some information set(s) that are subsets of Q_2^1. Then this process continues stage by stage. If for every S_i^j there exists t such that $S_i^j \subseteq Q_i^t$ or, in difference game notation, $j_i \in Q_i^t$, the game is called *difference game*. The inclusion $S_i^j \subseteq Q_i^t$ means that each player knows the stage of development of the game, i.e. he/she knows time. In Figure 5.1.1, $S_1^1 = Q_1^1$, $S_1^2 = Q_1^2$, and $Q_2^1 = S_2^1$. Moreover, if N is the length of the game Γ (i.e., the largest possible number of vertices), then $T_i \leq N/2$. In Figure 5.1.1, $T_1 = 2$ and $T_2 = 1$.

In order to provide a better insight into how a behavioral strategy of the difference game simplifies the enumeration issue, we shall consider the case in which the control sets are constant. The case of nonconstant control sets is not discussed because it is very cumbersome. Let us suppose that the ith player's pure strategy in the game Γ at the tth stage is denoted as $\tilde{u}_t^i$, which is an element of the ith player's control set, i.e., $\tilde{u}_t^i \in U_i$. Also, $\tilde{u}_t^i$ is the choice of the ith player in the information set $j_i \in Q_i^t$. Then any realization of the game Γ in terms of pure strategies of the ith player may be described as a sequence of elements $\tilde{u}_t^i \in U_i, t = 1, 2, \ldots, T_i$, and $i = 1, 2$. Therefore, instead of considering all possible strategies as is the case in games in extensive form, we can consider all possible choices of one information set at one stage.

Given this process of constructing pure strategies of the ith player (i.e., $\tilde{u}_t^i \in U_i$), we can consider a new game in normal form, $\tilde{\Gamma}$, which we shall call the general form of game Γ. In this game the set of pure strategies of the ith player, T_i is defined as $T_i = U_i \times \cdots \times U_i$, where U_i is multiplied by itself T_i times. In other words, the ith player can choose his/her strategy T_i times independently (i.e., his/her choice does not depend on previous choices for every $t \leq T_i$). Consequently, the pure strategies of the ith player form a sequence $(\tilde{u}_1^i, \tilde{u}_2^i, \ldots, \tilde{u}_{T_i}^i)$. That is, the ith player will use the strategy $\tilde{u}_t^i \in U_i$ as the tth element of his/her sequence whenever his/her position is in the set Q_1^t. If every player makes his/her choice in this manner the chosen strategies uniquely define a payoff for each player. Thus the game $\tilde{\Gamma}$ acquires a general form of the game Γ.

A pure strategy of the ith player in the game $\tilde{\Gamma}$ is called a *general strategy*, and his/her mixed strategy in $\tilde{\Gamma}$ is called a *mixed general strategy*, which is a mapping $\tilde{v}_i$ of the set T_i into $\Pi_i(T_i)$ (i.e., the set of all probability distributions on T_i) such that $\tilde{v}_i(T_i) \in \Pi_i(T_i)$.

The definition of a general strategy of the game $\tilde{\Gamma}$ is very involved if the admissibility of a control set of the ith player depends on his/her specific choice of moves, i.e., if the control sets of the players are not constant. This case will not be discussed here.

In Figure 5.1.1 the first player has four general strategies which are (LL), (LH), (HL), and (HH). Hence the matrix (i.e., normal form) of the general game $\tilde{\Gamma}$ of the difference game Γ is

	L	H
LL	−2	−4
LH	−3	−1
HL	−1	−6
HH	−5	0

.

Accordingly, his/her mixed general strategy is a vector $x = (x_1, x_2, x_3, x_4)$, where $x_j \geq 0$ and $\sum_{j=1}^{4} x_j = 1$. That player's behavioral strategies are $(S_1^1 \to L,\ S_1^2 \to L)$, $(S_1^1 \to L,\ S_1^2 \to H)$, $(S_1^1 \to H,\ S_1^2 \to L)$, $(S_1^1 \to H, S_1^2 \to H)$, and his/her mixed behavioral strategy is a pair (y_1, y_2), where $0 \leq y_j \leq 1$ and y_j is the probability of choosing L when the first player's move is in the information set S_1^j, $j = 1, 2$. Accordingly, there is the corresponding mixed general strategy

$$(y_1 y_2, y_1(1 - y_2), (1 - y_1)y_2, (1 - y_1)(1 - y_2)) \tag{5.1.1}$$

to the chosen mixed behavioral strategy pair (y_1, y_2).

By applying the technique illustrated in Figure 3.2.1 of Section 3.2, the optimal mixed general strategies of the first player is the vector $(0, \frac{5}{7}, \frac{2}{7}, 0)$. It is obvious that there is no mixed behavioral strategy pair of numbers (y_1, y_2) that makes the vector $(0, \frac{5}{7}, \frac{2}{7}, 0)$ conform to relation (5.1.1). This result is due to the first player's complete lack of memory as he/she cannot remember his/her first move when making the second move. This game will be modified in the following example to relax this result.

Example 5.1.2 Consider the game tree illustrated in Figure 5.1.2. In this game the first player remembers his/her first move. If he/she is in the set S_1^2, he/she remembers that his/her first move was L. If he/she is in set S_1^3, he/she remembers that his/her first move was H. In Figure 5.1.2 the relations $Q_1^1 = S_1^1$, $Q_1^2 = S_1^2 \cup S_1^3$, and $Q_2^1 = S_2^1$ do not show equalities between S_i^j and Q_i^t as in Figure 5.1.1. The first player's behavioral strategies are $(S_1^1 \to L,\ S_1^2 \to L)$, $(S_1^1 \to L,\ S_1^2 \to H)$, $(S_1^1 \to H,\ S_1^3 \to L)$, and $(S_1^1 \to H, S_1^3 \to H)$. His/her mixed behavioral strategy is a triple of numbers (y_1, y_2, y_3), where $0 \leq y_j \leq 1$ and y_j is the probability of choosing L in the

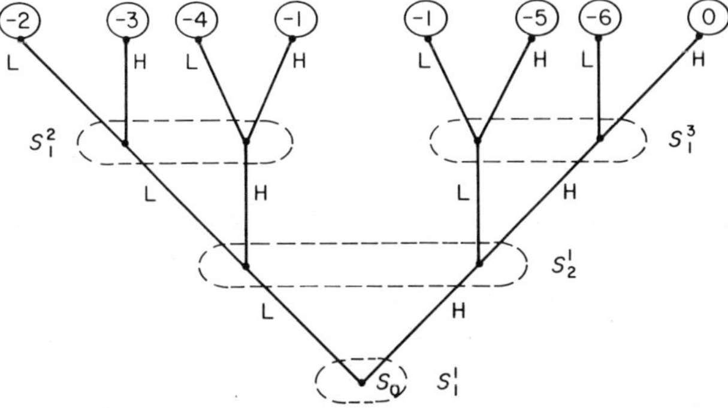

Figure 5.1.2

set S_1^j, $j = 1, 2, 3$. To a given mixed behavioral strategy (y_1, y_2, y_3), there corresponds the mixed general strategy

$$(y_1 y_2, y_1(1 - y_2), (1 - y_1)y_3, (1 - y_1)(1 - y_3)). \tag{5.1.2}$$

The optimal mixed general strategy for the first player can be written in the form (5.1.2). This is done by having $y_1 = \frac{5}{7}$, $y_2 = 0$, and $y_3 = 1$.

It is interesting to note that the general game $\tilde{\Gamma}$ in Examples 5.1.1 and 5.1.2 is the same. This is so because when the game $\tilde{\Gamma}$ is constructed from the game Γ, the structure of information sets in the sets Q_i^t does not affect the general strategies of $\tilde{\Gamma}$.

We shall prove the following existence theorem when the difference game Γ is finite.

Theorem 5.1.1 The finite difference game Γ has a solution in mixed behavioral strategies.

Proof Let us suppose that the set Q_i^t contains n_t^i information sets ($t = 1, 2, \ldots, T$, and $i = 1, 2$), which are enumerated by $j_i^t \in \{1, 2, \ldots, n_t^i\}$. Let us also suppose that the control set $U_i(j_i^t)$ associated with the number j_i^t has $m(j_i^t)$ elements. Any mixed strategy of the ith player at the tth stage is defined by n_t^i probability distributions, i.e., by the vectors $v_1^{it}, v_2^{it}, \ldots, v_{n_t^i}^{it}$ such that the sum of the components of each vector is equal to 1 (sometimes these vectors are called probability vectors). Moreover, the dimension of the vector v_j^{it} is equal to $m(j_i^t)$. We also define $v_i^t = (v_1^{it}, v_2^{it}, \ldots, v_{n_t^i}^{it})$ as a chance move of the ith player at the tth stage. Then v_i^t has the dimension $\sum_{j=1}^{n_t^i} m(j_i^t)$ and n_t^i subvector components. Furthermore, we define $v_i = (v_i^1, v_i^2, \ldots, v_i^{T_i})$, a mixed behavioral strategy vector of the ith player. Given the mixed behavioral strategies of both players, v_1 and v_2, and the terminal vertex z, the probability of going to that terminal vertex $p_{v_1 v_2}(z)$ and the expected payoff in mixed behavioral strategies

$$H(v_1, v_2) = \sum_{z \in E} p_{v_1 v_2}(z) f(z)$$

can be computed, where E is the set of terminal vertices and $f(z)$ is the payoff associated with the vertex z. If $(\bar{v}_1, \bar{v}_2)$ and $(\hat{v}_1, \hat{v}_2)$ are two pairs of strategies of both players, then the payoff H is linearly dependent on the convex combination of any subvector components v_i^t. In particular, let the above two pairs of strategies differ only in the j_0th subvector component of the mixed strategy of the first player, that is, in his/her chance move $v_{j_0}^{1t_0}$, where $j_0 \in \{1, 2, \ldots, n_{t_0}^1\}$. Consequently, the j_0th components of the mixed strategies of the first player, $\bar{v}_1$ and $\hat{v}_1$, are $\bar{v}_{j_0}^{1t_0}$ and $\hat{v}_{j_0}^{1t_0}$, respectively. The other components of these strategies are the same. Let us suppose that the unchanged part of the first player's mixed strategies is denoted by $\tilde{v}_1$. Also let

$$v_1(\lambda) = \lambda\bar{v}_1 + (1-\lambda)\hat{v}_1 \qquad \text{and} \quad v_{j_0}^{1t_0}(\lambda) = \lambda\bar{v}_{j_0}^{1t_0} + (1-\lambda)v_{j_0}^{1t_0},$$

where $\lambda \in [0, 1]$. Note that (by the above assumptions) $\tilde{v}_1(\lambda) = \tilde{v}_1$ (i.e., does not depend on λ) and $v_2 = \hat{v}_2 = \bar{v}_2$ (i.e., v_2 is constant). Then if $v_i(\lambda) = \lambda\bar{v}_i + (1-\lambda)\hat{v}_i$, $i = 1, 2$, the expected payoff is

$$\begin{aligned} H(v_1(\lambda), v_2(\lambda)) &= A(\tilde{v}_1, v_2)v_{j_0}^{1t_0}(\lambda) + B(\tilde{v}_1, v_2)(1 - v_{j_0}^{1t_0}(\lambda)) \\ &= \lambda\{A(\tilde{v}_1, v_2)\bar{v}_{j_0}^{1t_0} + B(\tilde{v}_1, v_2)(1 - \bar{v}_{j_0}^{1t_0})\} \\ &\quad + (1-\lambda)\{A(\tilde{v}_1, v_2)\hat{v}_{j_0}^{1t_0} + B(\tilde{v}_1, v_2)(1 - \hat{v}_{j_0}^{1t_0})\} \\ &= \lambda H(\bar{v}_1, \bar{v}_2) + (1-\lambda)H(\hat{v}_1, \hat{v}_2), \end{aligned}$$

where $A(\tilde{v}_1, v_2)$ and $B(\tilde{v}_1, v_2)$ are the parts of the payoff H that depend on $\tilde{v}_1$ and v_2, which are the parts of the mixed behavioral strategies of both players which, by assumption, have not been changed.

Now we can define the sets of optimal answers of the players on all fixed parts of mixed behavioral strategies of these players, excluding $v_{j_0}^{1t_0}$, the subvector component of the ith player on the tth stage, where $j_0 \in \{1, 2, \ldots, n_t^i\}$, $t = 1, 2, \ldots, T_i$, and $i = 1, 2$. It follows from above that these sets are convex-valued and, obviously, are closed. Also, the optimal answer mappings are u.h.c. [which follows from the continuity of the functions $A(\tilde{v}_1, v_2)$ and $B(\tilde{v}_1, v_2)$]. Then we can use the same reasoning developed in Theorem 4.1.3 and conclude with the help of the Kakutani theorem that the game Γ has a solution in mixed behavioral strategies. Q.E.D.

In the difference game Γ, solutions are computed by going backward from the terminal vertex to the initial vertex. Therefore, in Example 5.1.1 at the first stage the mixed behavioral strategy of the first player is fixed as y_1, i.e., the probability of L being taken by the first player at the first stage. The probability of L being chosen by the first player at the second stage is fixed at y_2. Similarly, for the second player. Then at the second stage both players will have a game in normal form, which is defined by the payoff matrix

	L	H
L	$-2y_1 - (1-y_1)$	$-4y_1 - 6(1-y_1)$
H	$-3y_1 - 5(1-y_1)$	$-y_1 - 0(1-y_1)$

,

where L and H are possibly pure strategies of the player. At the first entry of the matrix, both players choose L. Then the first player has two possible directions to follow. He/she can follow the first direction by choosing L with probability y_1 and hence can gain $-2y_1$ as a payoff. He/she can also take the second direction by choosing H with probability $(1 - y_1)$, realizing $-(1 - y_1)$ as a payoff. Then, at this entry, the first player's average payoff is $-2y_1 - (1 - y_1)$. Other entries of the payoff matrix can be computed similarly. By applying the techniques described in Section 3.2, the optimal strategies of the first player in this game are computed as $(\frac{1}{2}, \frac{1}{2})$ and the value of the game is $V = -(3 - \frac{1}{2}y_1)$. If $\bar{y}_1$ maximizes V, then $\bar{y}_1 = 1$ (i.e., at the first stage the first player is better off by choosing L with probability 1) and $\bar{V} = -2.5$.

Let us define $\tilde{V}$ as the value of the game $\tilde{\Gamma}$ (i.e., $\tilde{V}$ can be attained by mixed general strategies) and V as the value of the game Γ (i.e., V is attained by mixed behavioral strategies). The value of the game $\tilde{\Gamma}$ exists by Theorem 4.1.3 applied to finite game whereas the value of the game Γ exists by Theorem 5.1.1. In general, $\tilde{V} \neq V$. However, $V < \tilde{V}$ if the second player's set of mixed behavioral strategies coincides with his/her set of mixed general strategies and if the set of mixed behavioral strategies of the first player is of smaller dimension than his/her set of mixed general strategies. The latter may happen because by the definitions of mixed behavioral strategies of the first player, v_1, and of his/her mixed general strategies $\tilde{v}_1$, any v_1 can be realized as one of $\tilde{v}_1$. In Example 5.1.1 the second player's sets of strategies in the game Γ do not change after switching to the game $\tilde{\Gamma}$, but the first player's set of mixed general strategies is of greater dimension than his/her set of mixed behavioral strategies in the game Γ. Hence, in that example, $V = -2.5 < \tilde{V} = -2.43$.

In conclusion, since by Theorem 5.1.1 the game Γ has a solution in mixed behavioral strategies and the game $\tilde{\Gamma}$ has a solution in mixed general strategies, then if $V = \tilde{V}$, we say that the game Γ has a "full" solution. In Example 5.1.2, $V = \tilde{V}$. In Section 5.2 we shall show that under certain assumptions the existence of a "full" solution of a difference game is not accidental.

5.2 CONTINUOUS DIFFERENCE GAMES WITH CONSTANT CONTROL SETS

In Section 5.1 the information sets S_i^j were represented by numbers j_i, the jth state of the ith player. It was also assumed in that section that players make moves in turn and by stage. Then there exists a stage t such that the ith player's information set j_i^1 belongs to the set Q_i^t, and that player's control set at that stage is denoted as $U_i(j_i^t)$. Therefore, if the first player is entitled to the first move, he/she will make a move in the information set $j_1^1 \in Q_1^1$ and will make a choice in the control set $U_1(j_1^1)$. Then the second player makes his/her move in $j_2^1 \in Q_2^1$ and a choice in $U_2(j_2^1)$. This process continues stage by stage.

In this section we shall assume that the information sets in the game Γ will be represented by an n-dimensional vector of parameters, which will be called the *state* of the game. The nature and the dimension of this vector are defined by the "nature" of the conflict situation, which is mathematically described by a difference game. The determination of what kind of parameters should be used in specific situations is not within the realm of game theory, but is a "metatheory" question, and the decision depends only on the scientist (e.g., operations researcher) who must find a solution for the conflict situation using his/her judgment and experience. So in Example 1.1.1 (elementary poker) the information sets of the first player are described by a pair of numbers (α, β), where $\alpha \in \{1, 2, 3\}$, standing for the number of a card and $\beta \in \{1, 2\}$, standing for the number of the first player's move. However, we can only say that for every information set of the ith player j_i, there is one and only one state for that player $x(j_i)$. Therefore, we can use the parameters to describe information sets at every stage of the game. Let us define $x(j_i^t) = x_t^i$, $i = 1, 2$, where x_t^i is a vector of parameters describing the ith player's information set j_i^t at the tth stage. Then at the tth stage the ith player makes choices in his/her control set $U_i(x_t^i)$, $i = 1, 2$.

Next we shall consider possible connections between the information sets of both players at a given stage t. Let us suppose that the initial vertex belongs to the set S_1 (i.e., the first player makes the first move). Moreover, let x_{jt}^i stand for the jth information set of the ith player at the tth stage, where $jt = 1, 2, \ldots, n_t^i, i = 1, 2, t = 1, 2, \ldots$, and n_t^i is the number of information sets of the ith player at the tth stage. There are many possible sets of connections between the information sets of the first player and those of the second player, including those depicted in Figure 5.2.1. In this figure we schematically depict the sets Q_t of two possible difference games at stage t. Panel (a) depicts the set Q_t of one game that has $n_t^1 = 3$ and $n_t^2 = 4$. Panel (b) depicts the set Q_t of the other game with $n_t^1 = n_t^2 = 3$. The arrows represent a part of the branches of the game tree and connect the information sets of the players x_{jt}^i, $i = 1, 2$. Therefore, the major difference between panel (a) and panel (b) lies in the number of information sets accrued to the second player as a result of the moves made by the first player at some stage t.

In panel (a), by knowing the game tree (because every player knows the rules of the game at the onset) and by knowing the information sets he/she is going to, the second player can ascertain the moves made by the first player at the same stage t. For instance, if the second player is going to x_{1t}^2, then that player can identify those moves that originated from x_{1t}^1 and directed toward x_{1t}^2, in contrast to those directed toward x_{2t}^2. Thus at this stage the second player has an information advantage over the first player. Games with a tree

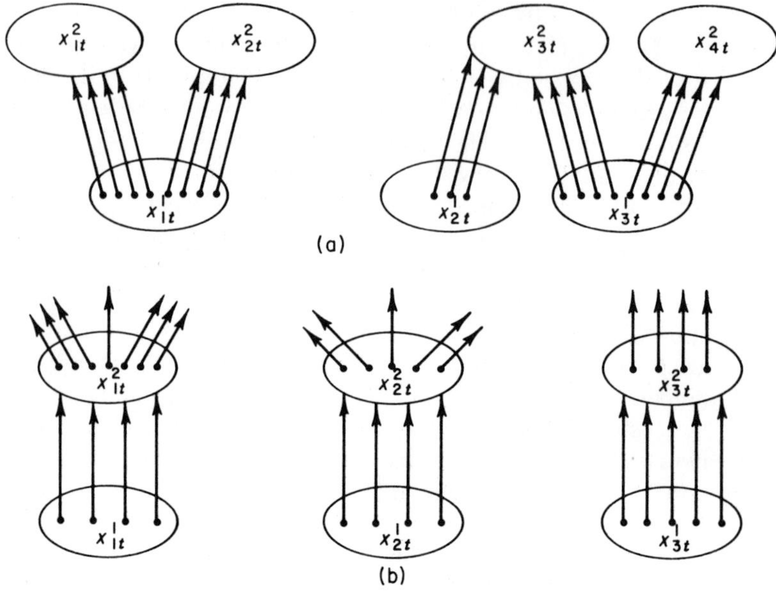

Figure 5.2.1

structure like that depicted in panel (a) are called games with discrimination at the tth stage (a more strict definition will be forthcoming).

In panel (b) the second player cannot ascertain the moves made by the first player at the given stage t, but he/she can get information about the first player's moves made at previous stages (i.e., $t^1 < t$). This follows from the one-to-one correspondence between information sets of both players (i.e., at stage t both players have an equal number of information sets).

The two-person difference games with one-to-one correspondence between the information sets of both players at every stage are called *games without discrimination.* Thus games that lack the correspondence are called *games with discrimination.* In the following discussion, only games without discrimination will be considered.

Noting that due to the one-to-one correspondence between information sets of the players, one can describe information sets using one vector x_{jt}, instead of two vectors x^1_{jt} and x^2_{jt}, where $jt = 1, 2, \ldots, n_t$ (because $n^1_t = n^2_t = n_t$ by the correspondence property). A typical tree of a difference game without discrimination is depicted in Figure 5.2.2. In this figure the game proceeds for two stages ($t = 1, 2$).

At the initial stage ($t = 1$) there are two information sets: one for each player, i.e., $n^1_1 = n^2_1 = n_1 = 1$. The pair of information sets is represented by one state x_1. At $t = 2$ there are three different pairs of information sets

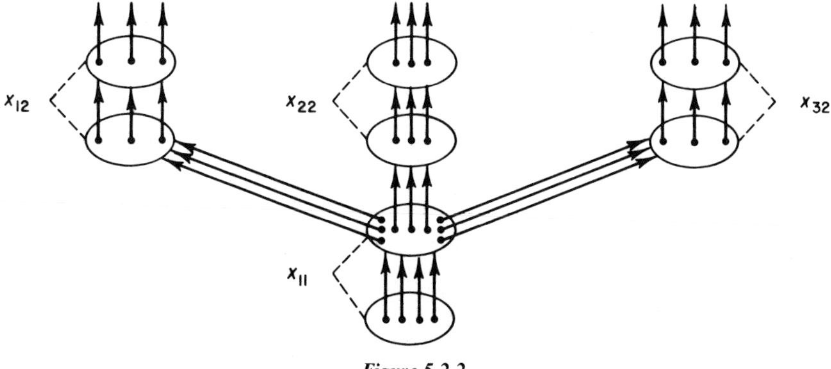

Figure 5.2.2

($n_2^1 = n_2^2 = n_2 = 3$) such that every one of the pairs is represented by the state x_{j2} ($j2 = 1, 2, 3$). Therefore, if the game (without discrimination) proceeds to T stages, the length of the game tree is $2T$. Also, two different versions in extensive form can be constructed, having the same rules as this game. This can be done by constructing two different trees. In the first tree the first player makes the first move and then proceeds on the tree to the end. That gives us the first version of this game in extensive form. The second tree is constructed by giving the second player the right to the first move, continuing on until the game is terminated. Therefore, we have the second version of this game in extensive form. This is again due to the one-to-one correspondence property.

Thus in games without discrimination both players have information only about the state of the game at the tth stage but not about each other's moves, as no player informs the other of his/her chosen move at that stage. However, at the $(t + 1)$th stage, these chosen moves lead to the formation of the state x_{t+1}, which players become familiar with. It is also required that moves at the tth stage be parameterized such that the moves chosen by the first player will be represented by the control vector $u \in R^m$ and those chosen by the second player will be represented by the control vector $w \in R^n$. Then at the tth stage $u_t \in U_1(x_t^1)$ and $w_t \in U_2(x_t^2)$. (For convenience, we shall drop the subscript t from these control vectors.)

Finally, the relation between the states x_t and x_{t+1} of the game may be written in the form

$$x_{t+1} = f_t(x_t, u, w), \tag{5.2.1}$$

where

$$u \in U_1(x_t), \qquad w \in U_2(x_t) \qquad \text{and} \quad t = 0, 1, 2, \ldots.$$

Example 5.2.1 Relation (5.2.1) can be applied to the von Neumann model of conflict interaction discussed in Section 4.2 by describing the continuation of conflict between M_1 and M_2 with time as

$$\begin{aligned} x_{t+1}^1 &= (B_1 u_1 - S_2 f_2)^+, \\ x_{t+1}^2 &= (B_2 u_2 - S_1 f_1)^+, \end{aligned} \tag{5.2.2}$$

where $U_i(x_t^1, x_t^2) = U_i(x_t^i) = \{(u_i, f_i) : x_t^i = A_i u_i - f_i;\ u_i \geq 0; f_i \geq 0\}$, A_i and B_i are the input and output matrices of model M_i, S_i is the interaction matrix of model M_i, and $B_i u_i = y_i$ for $i = 1, 2$.

Comparing relation (5.2.1) with this example, the state $x_t = (x_t^1, x_t^2)$, where x_t^i is the state of the ith model at the tth stage; the control vector $u = (u_1, f_1)$, where u_1 is the intensity vector of the model M_1 and f_1 is its inputs transferred to its military industry to annihilate the resources of M_2. Similarly for M_2, the control vector $w = (u_2, f_2)$. Thus each model has a continuum of control vectors (u_i, f_i), and the state of the game x_t is continuous.

For similicity we shall now consider only games that terminate exactly after T stages or games with finite length such that all vertices of the game tree that come after the $(T - 1)$ stages [i.e., $2(T - 1)$ steps on the tree] are terminal. These terminal vertices are also assumed to be described by a vector $x_T \in R^n$. Then relation (5.2.1) becomes

$$x_T = f_{T-1}(x_{T-1}, u, w),$$

where

$$u \in U_1(x_{T-1}), \qquad w \in U_2(x_{T-1}).$$

Since the game is antagonistic, the ith players payoff is defined by the function H: $R^n \to R$ such that $H(x_T)$ is the payoff associated with the terminal vertex x_T.

The game Γ is said to be a *continuous difference game with constant control set* (d.g.c.c.) if $U_i(x_t) = U_i$ and f and H are continuous functions, $i = 1, 2$. Example (5.2.1) would be an example of the d.g.c.c. Γ if the payoff function is continuous and in relations (5.2.2) the volumes of production of both models are constant and only the tactical moves $f_i, i = 1, 2$, are modified, as will be explained later.

Example 5.2.2 Let us consider two economies, each having constant production (i.e., the production set of the ith economy does not depend on inputs and can be described by N_i, which is a nonnegative n-tuple of constant levels of commodities available at the beginning of the conflict and which stays constant thereafter). S_1 and S_2 are interaction matrices and are defined as in Example 5.2.1. The tactical move vectors f_i at the tth stage are modified to become equal to the component[1] product $\phi^i \cdot x_t^i$, where $\phi^i = (\phi_1^i, \ldots, \phi_j^i, \ldots, \phi_n^i)$ and $0 \leq \phi_j^i \leq 1$. The vector ϕ^i represents the intensity of using the tth stage output x_t^i for the tactical moves. Then this conflict can be described as

$$\begin{aligned} x_{t+1}^1 &= (N_1 - S_2(\phi^2 \cdot x_t^2))^+, \\ x_{t+1}^2 &= (N_2 - S_1(\phi^1 \cdot x_t^1))^+, \\ 0 \leq \phi^i \leq I, \qquad & t = 0, 1, \ldots, T, \qquad \text{and} \quad i = 1, 2, \end{aligned} \tag{5.2.3}$$

where I is a vector whose components are equal to one and 0 is the zero vector.

There are two possible explanations for the occurrence of the constancy of products in relations (5.2.3). First, the conflict takes so little time that the two economies can use only the stock made before the start of the confrontation. This case may be termed "blitzkrieg." The second explanation is that the conflict is restricted to a part of each country (i.e., the frontier) but the rest of the territory supplies the confrontation zone with all commodities at the same constant level. This case can be dubbed "border war."

If the payoff function $H(x_T)$ is defined as in the static case of Section 4.2, i.e.,

$$H(x_T) = H(x_T^1, x_T^2) = \begin{cases} +1 & \text{if} \quad x_T^1 \in \mathring{R}_+^n \quad \text{and} \quad x_T^2 \in R_+^n \setminus \mathring{R}_+^n, \\ -1 & \text{if} \quad x_T^2 \in \mathring{R}_+^n \quad \text{and} \quad x_T^1 \in R_+^n \setminus \mathring{R}_+^n, \\ 0, & \text{otherwise,} \end{cases}$$

Example 5.2.2 will not be an example of a d.g.c.c. because $H(x_T)$ is not continuous. This problem can overcome by replacing $H(x_T)$ with a continuous function $\tilde{H}(x_T)$ defined similarly to $\tilde{H}(y_1, y_2)$ in Section 4.2.

As in Section 5.1, we shall consider the general form $\tilde{\Gamma}$ of the game Γ. The sequences $\{\tilde{u}_t\}_{t=0}^{t=T}$, where $\tilde{u}_t \in U_1$, and $\{\tilde{w}_t\}_{t=0}^{t=T}$, where $\tilde{w}_t \in U_2$, define the general strategies of the first and second players, respectively, in the game $\tilde{\Gamma}$. By the same token, the behavioral strategies of the first and second players in the game Γ are defined by the sequences $\{u_t\}_{t=0}^{t=T}$, where u_t is a function of R^n into U_1, and $\{w^t\}$, where w^t is a function of R^n into U_2. Accordingly, the sequence $\{v_t\}_{t=0}^{t=T}$, where v_t is a function of R^n into $\pi_1(U_1)$, and $\{\mu_t\}_{t=0}^{t=T}$, where μ is a function of R^n into $\pi_2(U_2)$, are the mixed behavioral strategies of the first and second players, respectively, in the game Γ. However, the mixed general

[1] If $x = (x_1, \ldots, x_n)$, $y = (y_1, \ldots, y_n)$ are two vectors, the component product of them $z = x \cdot y$ of these vectors is a vector $z = (z_1, \ldots, z_n)$ such that $z_i = x_i \cdot y_i$, $i = 1, \ldots, n$.

strategies of the game $\tilde{\Gamma}$ can be obtained by probabilistically mixing the elements of the set $(U_i)^T$ (i.e., $U_i \times \cdots \times U_i$ by T times).

Given the mixed behavioral strategies $\{v_t\}_{t=0}^{t=T}$ and $\{\mu_t\}_{t=0}^{T}$ of the first and second players, respectively, the payoff function of the first player is defined by going backward stage by stage. Here, at the tth stage, the state of the game is x_t and the first player's payoff is defined as

$$H_t(x_t) = \int_{U \times V} H_{t+1}\{f_t(x_y, \tilde{u}, \tilde{w})\}\, dv_t\, d\mu_t, \tag{5.2.4}$$

where $t = 1, 2, \ldots, T$. At the initial stage, the initial state is x_0 and the payoff is $H_1(x_0)$. At the terminal stage T, the terminal state is x_T and the terminal payoff is $H_{T+1}(x_T) = H(x_T)$. Note that $H_{t+1}(x_{t+1})$ in relations (5.2.4) is the first player's payoff when $(T + 1 - t)$ stages have elapsed. Once the player knows the payoff $H_{t+1}(x_{t+1})$, he/she tries to ascertain his/her payoff at the tth stage given his/her general strategy $\tilde{u}_t$ and the opponent's general strategy $\tilde{w}_t$, chosen with probabilities v_t and μ_t as their mixed strategies, respectively.

Before proving the next theorem, we recall the following fact on integrals.

Let f be a function of the product $U \times V$ into R, where the sets U and V are compact in R^m. Given any $u_n \in U$ and $w \in V$, then

$$\int_V f(x_0, u_n, w)\, dv_n \to \int_V f(x_0, u_0, w)\, dv_0$$

for any $u_n \to u_0$ and $v_n \xrightarrow{w} v_0$ if f is continuous. This fact follows from fact (iii) on measure space in Section 4.1.

In the proof of the theorem, we consider μ_n as an atomic measure concentrated in u_n, and μ_0 concentrated in u_0.[2] Then given any $u_n \in U$, $u_n \to u_0$ implies $\mu_n \xrightarrow{w} \mu_0$.

Theorem 5.2.1 The d.g.c.c. always has a solution in mixed behavioral strategies.

Proof Let us suppose that the initial state of the game Γ is x_0, but the stages are considered from $t = 1$. Also, let T be the length of the game Γ and $H_T(x_0)$ be the payoff function of the ith player in the game Γ which begins from the initial state x_0 and proceeds to no more than T stages. The proof is by induction on T. The induction hypothesis is that $H_T(x_0)$ is continuous in

[2] μ_n is an atomic measure defined on $U \subset R^m$ and concentrated in $u_n \in U$ if $\mu_n(U) = \mu(\{u_n\}) = 1$.

x_0, and the game, which is of length T, has a solution in mixed behavioral strategies.

Let Γ have length 1 (i.e., $T = 1$). If the first and second players take pure behavioral strategies u and w, respectively, then the payoff function is

$$H_1(x_1) = H\{f_1(x_0, u, w)\},$$

where x_0 is the initial state of the game. Note that $H\{f_1(x_0, u, w)\}$ is continuous in behavioral strategies u and w by the assumptions of the theorem and x_0 is constant since $T = 1$. Therefore, the existence of a solution in mixed behavioral strategies, denoted by $\bar{\nu}_1(x_0)$ and $\bar{\mu}_1(x_0)$, follows from Theorem 4.1.3. So we have to prove that the payoff function

$$H_1(x_0) = \int_{U_1 \times V_2} H_2\{f_1(x_0, u, w)\}\, d\bar{\nu}_1\,(x_0)\, \bar{\mu}_1(x_0)$$

is continuous in x_0, where $\bar{\nu}_1(x_0)$ and $\bar{\mu}_1(x_0)$ are optimal behavioral strategies of the first and second players, respectively, at the first state in the game Γ which has x_0 as the initial state and $H_2(x_2) = H(x_2)$. Then the payoff satisfies the inequalities

$$\begin{aligned}\int_{U_1 \times U_2} H_2\{f_1(x_0, u, w)\}\, d\nu_1\, d\bar{\mu}_1 &\le \int_{U_1 \times U_2} H_2\{f_1(x_0, u, w)\}\, d\bar{\nu}_1\, d\bar{\mu}_1\\ &\le \int_{U_1 \times U_2} H_2\{f_1(x_0, u, w)\}\, d\tilde{\nu}_1\, d\mu_1 \qquad (5.2.5)\end{aligned}$$

for any $\nu_1 \in \pi_1(U_1)$ and $\mu_1 \in \pi_2(U_2)$. Let us suppose that $x_n \to x_0$. Then by fact (iv) of Section 4.1, we can assume that

$$\nu_1(x_n) \xrightarrow{w} \bar{\nu}_1 \qquad \text{and} \quad \mu_1(x_n) \xrightarrow{w} \bar{\mu}_1$$

since the sets $\pi_1(U_1)$ and $\pi_2(U_2)$ are compact. Hence, for every n,

$$\begin{aligned}&\int_{U_1 \times U_2} H_2\{f_1(x_n, u, w)\}\, d\nu_1\, d\mu_1\,(x_n)\\ &\quad\le \int_{U_1 \times U_2} H_2\{f_1(x_n, u, w)\}\, d\nu_1\,(x_n)\, d\mu_1\,(x_n)\\ &\quad\le \int_{U_1 \times U_2} H_2\{f_1(x_n, u, w)\}\, d\nu_1\,(x_n)\, d\mu_1 \qquad (5.2.6)\end{aligned}$$

for every $\nu_1 \in \pi_1(U_1)$ and every $\mu_1 \in \pi_2(U_2)$. Then by taking the limit of inequalities (5.2.6), we have proved inequalities (5.2.5). Then

$$H_1(x_0) = \int_{U_1 \times U_2} H_2\{f_1(x_n, u, w)\}\, d\nu_1\,(x_n)\, d\mu_1\,(x_n) \rightarrow$$

$$\bar{H}_1(x_0) = \int_{U_1 \times U_2} H_2\{f_1(x_0, u, w)\}\, d\bar{\nu}_1\, d\bar{\mu}_1$$

and $(\bar{\nu}, \bar{\mu})$ is a saddle point of the game Γ as required.

Now let the game have length $T + 1$. As the first move is made, the game will have a length T. Then by the induction hypothesis, we say that the payoff function $H_2(x_1)$ exists, where x_1 is the state of the game at the second stage and the payoff $H_2(x_1)$ is a value in the game which begins from x_1 and proceeds to T stages. Therefore, for the final solution of the game with $T + 1$ stages we must now consider the game $\langle U_1, U_2, H\{f_1(x_0, u, w)\}\rangle$.

By the induction hypothesis, $H_2(x_1)$ is continuous and this game has a solution in mixed behavioral strategies, i.e., $\bar{\nu}_1(x_0)$ and $\bar{\mu}_1(x_0)$. These strategies together with the strategies existing by induction (i.e., $\{\bar{\nu}_2(\cdot), \ldots, \bar{\nu}_{T+1}(\cdot)\}$ and $\{\bar{\mu}_2(\cdot), \ldots, \bar{\mu}_{T+1}(\cdot)\}$) form the optimal behavioral strategies (solution) of the game Γ (i.e., $\{\bar{\nu}_1(\cdot), \ldots, \bar{\nu}_{T+1}(\cdot)\}$ and $\{\bar{\mu}_1(\cdot), \ldots, \bar{\mu}_{T+1}(\cdot)\}$). Q.E.D.

Theorem 5.2.1 also applies to nonantagonistic difference games.

Corollary Every nonantagonistic d.g.c.c. has a solution in mixed behavioral strategies (i.e., a Nash equilibrium).

The proof of this corollary is similar to that of Theorem 5.2.1 provided that the payoff function is redefined as $H^i(x_T)$, $i = 1, 2$.

It follows from Theorem 5.2.1 that the example of conflict interaction, Example 5.2.2, as defined by relations (5.2.3) and the continuous payoff function $\tilde{H}(x_T)$, has a solution.

Finally, we present the following theorem to characterize the definition of "full" solution, which was introduced in Section 5.1.

Theorem 5.2.2 The finite d.g.c.c. Γ without discrimination has a "full" solution (i.e., mixed general and behavioral strategies exist and their values coincide).

Proof Since Γ is finite, it satisfies the continuity conditions and hence has a solution in mixed behavioral strategies (a result that also follows from Theorem 5.2.1). Let us denote the value of the game Γ in mixed behavioral strategies, which begins from the initial state x_0 and continues for T stages by $V_T(x_0)$. Also, as pointed out in Section 5.1, the finite general game $\tilde{\Gamma}$ of the game Γ always has a solution because $\tilde{\Gamma}$ is always finite in normal form, regardless of the number of stages that Γ has. The value of $\tilde{\Gamma}$ will be denoted by $\tilde{V}_T(x_0)$. Our task is to show that $V_T(x_0) = \tilde{V}_T(x_0)$. This will be established by induction on the length of the game T.

Let Γ have length 1 (i.e., $T = 1$). The theorem is true because if $T = 1$, mixed behavioral and general strategies coincide since the game will be $\langle U_1, U_2, H\{f_1(x_0, \tilde{u}, \tilde{w})\}\rangle$, where the initial state x_0 is constant. In this game behavioral strategies do not depend on the state.

Now let Γ have length $(T + 1)$. Let us suppose that the cardinality of the set U_i is K_i and that the elements of this set are enumerated as $\tilde{u}_j$ and $\tilde{w}_j$, where $j = 1, 2, \ldots, K_i$, and $i = 1, 2$. Then any pure general strategies of the first player $(\tilde{u}_1, \tilde{u}_2, \ldots, \tilde{u}_T)$ may be written in the form $(\tilde{u}_{j1}, \tilde{u}_{j2}, \ldots, \tilde{u}_{jt}, \ldots, \tilde{u}_{jT})$, where jt is the number of the move of the first player at the tth stage and $1 \le t \le T$. Hence the full number of all possible pure general strategies of the first player is T^{K_1} and his/her mixed general strategy v_T is given by a sequence of numbers, i.e., $v_T = \{\alpha_{j1,\ldots,jT}\}$, where $0 \le \alpha_{j1,\ldots,jT} \le 1$ and $\sum_{j1=\cdots=jT=1}^{K_1} \alpha_{j1,\ldots,jT} = 1$. Here $\alpha_{j1,\ldots,jT}$ is the probability of the first player choosing the pure general strategy $(\tilde{u}_{j1}, \ldots, \tilde{u}_{jt})$ among all his/her pure general strategies.

Analogously, the second player's mixed general strategy μ_T is the sequence $\mu_T = \{\beta_{i1,\ldots,iT}\}$, where $0 \le \beta_{i1,\ldots,iT} \le 1$ and $\sum_{i1=\cdots=iT=1}^{K_2} \beta_{i1,\ldots,iT} = 1$.

$\beta_{i1,\ldots,iT}$ is the probability of choosing the pure strategy $(\tilde{w}_{i1}, \ldots, \tilde{w}_{iT})$ by the second player among all his/her pure general strategies $\{\beta_{i1,\ldots,iT}\}$.

If the first player chooses the mixed general strategy $v_T = \{\alpha_{j1,\ldots,jT}\}$ and the second player chooses the mixed general strategy $\mu_T = \{\beta_{i1,\ldots,iT}\}$, the payoff of the first player is defined as

$$H(v_T, \mu_T) = \sum_{j1=\cdots=jT=1}^{K_1} \sum_{i1=\cdots=iT=1}^{K_2} H(\tilde{u}_{j1}, \ldots, \tilde{u}_{jT}; \tilde{w}_{i1}, \ldots, \tilde{w}_{iT}) \times (\alpha_{j1,\ldots,jT}\beta_{i1,\ldots,iT}), \tag{5.2.7}$$

where

$$H_T(\tilde{u}_{j1}, \ldots, \tilde{u}_{jT}; \tilde{w}_{i1}, \ldots, \tilde{w}_{iT}) = H\{f_T(f_{T-1}(\cdots(f_1(x_0, \tilde{u}_{j1}, \tilde{w}_{i1}))\cdots), \tilde{u}_{jT-1}, \tilde{w}_{iT-1})\tilde{u}_{jT}, \tilde{w}_{iT})\}.$$

The right-hand side indicates consecutive iterations of states and payoffs; i.e., for $T = 1$ the payoff is

$$H_1(\tilde{u}_{j1}, \tilde{w}_{i1}) = H\{f_1(x_0, \tilde{u}_{j1}, \tilde{w}_{i1})\},$$

for $T_2 = 2$ the payoff is

$$H_2(\tilde{u}_{j1}, \tilde{u}_{j2}, \tilde{w}_{i1}, \tilde{w}_{i2}) = H\{f_2(f_1(x_0, \tilde{u}_{j1}, \tilde{w}_{i1}), \tilde{u}_{j2}, \tilde{w}_{i2})\},$$

and so on.

Let $\bar{v}_T = \{\bar{\alpha}_{j1,\dots,jT}\}$ and $\bar{\mu}_T = \{\beta_{i1,\dots,iT}\}$ be optimal mixed general strategies of both players.

Then (5.2.7) can be rewritten as

$$\bar{H}(\bar{v}_T, \bar{\mu}_T) = \sum_{i1=1}^{K_2} \sum_{j1=1}^{K_1} \left(\sum_{j2=\cdots=jT=1}^{K_1} \sum_{i2=\cdots=iT=1}^{K_2} H(\tilde{u}_{j1}, \dots, \tilde{u}_{jT}; \tilde{w}_{i1}, \dots, \tilde{w}_{iT}) \bar{\alpha}^{j1}_{j2,\dots,jT} \bar{\beta}^{i1}_{i2,\dots,jT} \right) \alpha_{j1} \beta_{i1}, \quad (5.2.8)$$

where

$$\bar{\alpha}_{j1} = \sum_{j2=\cdots=jT=1}^{K_1} \bar{\alpha}_{j1,\dots,jT}; \; \bar{\beta}_{i1} = \sum_{i2=\cdots=iT=1}^{K_2} \bar{\beta}_{i2,\dots,iT};$$

$$\bar{\alpha}^{j1}_{j2,\dots,jT} = \bar{\alpha}_{j1,\dots,jT} \Big/ \sum_{j2=\cdots=jT=1}^{K_1} \bar{\alpha}_{j1,\dots,jT};$$

and

$$\bar{\beta}^{i1}_{i2,\dots,iT} = \bar{\beta}_{i2,\dots,iT} \Big/ \sum_{i1=\cdots=iT=1}^{K_2} \bar{\beta}_{i1,\dots,iT}.$$

The number $\bar{\alpha}_{j1}$ is interpreted as the probability that the first player will take $\tilde{u}_{j1}$ as his/her first move and $\bar{\alpha}^{j1}_{j2,\dots,jT}$ is the relative probability, i.e., the probability that the first player will choose the moves $(\tilde{u}_{j2}, \dots, \tilde{u}_{jT})$ if his/her first move is $\tilde{u}_{j1}$. For the second player, the numbers $\bar{\beta}_{i1}$ and $\bar{\beta}^{i1}_{i2,\dots,iT}$ are interpreted similarly. All these probabilities are calculated at the optimum.

Now let us prove that $\{\bar{\alpha}^{j1}_{j2,\dots,jT}\}$ and $\{\bar{\beta}^{i1}_{i2,\dots,iT}\}$ are optimal mixed general strategies in the subgame $\tilde{\Gamma}_{j1,i1}$ of the game $\tilde{\Gamma}$. We shall prove this by contradiction. The game $\tilde{\Gamma}_{j1,i1}$ has remained after the first moves $j1$, $i1$ are made by the first and second players. Specifically, given moves $\bar{j}1$ and $\bar{i}1$, strategies

$\{\bar{\alpha}^{j1}_{j2,\ldots,jT}\}$ and $\{\beta^{i1}_{i2,\ldots,iT}\}$ are not optimal. If we can find a strategy $\tilde{\alpha}^{\bar{j}1}_{j2,\ldots,jT}$ such that

$$\sum_{j2=\cdots=jT=1}^{K_1} \sum_{i1=\cdots=iT=1}^{K_2} H(\tilde{u}_{j1},\ldots,\tilde{u}_{jT};\tilde{w}_{i1},\ldots,\tilde{w}_{iT})\tilde{\alpha}^{\bar{j}1}_{j2,\ldots,jT}\beta^{\bar{i}1}_{i2,\ldots,jT}$$

$$> \sum_{j2=\cdots=jT=1}^{K_1} \sum_{i2=\cdots=iT=1}^{K_2} H(\tilde{u}_{i1},\ldots,\tilde{u}_{jT};\tilde{w}_{i1},\ldots,\tilde{w}_{iT})\bar{\alpha}^{\bar{j}1}_{j2,\ldots,jT}\bar{\beta}^{\bar{i}1}_{i2,\ldots,iT}, \tag{5.2.9}$$

then we can construct a new strategy $\tilde{\alpha}_{j1,\ldots,jT}$, taking the relative probability as $\bar{\alpha}^{j1}_{j2,\ldots,jT}$, which is defined by the optimal strategy $\{\tilde{\alpha}_{j1,\ldots,jT}\}$ after any first move except the move $\bar{j}1$ and the relative probability $\tilde{\alpha}^{\bar{j}1}_{j2,\ldots,jT}$. In the case of the move $\bar{j}1$, we get a new mixed general strategy $\{\tilde{\alpha}_{i1,\ldots,jT}\}$ such that, according to (5.2.8),

$$\sum_{j1=\cdots=jT=1}^{K_1} \sum_{i1=\cdots=iT=1}^{K_2} H(\tilde{u}_{j1},\ldots,\tilde{u}_{jT};\tilde{w}_{i1},\ldots,\tilde{w}_{iT})\tilde{\alpha}_{j1,\ldots,jT}\bar{\beta}_{i1,\ldots,iT}$$

$$> \sum_{j1=\cdots=jT=1}^{K_1} \sum_{i1=\cdots=iT=1}^{K_2} H(\tilde{u}_{j1},\ldots,\tilde{u}_{jT};\tilde{w}_{i1},\ldots,\tilde{w}_{iT})\bar{\alpha}_{j1,\ldots,jT}\bar{\beta}_{i1,\ldots,iT}.$$

This contradicts the definition of $\{\bar{\beta}^{i1}_{i1,\ldots,iT}\}$. Hence we proved the optimality of $\{\bar{\beta}^{i1}_{i2,\ldots,iT}\}$ in the subgame $\tilde{\Gamma}_{\bar{j}1,\bar{i}1}$. By the same reasoning, the optimality of $\{\bar{\alpha}_{j2,\ldots,jT}\}$ in the subgame $\tilde{\Gamma}_{\bar{i}1,\bar{j}1}$ can be shown. Thus we can rewrite (5.2.9) in the form

$$\tilde{H}(\bar{v}_T,\bar{\mu}) = \sum_{j1=1}^{K_1}\sum_{i1=1}^{K_2} \tilde{H}_{T-1}(x_{j1,i1})\bar{\alpha}_{j1}\bar{\beta}_{i1}, \tag{5.2.10}$$

where $\tilde{H}_{T-1}(x_{j1,i1})$ is the value of the general game $\tilde{\Gamma}_{j1,i1}$, which is derived from the game Γ after the first stage and $\tilde{\Gamma}_{j1,i2}$ goes to the state $x_{j1,i1} = f(x_0, \tilde{u}_{ji}, \tilde{w}_{i1})$. But this game has length $(T-1)$. Then by the induction hypothesis $\tilde{H}_{T-1}(x_{j1,i1}) = H(x_{j1,i1})$, where $H(x_{j1,i1})$ is the value of the subgame $\Gamma_{j1,i1}$ derived from the game Γ after the first moves $\tilde{u}_{j1}$ and $\tilde{w}_{i1}$ are made by the first and second players, respectively. Hence

$$\tilde{H}(\bar{v}_T,\bar{\mu}_T) = \sum_{j1=1}^{K_1}\sum_{i1=1}^{K_2} H(x_{j1,i1})\bar{\alpha}_{i1}\bar{\beta}_{i1}.$$

As discussed above (i.e., $T = 1$), in a one-stage game optimal mixed behavioral strategies and optimal mixed general strategies of both players coincide. The same reasoning used to show the optimality of strategies $\{\bar{\alpha}_{j1}\}$ and $\{\bar{\beta}_{i1}\}$ in relation (5.2.10) can be used to show the optimality of strategies $\{\bar{\alpha}^{j1}_{j2,\ldots,jT}\}$ and $\{\bar{\beta}^{i1}_{i2,\ldots,iT}\}$. Therefore,

$$\tilde{H}(\bar{\nu}_T, \bar{\mu}_T) = H_T(x_0). \quad \text{Q.E.D.}$$

CHAPTER

6

Difference Games with Variable Control Sets

The assumption that control sets are independent of the state of the game is a restrictive requirement and does not accommodate interesting and real conflict situations. In reality, options of available controls depend on the prevailing achieved states, the stock of commodities available in the economy, money supply if the prescribed game is connected with markets, etc. In particular, this assumption is more restrictive when the game describes a conflict situation between two economies. As seen before, the ability of one economy to use a specific quantity of its resources to efficiently influence the other economy depends on the available stock or on the prevailing achieved state. Therefore, it is important to develop a theory for the case of variable control sets. In Section 6.1 we shall describe a class of games in which the control sets continuously depend on the state of the game and show that these games have solutions in mixed behavioral strategies. This theory will then be applied to a war between two economies that are described by von Neumann models. In Section 6.2 we shall present a complete solution of a game that describes a war between two one-commodity Leontief models. This game is representative of continuous difference games with control sets that continuously depend on the state of the game.

6.1 CONTINUOUS DIFFERENCE GAMES WITH STATE-DEPENDENT CONTROL SETS

Theorem 5.2.1, which shows the existence of solutions for difference games with constant control sets, is not a satisfactory framework for analyzing interesting economic cases. Therefore, alternative games that allow dependence of control sets on states are more desirable. This type of game can be defined as follows: Let Γ be a difference game defined by

$$x_{t+1} = f_t(x_t, u_t, w_t),$$

where $u_t \in U_1(x_t)$ and $w_t \in U_t(x_t)$. Moreover, let the function f_t be continuous and the control sets of the first and second players $U_1(x_t)$ and $U_2(x_t)$ be continuous mappings of R^n into 2^{R^m} and of R^n into 2^{R^l}, respectively (a strict definition of the continuity of this kind of mappings will be provided later in this section). Then Γ is called a *continuous difference game* (without discrimination). The problem in this section is to show the existence of a solution in the game Γ.

Recall that the proof of Theorem 5.2.1, concerning the existence of a solution in a continuous difference game with constant control sets, is based on the fact that the function

$$F(x) = \max_{\nu \in \pi_1(U_1)} \min_{\mu \in \pi_2(U_2)} \int_{U_1 \times U_2} f(x, u, w)\, d\nu\, d\mu$$

is continuous in x. This fact was needed for the proof by "backward" induction. In this section we shall prove a similar fact (i.e., Lemma 6.1.1), taking into account the fact that the control sets U_i, $i = 2$, are continuous mappings of R^n into 2^{R^m} and of R^n into 2^{R^l}. But, first, we shall introduce some definitions.

Let U be any closed, nonempty subset of R^n. The *distance between a point $x \in R^n$ and the set U* is defined by

$$d(x, U) = \min_{y \in U} d(x, y),$$

and the *closed ε neighborhood* of the set U is defined by

$$B_\varepsilon(U) = \{x \in R^n : d(x, U) \leq \varepsilon\},$$

where $\varepsilon > 0$. These definitions are illustrated in Figure 6.1.1. In panel (a), $d(x, U)$ is equal to the distance between α and x. In panel (b), the distance between the set U and the neighbor $B_\varepsilon(U)$ is ε.

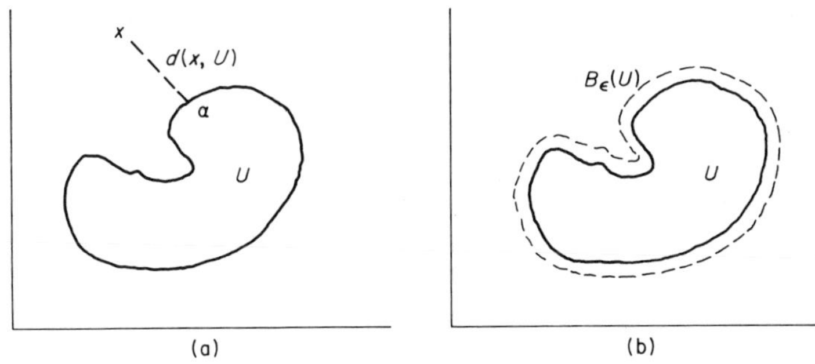

Figure 6.1.1

Let U and V be nonempty subsets of R^n. The distance

$$\delta(U, V) = \inf\{\varepsilon \in (0, \infty) : U \subset B_\varepsilon(V), V \subset B_\varepsilon(U)\}$$

is called the *Hausdorf distance* between the sets U and V. It turns out that the Hausdorf distance defines a metric space on the set of all compact nonempty subsets of R^n.

Let U be a mapping of R^n into the set of all compact nonempty subsets of R^n and $U(x_n)$ and $U(x_0)$ be the images of $x_n, x_0 \in R^n$, respectively. Then the mapping U is said to be *continuous* at x_0 (in the sense of the Hausdorf distance) if $x_n \to x_0$ implies $\delta(U(x_n), U(x_0)) \to 0$ as $n \to \infty$. In other words, the images of x_n and x_0 converge. U is continuous if it is continuous at every point in R^n.

The following facts of measure theory will be used in proving Lemma 6.1.1.

(i) Let V be a compact subset of R^n and let f be a continuous function of R^n into R. Then for any $\varepsilon > 0$, there exists $\delta(\varepsilon)$ such that for any partition $V = \{S_i\}$, $i = 1, 2, \ldots, k$, with the diameter of S_i less than $\delta(\varepsilon)$,[1]

$$\left| \sum_{i=1}^{k} f(x_i)\nu(S_i) - \int_V f(x)\, d\nu \right| < \varepsilon, \tag{6.1.1}$$

where $x_i \in S_i$.

(ii) Let $V \subset R^n$ and let $S \subset V$ be a Borel measurable set. If $\nu_n \in \pi(V)$ such that $\nu_n \xrightarrow{w} \nu_0$ and $\nu_0(\partial S) = 0$, where ∂S is the boundary of the set S, then $\nu_n(S) \to \nu_0(S)$.

[1] The diameter of $S_i \subset R^n$ is the number $d(S_i) = \max_{x, y \in S_i} d(x, y)$.

Let $\nu \in \pi(V)$ and $V = \{S_i\}$, $i = 1, 2, \ldots, k$, such that $S_i \cap S_j = \varnothing$ if $i \neq j$. Then for any $x_i \in S_i$, measure $\nu_S = \sum_{i=1}^{k} \lambda_i \nu_{x_i}$, where $\nu_S = \nu(S)$ and ν_{x_i} is an atomic measure concentrated on the point $x_i \in S_i$ (i.e., $\nu_{x_i}(V) = \nu_{x_i}(\{x_i\}) = 1$) and $\lambda_i = \nu(S_i)$ is called a *discretization of measure* ν. In other words, instead of considering measure ν, we consider a discrete approximation of it. It follows from the definition of measure that $\sum_{i=1}^{k} \lambda_i = 1$.

With the use of discretization, relation (6.1.1) may be written as

$$\left| \sum_{i=1}^{k} f(x_i)\lambda_i \nu_{x_i} - \int_V f(x)\, d\nu \right| < \varepsilon, \tag{6.1.2}$$

where $\lambda_i = \nu(S_i)$.

The above definitions and facts should lay the groundwork for the following lemma, which is used in the proof of the next theorem.

Lemma 6.1.1 Let U be a mapping of R^n into 2^{R^m}, and for every $x \in R^n$, the image set $U(x)$ is continuous and compact valued. Moreover, let f be a continuous function of R^n into R. Then given any $x_n, x_0 \in R^n$, $x_n \to x_0$ implies

$$\max_{\nu \in \pi(U(x_n))} \int_{U(x_n)} f\, d\nu \to \max_{\nu \in \pi(U(x_0))} \int_{U(x_0)} f\, d\nu$$

(in other words, the function

$$I(x) = \max_{\nu \in \pi(U(x))} \int_{U(x)} f\, d\nu$$

is continuous at the point x_0).

Proof We can assume without loss of generality (because of the continuity of f and the compact valuedness of $U(\cdot)$) that there exists a compact set V such that $U(x_n) \subset V$ for all $n = 0, 1, \ldots$ (i.e., $\bigcup_{n=0} U(x_n) \subset V$). Then it follows from fact (iv) of Section 4.1 (as shown in the proof of Theorem 5.2.1) that there exists a measure $\bar{\nu}_n \in \pi(U(x_n))$ such that

$$\max_{\nu \in \pi(U(x_n))} \int_{U(x_n)} f\, d\nu = \int_{U(x_n)} f\, d\bar{\nu}_n$$

(i.e., $\bar{\nu}_n$ is an optimal measure). Moreover, since $U(x_n) \subset V$, we can consider $\nu_n \in \pi(V)$. So from weakly compactness of $\pi(V)$ we can assume $\bar{\nu}_n \xrightarrow{w} \bar{\nu}$. Thus we wish to show that

$$\int_{U(x_n)} f\, d\bar{\nu}_n \to \int_{U(x_0)} f\, d\bar{\nu}. \tag{6.1.3}$$

To this end, for any $\varepsilon > 0$, we shall take the partition $V = \{S_i\}$, $i = 1, 2, \ldots, k$, satisfying the following conditions:

(a) the diameter of S_i is less than $\delta(\varepsilon)$, $i = 1, 2, \ldots, k$;
(b) $\bar{v}(\partial S_i) = 0$, $i = 1, 2, \ldots, k$;
(c) if $S_i \cap U(x_0) \neq \varnothing$, then there is a number N such that for all $n \geq N$, $S_i \cap U(x_n) \neq \varnothing$; and
(d) S_i is Borel measurable.

Condition (b) can be satisfied by the countability of the set of atoms of the measure $\bar{v}$.[2] Condition (c) can be satisfied since $U(x_n)$ converges to $U(x_0)$ and $U(x_0)$ is compact.

Relation (6.1.2) may be written as

$$\int_{U(x_n)} f\, dv_n = \sum_{i=1}^{k} f(x_i)\lambda_i^n v_{x_i^n} + r_1, \tag{6.1.4.}$$

where $|r_1| < \varepsilon$ and the points x_i^n are chosen such that $x_i^n \in S_i \cap U(x_n)$ and $x_i^n \to x_i^0$, where $x_i^0 \in U(x_0)$. Such points exist due to condition (c). We can also assume $\lambda_i^n \to \lambda_i^0$ without loss of generality. Then

$$\lambda_i^n v_{x_i^n} \to \lambda_i^0 v_{x_i^0}$$

and the measure

$$\sum_{i=1}^{k} \lambda_i^0 v_{x_i^0} \in \pi(U(x_0)).$$

By fact (ii) of this section, we have

$$\lambda_i^n v_{x_i^n} = v_n(S_i) \to \bar{v}(S_i).$$

Then

$$\sum_{i=1}^{k} f(x_i)\lambda_i^n v_{x_i^n} \to \sum_{i=1}^{k} f(x_i)\bar{v}(S_i) = \int_{U(x_0)} f\, d\bar{v} + r_2, \tag{6.1.5}$$

where $|r_2| < \varepsilon$. Note that the equality in relation (6.1.5) holds by fact (i).

[2] A point $x_0 \in V$ is called an *atom* of the measure $\bar{v}$ if $\bar{v}(U) \neq 0$ for any measurable set $U \subset V$ such that $x_0 \in U$. If the measurable set U does not contain any atoms of the measure v on its boundary, then $\bar{v}(\partial U) = 0$.

Now let us choose a number $N(\varepsilon)$ such that for any $n > N(\varepsilon)$,

$$\left| \sum_{i=1}^{k} f(x_i)\lambda_i^n v_{x_i^n} \to \sum_{i=1}^{k} f(x_i)\lambda_i^0 \bar{v}_{x_i^0} \right| < \varepsilon. \tag{6.1.6}$$

Then, substituting (6.1.3) and (6.1.4) in (6.1.6), we get

$$\left| \int_{U(x_n)} f\, dv_n - \int_{U(x_0)} f\, d\bar{v} \right| < 3\varepsilon \tag{6.1.7}$$

for any $v \in \pi(U(x_n))$. Owing to the arbitrariness of ε, we can see that relation (6.1.3) holds.

Now we shall show that $\bar{v}$ is a maximizing measure. By fact (i), for any $\varepsilon > 0$ and any $v \in \pi(U(x_0))$,

$$\int_{U(x_0)} f\, dv = \sum_{i=1}^{k} f(x_i^n)\lambda_i^n v_{x_i^n} + r_3,$$

where $x_i^n \in S_i \cap U(x_n)$ and $|r_3| < \varepsilon$. This is so because $v \in \pi(U(x_0))$ and the partition $\{S_i\}$ is chosen such that from $S_i \cap U(x_0) \neq \varnothing$ implies $S_i \cap U(x_n) \neq \varnothing$. Again by condition (c) we can find $x_i^n \in U(x_n)$ such that

$$\sum_{i=1}^{k} f(x_i^n)\lambda_i^0 v_{x_i^n} = \sum_{i=1}^{k} f(x_i^n)\lambda_i^0 v_{x_i^0}.$$

The measure $\sum_{i=1}^{k} \lambda_i^0 v_{x_i^n}$ is a discretization of a measure $v_n \in \pi(U(x_n))$, and [due to (ii)] it satisfies

$$\sum_{i=1}^{k} f(x_i)\lambda_i^0 v_{x_i^n} = \int_{U(x_n)} f\, dv_n + r_n,$$

where $|r_n| < \varepsilon$. But since $\bar{v}_n$ is a maximizing measure, we have

$$\int_{U(x_n)} f\, d\bar{v}_n \geq \int_{U(x_n)} f\, dv_n.$$

Again, by substitution in (6.1.7), we get

$$\int_{U(x_0)} f\, d\bar{v} > \int_{U(x_0)} f\, dv + r_{n+1}$$

for any $v \in \pi(U(x_n))$, where $|r_{n+1}| < 5\varepsilon$. Hence, due to the arbitrariness of ε, we can choose it so small that

$$\int_{U(x_0)} f\,d\bar{v} = \max_{v \in \pi(U(x_0))} \int_{U(x_0)} f\,dv. \quad \text{Q.E.D.}$$

Corollary Let U_1 and U_2 be mappings of R^n into 2^{R^m} and of R^n into 2^{R^l}, respectively, such that for every $x \in R^n$, the image sets $U_i(x)$, $i = 1, 2$ are continuous and compact valued. Moreover, let f be a continuous function of R^{n+m+l} into R. Then given any $x_n, x_0 \in R$, $x_n \to x_0$ implies

$$\max_{v \in \pi_1(U_1(x_n))} \min_{\mu \in \pi_2(U_2(x_n))} \int_{U_1(x_n) \times U_2(x_n)} f(x, u, w)\,dv\,d\mu$$

$$\to \max_{v \in \pi_1(U_1(x_0))} \min_{\mu \in \pi_2(U_2(x_0))} \int_{U_1(x_n) \times U_2(x_n)} f(x, u, w)\,dv\,d\mu.$$

Proof The same as in Lemma 6.1.1.

Based on Lemma 6.1.1 and its corollary and by the reasoning developed in proving Theorem 5.2.1, one can prove the following theorem.

Theorem 6.1.1 Any continuous difference game Γ has a solution in mixed behavioral strategies.

This theorem can be used to show the existence of a solution in Example 5.2.2 with the control sets modified to become continuous mappings. To this end, we must check that the assumptions of the theorem are satisfied. This means that we shall make sure that the control sets U_1 and U_2 are continuous mappings.

Recall that the control set of the first player is

$$U_1(x) = \{(u_1, f_1) : x_1 = A_1 u_1 - f_1; u_1 \geq 0; f_1 \geq 0\}, \qquad (6.1.8)$$

where $(u_1, f_1) = u \in R^{m+n}$.

Lemma 6.1.2 The mapping U_1 of R^n_+ into R^{m+n}_+, which is defined by relation (6.1.8), is continuous.

Proof The strategy of the proof will be to show that $U_1(\cdot)$ is upper semicontinuous (u.s.c.) and lower semicontinuous (l.s.c.).[3] Then u.s.c. and l.s.c. imply that U_1 is continuous.

The u.s.c. of $U_1(x)$ is straightforward. Let $x_1^n \to x_1^0$, and for $(u_n, f_n^n) \in U_1(x_1^n)$. Let $u_n \to u_0$ and $f_n^n \to f_1^0$ as $n \to \infty$. Then

$$x_1^n = A_1 u_n - f_n^n \to x_1^0 = A_1 u_0 - f_1^0$$

as $n \to \infty$, where $u_0 \geq 0$ and $f_1^0 \geq 0$. Therefore, $(u_0, f_1^0) \in U_1(x_0)$, which proves that U_1 is u.s.c.

Now we shall show that $U_1(x)$ is l.s.c. Let $x_m \to x_0$ with $x_m = \sum_{i=1}^n x_m^i e_i$ and $x_0 = \sum_{i=1}^n x_0^i e_i$, where e_i is the ith unit vector and x_m^i and x_0^i are the coordinates of the vectors x_m and x_0, respectively. Moreover, let us define $L_m = \min_{i \in I}(x_m^i / x_0^i)$, where I is the set of indices such that $x_0^i > 0$. Then it follows from $x_m \to x_0$ that $x_m^i \to x_0^i$, $i = 1, 2, \ldots, n$, and $L_m \to 1$. Hence

$$x_m = \sum_{i=1}^n x_m^i e_i = \sum_{i=1}^n [L_m x_0^i + (x_m^i - L_m x_0^i)] e_i = L_m x_0 + \Delta_m,$$

where $\Delta_m = \sum_{i=1}^n (x_m^i - L_m x_0^i) e_i \geq 0$. Note that $\Delta_m \to 0$ as $m \to \infty$. But from the definition of U_1, for any $x_1^1, x_1^2 \in R_+^n$,

$$U_1(x_1^1 + x_1^2) \supset U_1(x_1^1) + U_1(x_1^2).$$

Thus

$$U_1(x_m) = U_1(x_0 L_m + \Delta_m) \supset U_1(x_0 L_m) + U_1(\Delta_m) = L_m U_1(x_0) + U_1(\Delta_m).$$

Moreover, due to the nonnegativeness of the matrix A_1, if $(\Delta u_m, \Delta f_1^m) \in U_1(\Delta_m)$ and $\Delta_m \to 0$, then $(\Delta u_m, \Delta f_1^m) \to 0$.

Now let us take an element $(\Delta u_m, \Delta f_1^m)$ from the set $U_1(\Delta_m)$ and let us consider the sequence

$$L_m(u_0, f_1^0) + (\Delta u_m, \Delta f_1^m) = (L_m u_0 + \Delta u_m, f_1^0 + \Delta f_1^m) = (u_m, f_1^m).$$

Then

$$(u_m, f_1^m) \in L_m U_1(x_0) + U_1(\Delta_m) \subset U_1(x_m)$$

[3] $\phi(x)$ is l.s.c. at the point x_0 if, given any $x_n \to x_0$, where $x_n, x_0 \in R^n$, and a point $y_0 \in \phi(x_0)$, there exists a sequence $\{y_n\}$ such that $y_n \to y_0$, where $y_n \in \phi(x_n)$.

and

$$(u_m, f_1^m) \to (u_0, f_1^0).$$

Therefore U is l.s.c. Q.E.D.

Hence we can conclude that Example 5.2.2 with state-dependent control sets has a solution.

6.2 A SOLUTION OF THE DIFFERENCE GAME: "WAR BETWEEN ONE-COMMODITY MODELS"

The game to be described in this section does not belong to the class of games discussed before because the payoffs in these games are discontinuous. The game is a difference game of survival (with discrimination).

In applying a difference game of survival to a conflict between two one-commodity models, our objective is to demonstrate once more the usefulness of the method of going backward from terminal situations in finding solutions. This method was used in the proofs of existence theorems 5.1.1 and 5.2.1. We shall consider the case where players move in turn and the first player is entitled to the first move.

The models (economies) involved in the conflict are of the simplest von Neumann (i.e., Leontief) variety and will be denoted by i, $i = 1, 2$. The technology mapping of model i is defined by the growth factors α_i and has the form

$$a_i(x) = \{y : 0 \leq y \leq \alpha_i x\},$$

where $i = 1, 2$.

Given the initial states of the first and second models, $x_1(0)$ and $x_2(0)$, respectively, then at the first stage, the first model will make the first move, followed by the second model according to the rules:

$$\begin{aligned} x_1(1) + f_1(1) &\leq \alpha_1 x_1(0), \\ x_2(1) &= x_2(0) - s_1 f_1(1), \end{aligned} \tag{6.2.1}$$

where $x_1(1)$ and $x_2(1)$ are the states of the first and second models at the first stage, respectively. The economic interpretation of these equations is similar to that given in previous sections. In the first equation, given the initial state $x_1(0)$, the first model's resource available at the first stage should not exceed its economic productive capacity based on the initial stock. It will assign part of this existing resource to its military industry as its interaction resource with the second model. So by choosing $f_1(1) \geq 0$, the first model makes its first tactical move. Its economic move is embodied in choosing the state $x_1(1)$ which, with the growth factor, determines the model's economic productive capacity at the second stage. However, once the first model determines its tactical move and $f_1(1)$ is chosen, the determination of the economic move $x_1(1)$ becomes a simple matter. It should be chosen as large as possible, that is,

$$x_1(1) = \alpha_1 x_1(0) - f_1(1).$$

This choice accommodates the first model's best interest because $x_1(1)$ is its state at the first stage, and with the growth factor α_1 it determines the model's prevailing and future productive capacities. Otherwise, the first model is cutting itself off (intentionally or unintentionally) and is helping its opponent. In this case s_1 is the interaction coefficient of the first model and has the same interpretation as the interaction matrix S_1 in previous sections. It represents the efficiency of the military industry of the first model by allowing a comparison between the amount of damage that the first model can inflict on the second model and the amount of the resource stock of the latter which it spared by choosing not to attack the first model. Thus the first tactical move of the first model f_1 is made to inflict damage worth $s_1 f_1$ commodities to the second model's resource at the first stage. Therefore, the second model's state at the first stage is the resource that is left unharmed by the attack of the first model.

As before, we shall say that the first model is the winner at the first stage if $x_1(1) > 0$ and $x_2(1) \leq 0$ [we allow $x_2(1) < 0$ to keep the mathematical analysis simple, and it is economically equivalent to $x_2(1) = 0$]. If the first model wins, the game terminates at this stage. That is, the game is over. The difference between this game at the first stage and similar games in previous sections lies in the passivity of the second model at this stage.

If the first model does not win, the game will continue to the second stage. At this stage, the first model is passive and it is the second model's turn to make the moves, transferring the game to the new states $x_1(2)$ and $x_2(2)$ such that

$$x_1(2) = x_1(1) - s_2 f_2(2),$$

$$x_2(2) + f_2(2) \leq \alpha_2 x_2(1).$$

Similarly, if $x_1(2) \leq 0$ and $x_2(2) > 0$, we say that the second model is the winner and the game terminates at the second stage.

In general, the game proceeds as follows. If the stage is odd, the second model is passive and it is the first model's turn to make the moves, resulting in the states $(x_1(t), x_2(t))$ such that

$$x_1(t) + f_1(t) \leq \alpha_1 x_1(t-1),$$

$$x_2(t) = x_2(t-1) - s_1 f_1(t).$$

If the stage is even, the first model is passive and it is the second model's turn to make the moves and the realized states $(x_1(t+1), x_2(t+1))$ are governed by the equations

$$x_1(t+1) = x_1(t) - s_2 f_2(t),$$

$$x_2(t+1) + f_2(t+1) \leq \alpha_2 x_2(t).$$

If at any of the odd stages, $x_1(t) > 0$ and $x_2(t) \leq 0$, the first model will win. If $x_1(t+1) \leq 0$ and $x_2(t+1) > 0$, the second model will win at an even stage. This is due to the rules of the game. At odd stages the first model attacks the second model, and the latter stays passive. So the resource stock of the first model does not "vanish" at the odd (tth) stages. Therefore, when the first model makes its tactical move at these stages, it has to save a positive part of its resource to constitute its state at the next (even) stage. The opposite holds for the even ($(t+1)$th) stages.

Given the initial stages $(x_1(0), x_2(0))$, let us first consider the case in which the first model wins at the first stage, i.e., $x_1(1) > 0$ and $x_2(1) \leq 0$. Then

$$f_1(1) < \alpha_1 x_1(0),$$

$$x_2(0) - s_1 f_1(1) \leq 0,$$

which by substitution yield

$$x_2(0) < s_1 \alpha_1 x_1(0). \tag{6.2.2}$$

If the tactical strategy $f_1(1)$ completely destroys the initial stock of the second model, then $f_1(1)$ will be called a victory strategy of the first player. Also since the first model is the winner, the set of initial states $(x_1(0), x_2(0))$, which satisfy relation (6.2.2), will be called the victory set of the first model at the first stage and will be denoted by V_1^1 (where the superscript stands for the stage and the subscript for the model). This set is illustrated in Figure 6.2.1.

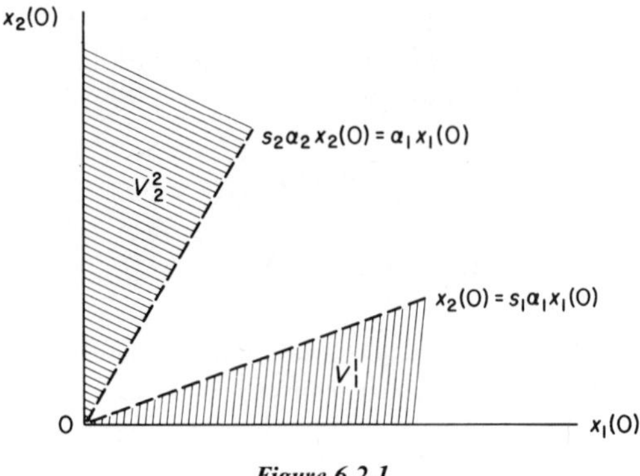

Figure 6.2.1

Then its victory strategy is defined on V_1^1 and is equal to

$$f_1(x_1(0), x_2(0)) = x_2(0)/s_1.$$

Now let us consider the alternate case in which $(x_1(0), x_2(0)) \notin V_1^1$ and $T = 2$, i.e., the first player is not the victor at the first stage and the game proceeds to the second stage where the second model wins. Then $x_1(2) \leq 0$ and $x_2(2) > 0$. The relevant states at this stage are $(x_1(1), x_2(1))$. So the victory set of the second model at the first stage, expecting to win at the second stage, consists of the states $(x_1(1), x_2(1))$ such that

$$x_1(1) < s_2\alpha_2 x_2(1) \tag{6.2.3}$$

and is denoted by $\tilde{V}_2^1$. In this inequality $x_1(1)$ and $x_2(1)$ are substituted for from relation (6.2.1). However, as was already pointed out, we consider

$$x_1(1) = \alpha_1 x_1(0) - f_1(1)$$

because once $f_1(1)$ is chosen, the first model will be better off taking $x_1(1)$ at its maximum to lessen the impact of the second model's attack at the next stage [i.e., to increase $x_1(2)$]. Then relation (6.2.3) becomes

$$\alpha_1 x_1(0) - f_1(1) < s_2\alpha_2[x_2(0) - s_1 f_1(1)]$$

or

$$s_2\alpha_2 x_2(0) > \alpha_1 x_1(0) + [s_2\alpha_2 s_1 - 1]f_1(1). \tag{6.2.4}$$

If the initial states of the game, $(x_1(0), x_2(0))$, and the tactical move of the first model at the first stage, $f_1(1)$, satisfy relation (6.2.4), then the second model can win at the second stage [because it implies (6.2.3), which means that the second model will be the victor at the second stage]. Therefore, the first model should choose its move $f_1(1)$ in such a way that the set of initial states that satisfy (6.2.4) would be at the minimum. In fact, the first model's optimal behavior depends on the relationships among the different parameters used in the description of the game [i.e., on the signs of $(s_2\alpha_2 s_1 - 1)$ and $(\alpha_1 - \alpha_2)$].

We shall consider only one case. That is, when $\alpha_1 > \alpha_2$ and $d_1 = s_1\alpha_1 s_2 - 1 < 0$. The first inequality may be interpreted as this: The first model is economically stronger (more productive) than the second model. The second inequality is a little less obvious. Let us assume that the second model uses δ of its resource stock to attack the first model. Then the amount of the damage to the first model's resource stock is $s_2\delta$. But if the second model chooses not to use δ, sparing $s_2\delta$ of the first model's stock, then the latter can use this amount of its resource in its manufacturing industry and can produce $\alpha_1 s_2\delta$. Then the first model can transfer the quantity $\alpha_1 s_2\delta$ into its military industry and can annihilate $s_1\alpha_1 s_2\delta$ of the stock of the second model. By comparing the amount $s_1\alpha_1 s_2\delta$ that it could suffer if it chooses not to attack the first model with the amount δ that it could waste in weaponry if it decides to attack, the second model can evaluate the military-economic capability of the first model with respect to its own capability. Thus the second model has to consider

$$(s_1\alpha_1 s_2 - 1)\delta = d_1\delta.$$

If $d_1 < 0$, then $s_1\alpha_1 s_2\delta < \delta$. This means that the second model's disinclination to use δ against the first model is warranted because the second model's loss would be no more than $s_1\alpha_1 s_2\delta$, which is less than the initial quantity δ which it could use to produce $\alpha_2\delta$ during the initial stage. Thus the interpretation of $s_1\alpha_1 s_2\delta - 1 < 0$ is that the first model is militarily economically inefficient in its interaction with the second model. If $d_1 = s_1\alpha_1 s_2 - 1 < 0$ and $\alpha_1 > \alpha_2$, then $d_2 = s_2\alpha_2 s_1 - 1 < 0$, i.e., the second model is also militarily economically inefficient with respect to the first model.

If $d_1 \geq 0$, the opposite is true. In this case the second model's disinclination to use δ of its stock to annihilate $s_2\delta$ of the first model's stock would give the latter the chance to use it as a stock in its military industry and to do harm to the second model at least equal to δ (i.e., $s_1\alpha_1 s_2\delta \geq \delta$). Thus $d_1 \geq 0$ may have the interpretation that the first model is militarily economically efficient with respect to the second model.

Returning to relation (6.2.4), it should be recalled that the first model should choose $f_1(1)$ such that the set of initial states satisfying (6.2.4) will be minimized. Since $d_1 < 0$, $d_2 = s_2\alpha_2 s_1 - 1 < 0$. Then the first model's best tactical choice is $f_1(1) = 0$. Hence we get

$$s_2\alpha_2 x_2(0) > \alpha_1 x_1(0). \tag{6.2.5}$$

The set of initial states that satisfy relation (6.2.5) is the smallest set that insures victory for the second model at the second stage and will be denoted by V_2^2. This set is depicted in Figure 6.2.1. Note that if the second model scores a victory at the second stage with $f_1(1) > 0$, then (6.2.4) holds. Also, any initial states that satisfy (6.2.5) belong to V_2^2. So if $(x_1(0), x_2(0))$ satisfies relation (6.2.5) [i.e., $(x_1(0), x_2(0) \in V_2^2$], the first player cannot win at the first stage because V_1^1 and V_2^2 are disjoint, which can be seen by comparing the slopes of (6.2.2) and (6.2.5). It also follows from (6.2.5) that the second model can win at the second stage regardless of what tactical moves the first model will make. This is due to $d_2 = s_2\alpha_2 s_1 - 1 < 1$, which transforms (6.2.5) into

$$s_2\alpha_2 x_2(0) > \alpha_1 x_1(0) + (s_2\alpha_2 s_1 - 1)f_1(1),$$

which is identical to (6.2.4). Then by making a simple arrangement and substituting $x_1(1)$ and $x_2(1)$, relation (6.2.5) yields relation (6.2.3). If the second model chooses $f_2(2) = \alpha_2 x_2 - \varepsilon$, where ε is arbitrarily small, then $x_1(0) < 0$ and $x_2(2) > 0$, which means that the second model wins at the second stage.

If the initial states do not belong to $V_1^1 \cup V_2^2$, then the game continues to the third stage. If the first model wins the game at this stage, its victory set at this stage will be V_1^3. Therefore, in a game which develops over three successive stages we have $(x_1(2), x_2(2)) \in V_1^1$, $(x_1(1), x_2(1)) \notin \tilde{V}_2^1$, and $(x_1(0), x_2(0)) \notin V_1^1$. In other words, for achieving victory at the third stage ($T = 3$), the first model should choose its first stage tactical moves such that after changing moves, the states of the game at the second stage ($t = 2$) belong to V_1^1, i.e.,

$$(x_1(2), x_2(2)) \in V_1^1.$$

Moreover, since the first model wins the game at the third stage, neither model can win at an earlier stage. The second model cannot win at the second stage because of the first model's tactical counterstrategy at the first stage ($t = 1$). Otherwise the first-stage state will belong to $\tilde{V}_2^1$, i.e.,

$$(x_1(1), x_2(1)) \in \tilde{V}_2^1.$$

Also, the first model cannot win the game at the first stage, i.e.,

$$(x_1(0), x_2(0)) \notin V_1^1.$$

Otherwise, we do not need to define V_1^3. Finally, at the third stage, the first model can choose its last strategy $f_1(3)$, which brings victory at this stage regardless of what tactical strategy the second model has chosen at the second stage.

Since the condition of winning at the third stage is $(x_1(2), x_2(2)) \in V_1^1$, then by the definition of V_1^1,

$$x_2(2) < s_1\alpha_1 x_1(2)$$

or

$$\alpha_2 x_2(1) - f_2(2) < s_1\alpha_1[x_1(1) - s_2 f_2(2)]. \tag{6.2.6}$$

Given $s_1\alpha_1 s_2 < 1$ (i.e., $d_1 < 0$), the second model can counter the first model and narrow the latter's set of first-stage victory states that satisfy (6.2.6) if the second model chooses $f_2(2) = 0$. So (6.2.6) becomes

$$\alpha_2 x_2(1) < s_1\alpha_1 x_1(1). \tag{6.2.7}$$

Let us define the set of the first-stage states that satisfies (6.2.7) as

$$\tilde{V}_1^1 = \{(x_1, x_2) : \alpha_2 x_2 < s_1\alpha_1 x_1\}$$

(the first model's set of first stage states that realizes victory after two stages). Then if $d_2 = s_2\alpha_2 s_1 - 1 < 0$ (and $\alpha_1 > \alpha_2$), it follows that the states that belong to $\tilde{V}_1^1$ do not belong to

$$\tilde{V}_2^1 = \{(x_1, x_2) : s_2\alpha_2 x_2 > x_1\}.$$

That is, $\tilde{V}_2^1$ and $\tilde{V}_1^1$ are disjoint. Thus, if (6.2.7) holds, then

$$(x_1(1), x_2(1)) \notin \tilde{V}_2^1 \qquad \text{and} \quad (x_1(2), x_2(2)) \in V_1^1.$$

After substituting $x_1(1)$ and $x_2(1)$, (6.2.7) becomes

$$x_2(0) - s_1\alpha_1 \frac{\alpha_1}{\alpha_2} x_1(0) < s_1\left(1 - \frac{\alpha_1}{\alpha_2}\right) f_1(1). \tag{6.2.8}$$

Since $\alpha_1 > \alpha_2$, the first model's best tactical move at $t = 1$ for countering the second model's above behavior is to choose $f_1(1) = 0$, which expands to the maximum the long range of initial stages satisfying (6.2.8), and so

$(x_1(2), x_2(2)) \in V_1^1$, i.e., the range of initial states that bring victory to the first model at $t = 3$. Thus V_1^3 takes up the space adjacent to V_1^1:

$$V_1^3 = \left\{(x_1, x_2) : s_1\alpha_1 x_1 \leq x_2 < s_1\alpha_1 \frac{\alpha_1}{\alpha_2} x_1\right\}.$$

These victory sets are depicted in Figure 6.2.2.

The optimal behavioral strategy (solution) of the first player over the three stages is its victory strategy $f_1(x_1, x_2)$ defined on $V_1^1 \cup V_1^3$ (regardless of time) such that

$$f_1(x_1, x_2) = \begin{cases} 0 & \text{if } s_1\alpha_1 x_1 \leq x_2 \leq \dfrac{\alpha_1}{s_2\alpha_2} x_1, \\ \dfrac{x_2}{s_1} & \text{if } 0 \leq x_2 < s_1\alpha_1 x_1. \end{cases}$$

That is, the first model should choose its best tactical strategy to be zero if t is an even number and the tth state of the game, $(x_1(t), x_2(t))$, lies in V_1^3. This choice transfers the tth state up through two stages such that $(x_1(t + 2), x_2(t + 2)) \in V_1^1$,[4] which is the necessary and sufficient condition for winning at the third stage beginning from $(x_1(t), x_2(t))$. Once this state is in V_1^1, the choice of the tactical move by the first model of $f_1(x_1(t + 2), x_2(t + 2)) = x_2(t + 2)/s_1$ realizes victory at the next stage. The second model's optimal

[4] It is easy to show that if $(x_1(t), x_2(t)) \in V_1^3$, then, by taking $f_1(t + 1) = 0$, the state $(x_1(t + 2), x_2(t + 2)) \in V_1^1$, i.e., if $(x_1(t), x_2(t)) \in V_1^3$, then

$$s_1\alpha_1 x_1(t) \leq x_2(t) < s_1\alpha_1\left(\frac{\alpha_1}{\alpha_2}\right)x_1(t). \tag{1}$$

By taking $f_1(t + 1) = 0$, Eq. (1) becomes

$$x_2(t + 1) < \frac{s_1\alpha_1}{\alpha_2} x_1(t + 1), \tag{2}$$

i.e., $(x_1(t + 1), x_2(t + 1)) \in \tilde{V}_1^1$. Furthermore, since $f_2(t + 2)$ should be taken less than $\alpha_2 x_2(t + 1)$, and $(1 - s_1\alpha_1 s_2) > 0$, then (2) yields

$$\alpha_2 x_2(t + 1) - f_2(t + 2) < s_1\alpha_1[x_1(t + 1) - s_2 f_2(t + 2)]$$

or

$$x_2(t + 2) \leq s_1\alpha_1 x_1(t + 2).$$

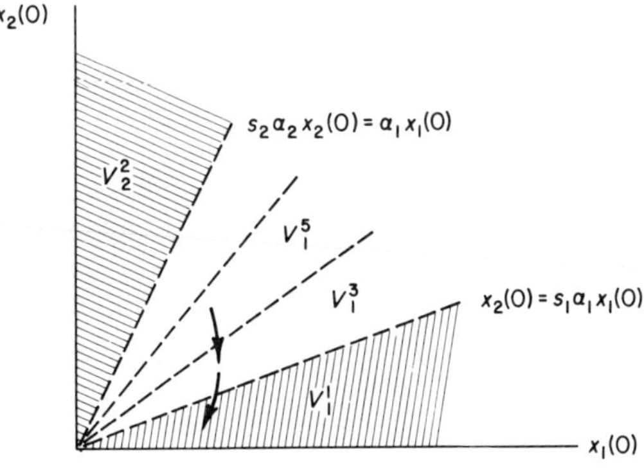

Figure 6.2.2

counterstrategy in $\tilde{V}_1^1$ is zero. Otherwise the second model may lose at the next stage (i.e., it may jump to V_1^1).

In the remaining part of this section we shall show that the line

$$s_2 \alpha_2 x_2(0) = \alpha_1 x_1(0)$$

that bounds V_2^2 in Figure 6.2.2 is a barrier that the first model cannot traverse, i.e., $V_2^4 = \cdots = V_2^T = \varnothing$ (where T is even) because $V_2^2 \neq \varnothing$ or $\overline{V}_2^4 = \overline{V}_2^6 = \cdots = \overline{V}_2^T = \overline{V}_2^2 = V_2^2$, where $\overline{V}_2^{2k}$ $(k = 2, 3, \ldots)$ is the set of initial states of the game that realize victory for the second model, in at most $2k$ stages, beginning from the first stage. Then we shall construct the first model's victory set at the fifth stage V_1^5 and define the maximum number of stages which it takes to achieve victory over the second model.

We shall show first that $V_2^2 = \overline{V}_2^4$ (i.e., $V_2^4 = \varnothing$). Suppose that the second player will win at the fourth stage $(T + 1 = 4)$. Then

$$(x_1(0), x_2(0)) \in V_2^4. \tag{6.2.9a}$$

This means that neither of the models can win at an earlier stage. So the second model cannot win at the second stage $(t = 2)$. Hence

$$(x_1(0), x_2(0)) \notin V_2^2, \tag{6.2.9b}$$

but

$$(x_1(2), x_2(2)) \in V_2^2. \tag{6.2.9c}$$

Also, the first model cannot win at the third stage ($t = 3$). Therefore,

$$(x_1(1), x_2(1)) \notin \tilde{V}_1^1, \tag{6.2.9d}$$

where $\tilde{V}_1^1$ is defined above, that is, the first model's set of first-stage states that realize victory in two stages ($t = 3$). By the definition of V_2^2, (6.2.9a) implies that

$$s_2 \alpha_2 x_2(2) > \alpha_1 x_1(2),$$

which by substitution for $x_1(2)$ and $x_2(2)$ yields

$$s_2 \alpha_2[\alpha_2 x_2(1) - f_2(2)] > \alpha_1[x_1(1) - s_2 f_2(2)] \tag{6.2.10}$$

or

$$(\alpha_1 - \alpha_2) s_2 f_2(2) > \alpha_1 x_1(1) - s_2 \alpha_2^2 x_2(1). \tag{6.2.11}$$

Since $\alpha_1 > \alpha_2$, it is in the best interest of the second model to launch a full attack on the first model so that the second model can stretch its victory range defined by relation (6.2.11) to the full length. Thus the second model should choose its second-stage tactical move to be

$$f_2(2) = \alpha_2 x_2(1) - \varepsilon,$$

where $\varepsilon > 0$ is an arbitrarily small number, which will transform relation (6.2.11) into

$$s_2 \alpha_2 x_2(1) \geq x_1(1) \tag{6.2.12}$$

(equality is due to the arbitrariness of ε). Note that if the state $(x_1(1), x_2(1)) \in \tilde{V}_2^1$, it satisfies relation (6.2.12), too. The set $\tilde{V}_2^1$ differs from the set of states that satisfy (6.2.12) by excluding the states that lie on the boundary of the latter, which is defined by $s_2 \alpha_2 x_2(1) = x_1(1)$ (this means that if the second model wins at the second stage, the first model cannot win at the third stage), so we get (6.2.9d). The substitution for $x_1(1)$, $x_2(1)$, and $f_2(2)$ in relation (6.2.11) gives

$$\alpha_1^2 x_1(0) - s_2 \alpha_2^2 x_2(0) \leq (\alpha_1 - s_2 \alpha_2^2 s_1) f_1(1). \tag{6.2.13}$$

Similarly, $\alpha_1 > s_2 \alpha_2^2 s_1$ since $\alpha_1 > \alpha_2$ and $d_1 < 0$. The first model will reduce its loss (defeat) region if it chooses its tactical move $f_1(1)$ at the maximum, i.e.,

$$f_1(1) = \alpha_1 x_1(0) - \varepsilon,$$

where $\varepsilon > 0$. Relation (6.2.13) becomes

$$\alpha_1^2 x_1(0) \leq s_2 \alpha_2^2 x_2(0), \tag{6.2.14}$$

which defines V_2^4. It should be seen by comparing the slopes of relations (6.2.5) and (6.2.14) that all initial states in V_2^4 belong to V_2^2, which contradicts (6.2.9b). So $V_2^4 = \varnothing$. In other words, the first model's loss (defeat) set of initial states does not expand as the game proceeds over additional stages. Therefore, $\bar{V}_2^2 = \bar{V}_2^4 = \bar{V}_2^6 = \cdots = \bar{V}_2^{T+1}$ (where T is odd), which implies $\tilde{V}_2^1 = \tilde{V}_2^3 = \cdots = \tilde{V}_2^k = \cdots = \tilde{V}_2^T$, where $\tilde{V}_2^k$ is the set of the first-stage states that bring victory for the second model in at most k stages, beginning from the first stage. That is, the second model may win if the initial state of the game (or any state of the game at an even stage) belongs to the range above the barrier line.

Now we shall construct V_1^5, i.e., the set in which the first model can win at the fifth stage. That is,

$$(x_1(0), x_2(0)) \in V_1^5. \tag{6.2.15a}$$

Then neither of the models can win at an earlier stage ($t < 5$). By (6.2.15a) it should be seen that

$$(x_1(2), x_2(2)) \in V_1^3, \tag{6.2.15b}$$

i.e., the first model must find the desirable tactical move $f_1(1)$ (which will be shown to equal zero), which implies, regardless of any tactical move made by the second model, that $(x_1(2), x_2(2))$ should belong to V_1^3. Such a move will inevitably provide the first model with a victory in two stages; that is, at the fifth stage. Moreover, the first model should choose its moves such that the second model will have no opportunity to win after the first move. Then

$$(x_1(1), x_2(1)) \notin \tilde{V}_2^3, \tag{6.2.15c}$$

where $\tilde{V}_2^3$ is the second model's set of the third-stage states that realize victory at the fourth stage. Also, (6.2.15a) means that neither model can win at a stage earlier than the fifth stage. So the first model cannot win at stages one through four. Hence

$$(x_1(0), x_2(0)) \notin V_1^3. \tag{6.2.15d}$$

By definition of V_1^3, (6.2.15b) implies that

$$x_2(2) < s_1\alpha_1\left(\frac{\alpha_1}{\alpha_2}\right)x_1(2),$$

or, by substitution for $x_1(2)$ and $x_2(2)$,

$$\alpha_2 x_2(1) - s_1\alpha_1\left(\frac{\alpha_1}{\alpha_2}\right)x_1(1) < \left[1 - s_1\alpha_1\left(\frac{\alpha_1}{\alpha_2}\right)s_2\right]f_2(2). \qquad (6.2.16)$$

If $[1 - s_1\alpha_1(\alpha_1/\alpha_2)s_2] > 0$, it is optimal for the second model to take $f_2(2) = 0$. Then relation (6.2.16) becomes

$$\alpha_2 x_2(1) < s_1\alpha_1\left(\frac{\alpha_1}{\alpha_2}\right)x_1(1). \qquad (6.2.17)$$

This defines the set of all possible first-stage states that contain the set of states realizing victory for the first model at the fifth stage. Again, by substituting for $x_1(1)$ and $x_2(1)$ and by choosing $f_1(1) = 0$ (it is the best choice since $\alpha_1 > \alpha_2$), relation (6.2.17) yields the first model's victory set at the fifth stage, i.e.,

$$V_1^5 = \left\{(x_1, x_2) : s_1\alpha_1\left(\frac{\alpha_1}{\alpha_2}\right)x_1 \le x_2 < s_1\alpha_1\left(\frac{\alpha_1}{\alpha_2}\right)^2 x_1\right\},$$

so V_1^5 takes up the space adjacent to V_1^3 in Figure 6.2.2.

If $[1 - s_1\alpha_1(\alpha_1/\alpha_2)s_2] < 0$, the second model should choose $f_2(2)$ as large as possible, i.e.,

$$f_2(2) = \alpha_2 x_2(1) - \varepsilon,$$

where $\varepsilon > 0$ is arbitrary. Then relation (6.2.16) gives

$$s_2\alpha_2 x_2(1) \le x_1(1), \qquad (6.2.18)$$

which by substituting for $x_1(0)$ and $x_2(0)$ and by choosing $f_1(1) = 0$ yields

$$s_2\alpha_2 x_2(0) \le \alpha_1 x_1(0).$$

This equation defines all the states that belong to the set V_2^2, including those states on the border line

$$s_1\alpha_2 x_2(0) = \alpha_1 x_1(0)$$

that bounds that set. Therefore, V_1^5 is the space that is sandwiched between V_1^3 and V_2^2, i.e.,

$$V_1^5 = \left\{(x_1, x_2) : s_1\alpha_1\left(\frac{\alpha_1}{\alpha_2}\right)x_1 < x_2 < \frac{\alpha_1}{s_2\alpha_2}x_1\right\}.$$

But since $\overline{V}_2^2 = \overline{V}_2^4 = \overline{V}_2^6 = \cdots = \overline{V}_2^{T+1}$ (where T is odd), which implies that $\tilde{V}_2^1 = \tilde{V}_2^3 = \tilde{V}_2^5 = \cdots = \tilde{V}_2^T$, the first model cannot traverse the line

$$\alpha_1 x_1(0) = s_2\alpha_2 x_2(0),$$

either. Hence in the case of $[1 - s_1\alpha_1(\alpha_1/\alpha_2)s_2] < 0$, $V_1^7 = V_1^9 = \cdots = V_1^T = \varnothing$ (where T is odd) or $\overline{V}_1^5 = \overline{V}_1^7 = \overline{V}_1^9 = \cdots = \overline{V}_1^T$, where $\overline{V}_1^T$ is also the set of initial states from which the first model can win in at most T stages. If the initial state $(x_1(0), x_2(0))$ lies on the barrier line

$$s_2\alpha_2 x_2(0) = \alpha_1 x_1(0),$$

the first model can win because

$$\begin{aligned} s_2\alpha_2 x_2(1) - x_1(1) &= s_2\alpha_2 x_2(0) - \alpha_1 x_1(0) + (s_2\alpha_2 s_1 - 1)f_1(1) \\ &= (s_2\alpha_2 s_1 - 1)f_1(1) < 0, \end{aligned}$$

i.e., $(x_1(1), x_2(1)) \notin \tilde{V}_2^1$. So the second model cannot win at the second stage, and the states of the game belong to the range in which the first model can win. So, for instance, in the case of $[1 - s_1\alpha_1(\alpha_1/\alpha_2)s_2] < 0$, the barrier line should belong to V_1^5, i.e., this set may be written as

$$V_1^5 = \left\{(x_1, x_2) : s_1\alpha_1\left(\frac{\alpha_1}{\alpha_2}\right)x_1 < x_2 \leq \frac{\alpha_1}{s_2\alpha_2}x_1\right\}.$$

It can be shown that

$$V_1^7 \neq \varnothing \qquad \text{and} \quad \overline{V}_1^7 \supset \overline{V}_1^5.$$

In general, it can also be shown by the same reasoning developed above that the maximum number of stages that it takes the first model to achieve victory, $k_0 + 2$, where k_0 is defined by

$$s_1\alpha_1\left(\frac{\alpha_1}{\alpha_2}\right)^{k_0-1} s_2 < 1,$$

$$s_1\alpha_1\left(\frac{\alpha_1}{\alpha_2}\right)^{k_0} s_2 < 1.$$

Thus, despite the inefficiency of its military industry, the first model can increase its resource stock after k_0 stages, due to its higher economic growth ($\alpha_1 > \alpha_2$), to the point that is sufficient for victory. From another point of view, we can say that if at the onset of the game the first model was inefficient (i.e., $d_1 = s_1\alpha_1 s_2 - 1 < 0$), but did not lose immediately because of superior initial resource stock in comparison with that of its opponent, its efficiency would grow stage by stage according to $s_1\alpha_1(\alpha_1/\alpha_2)^k s_2$. Moreover, the first model will reach a stage k_0 at which it will be efficient everywhere below the barrier line. In this case

$$k_0 = \left[\frac{\alpha_2}{\alpha_1} \ln \frac{1}{s_1\alpha_1 s_2}\right] + 1.$$ [5]

However, the problem is very simple for the second model: to win at its first move (i.e., $T + 1 = 2$). In the future, it will never have a better opportunity to win since $V_2^2 = V_2^4 = V_2^6 = \cdots = V_2^{T+1}$.

In general, the optimal strategy of the first player is

$$f_1(x_1, x_2) = \begin{cases} 0 & \text{if } s_1\alpha_1 x_1 \le x_2 \le \dfrac{\alpha_1}{s_2\alpha_2} x_1, \\[2ex] \dfrac{x_2}{s_1} & \text{if } 0 \le x_2 < s_1\alpha_1 x_1, \\[2ex] \text{either of the above if} & x_2 > \dfrac{\alpha_1}{s_2\alpha_2} x_1. \end{cases}$$

If $(x_1(0), x_2(0)) \in V_1^T$, where T is odd and greater than one, then by taking $f_1(x_1, x_2) = 0$ the first model transfers the state of the game to V^{T-2}, regard-

[5] $[y]$ denotes the integer part of y.

less of the moves of the second model. If $T - 2 > 1, f_1(x_1, x_2) = 0$ transfers the state of the game to V_1^{T-4}, and so on. This backward process is illustrated by the arrows in Figure 6.2.2. For the second model, the optimal strategy is

$$f_2(x_1, x_2) = \begin{cases} 0 & \text{if} \quad s_2\alpha_2 x_2 < x_1 \leq \dfrac{\alpha_2}{s_1\alpha_1} x_2, \\ \dfrac{x_1}{s_2} & \text{if} \quad 0 \leq x_1 \leq s_2\alpha_2 x_2, \\ \text{either of the above if} & x_1 > \dfrac{\alpha_2}{s_1\alpha_1} x_2 \end{cases}$$

(recall that the second model makes its moves at odd stages and the first model at even stages).

Other cases that show different relationships among the parameters can be analyzed similarly (Poletaev, 1970).

PART

III

Differential Games

CHAPTER

7

Differential Games: Basic Definitions

A differential game, like a finite difference game, is a situation of conflict (or cooperation) in which players choose their strategies over time. However, in continuous finite difference games, discussed in Chapter 6, there is a continuum (i.e., an infinite number) of states of both players, but the number of stages on the game tree is finite or countable. Thus time is measured in discrete units. In contrast to a continuous finite difference game, in a differential game the players make their moves over an interval of time, so not only are the numbers of moves, stages, and states infinite, but the number of time periods is also infinite (i.e., there is an initial time and a terminal time, and the time is measured in continuous units). Thus the state of the game is governed by a system of differential equations. However, the tools that deal with this kind of system, although sophisticated, make it possible to explore the existence, properties, and calculation of solutions (i.e., continuous optimal paths) of differential games.

Additionally, in contrast to difference games, differential games must operate with behavioral strategies that define the control functions of the players as functions of the state which is reached by the game at a given moment of time. However, these behavioral strategies, especially optimal strategies, are discontinuous functions of the states of the game. In other words, due to the imperfect nature of describing real-life situations using infinitesimal differential equations, at the optimum players must instantly change controls, giving rise to sets of surfaces of switching and reswitching of controls. Therefore, the discontinuity of behavioral strategies yields discontinuity of the right-hand side of the system of differential equations, which defines the differential game. Moreover, in general a system of differential equations with a discontinuous right-hand side has no solution. Thus the problem that arises is how to define strategies of players in differential games and how to define the solution of a system of differential equations such that the solution exists even if the right-hand side of the system is discontinuous. The first of these questions will be discussed in Section 7.1. The second question will be treated in Section 7.2. Finally, the chapter will be concluded with a description of some restrictions on behavioral strategies so that it becomes possible to develop methods of defining solutions of many differential games.

7.1 STRATEGIES AND SOLUTIONS

To understand the strategies and the solution of a differential game, we shall go back to relation (5.2.1) of Section 5.2. This relation, which defines a continuous difference game, may be written in the form

$$\frac{(x_{t+1} - x_t)}{\Delta} = \phi(t, x_t, u, w), \tag{7.1.1}$$

where $\Delta = 1$, $x_t \in R^n$, $u \in U_1(x_t) \subset R^l$, $w \in U_2(x_t) \subset R^m$, and

$$\phi(t, x_t, u, w) = f_t(x_t, u, w) - x_t.$$

If Δ can be taken as small as possible, then in the limit, relation (7.1.1) becomes

$$\dot{x} = \frac{dx}{dt} = \phi(t, x, u, w), \tag{7.1.2}$$

starting from the given initial vector $x(t_0) = x_0$, where t_0, the initial time, is given, $x \in R^n$, $u \in U_1(t, x) \subset R^l$, and $w \in U_2(t, x) \subset R^m$. These differential equations are called the *kinematic equations* or the *equations of motion.* As in the last chapter, the vector $x \in R^n$ is known as the *state variables* and the vectors $u \in R^l$ and $w \in R^m$, which are generally subject to some constraints, are called the *control variables* of the first and second players, respectively. These control variables belong to the given *control sets* $U_1(t, x)$ and $U_2(t, x)$. The differential game continues according to the kinematic equations until the termination time.

The (behavioral) strategy of the ith player, $i = 1, 2$, is generally considered a rule for determining that player's control vector at any time as a function of time and of the state variables at that time. Analogously with difference games, we shall, however, consider two kinds of pure strategies: pure general strategies $\tilde{u}(t)$ and $\tilde{w}(t)$, which are functions of $[t_0, T]$ into R^l and R^m, respectively, such that $\tilde{u} \in U_1(t)$ and $\tilde{w}(t) \in U_2(t)$, where t_0 is the initial time and T is the terminal time that may be infinite, and pure behavioral strategies $u(t, x)$, $w(t, x)$ of $[t_0, T] \times R^n$ into R^l and R^m, respectively, such that $u(t, x) \in U_1(t, x)$ and $w(t, x) \in U_2(t, x)$, where $x \in R^n$. In differential games, $\tilde{u}$ and $\tilde{w}$ are called *program strategies*. Any solution in program strategies implies that the ith player, $i = 1, 2$, seeks the answer as a function of time, regardless of the state of the game at that time. This is an awkward strategy. For instance, suppose the differential game describes a fight between two jet fighters. Then it is impossible to think that each pilot decides his/her strategy beforehand by making choices at any time as a function of that time, regardless of the contemporaneous situation, as summarized by state vector at that time.

If the pure general strategy of the second player is fixed, the first player can achieve the best results by taking a probabilistic mixture of his/her pure general strategies. However, although the consideration of mixed general strategies, especially in the finite case, is reasonable, the meaning of taking probabilistic mixtures of whole functions is incomprehensible from the standpoint of both mathematics and common sense. Therefore, in differential games it is absolutely necessary to consider behavioral strategies in addition to general strategies. But in this way, additional difficulties arise in conjunction with the solution of relation (7.1.2).

The kinematic equations together with the initial condition $x(0) = x_0$ and the control vectors chosen by the players determine the state vector. So given the pure behavioral strategies of both players, $u(t, x)$ and $w(t, x)$, the solution of relation (7.1.2) is a differentiable vector function $x(t)$ such that

$$\dot{x}(t) = \phi(t, x(t), u(t, x(t)), w(t, x(t))), \tag{7.1.3}$$

where $x(t_0) = x_0$, $u(t, x(t)) \in U_1(t, x(t))$, $w \in U_2(t, x(t))$, for all $t \in [t_0, T]$. It turns out that in almost all interesting cases, both players choose their behavioral strategies such that the right side of relation (7.1.3) is discontinuous, even if the function $\phi(t, x, u, w)$ is continuous. Thus we shall first consider the case in which the kinematic equations have no control vectors, i.e.,

$$\dot{x} = F(t, x), \tag{7.1.4}$$

where $x(t_0) = x_0$ and $x \in R^n$. Then by introducing a new variable x_{t+1} such that $x_{n+1}(t) = t$ and $x_{n+1}(t_0) = t_0$, relation (7.1.4) becomes

$$\dot{x} = F(x), \tag{7.1.5}$$

where $x(t_0) = x_0$ and $x \in R^{n+1}$. The first theorem of this chapter will characterize the existence of the solution of relation (7.1.5).

Theorem 7.1.1 Let F be a function of R^{n+1} into R^{n+1} that satisfies the conditions

(i) $|F(x)| \leq k_2(k_1 + |x|)$,
(ii) $|F(x_1) - F(x_2)| \leq k_3|x_1 - x_2|$,

where x, x_1, and x_2 are points in R^{n+1} and k_1, k_2, and k_3 are positive constants and $|x| = (\sum_{i=1}^{n+1} (x_i)^2)^{1/2}$. Then relation (7.1.5) has a unique solution.

The proof of this theorem can be found in standard books on differential equations.[1]

Note that if the solution of relation (7.1.5), $x(t)$, which sometimes is called a trajectory starting from x_0, belongs to a bounded region of R^{n+1} (e.g., to a sphere with a finite diameter), then condition (i) holds. This result is due to the continuity of $F(x(t))$, which follows from condition (ii). This condition is called Lipschitz's condition. It is stronger than the continuity of $F(x)$ but weaker than the differentiability of $F(x)$.

An analog of Theorem 7.1.1 is that if $F(x)$ does not satisfy Lipschitz's conditions but is continuous, relation (7.1.5) will have a solution but it may not be unique.

As we pointed out before, the right-hand side of relation (7.1.5) may be discontinuous, which may negate the possibility of constructing a solution. This problem frequently is encountered by students of differential equations and will be illustrated by the following example.

Let $F(x)$ be a function of R into R such that

$$F(x) = \begin{cases} +1 & \text{if } x < 0, \\ -1 & \text{if } x \geq 0. \end{cases} \tag{7.1.6}$$

Making use of this example, if we integrate both sides of (7.1.5), with $t_0 = 0$, we get the solution

$$x(t) = \begin{cases} t + x_0 & \text{if } x_0 < 0, \\ x_0 - t & \text{if } x_0 \geq 0. \end{cases}$$

If the initial point $x_0 < 0$, the trajectory (solution) $x(t)$ continues to increase until it reaches $x(\bar{t}) = 0$ and cannot go any further. So $x(\bar{t}) = 0$, which

[1] See, for example, Coddington and Levinson (1955).

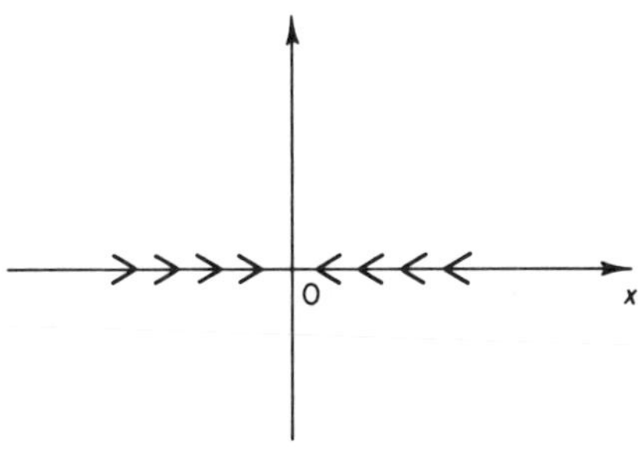

Figure 7.1.1

implies that $\bar{t} = -x_0$. The opposite is true if $x_0 \geq 0$. The solution continues to decrease until it stops at $x(\bar{t}) = 0$. In this case, $\bar{t} = x_0$. This phenomenon should be understandable by considering the field of directions of the trajectories that are defined by $F(x)$, or the isoclinic lines which are points on the x axis in the above example. This is illustrated in Figure 7.1.1, (i.e., the directions of the trajectory at both sides of the origin are opposite to each other). If $x_0 = 0$, no trajectory can be constructed from either direction because it will violate the above cases. Therefore, if $x_0 = 0$, the solution of this example will not exist.

It is worth noting that relation (7.1.5) and the above example can be embodied in a very simple controlled system, e.g.,

$$\dot{x} = u$$

if the player, who chooses the control function $u(x)$, applies the following behavioral strategy

$$u(x) = \begin{cases} +1 & \text{if} \quad x < 0, \\ -1 & \text{if} \quad x \geq 0. \end{cases}$$

Furthermore, the right-hand side of $\dot{x} = u$ is differentiable in x and u. The discontinuity of this controlled system emerges from especially chosen controls.

The set of points at which the right-hand side of (7.1.5), $F(x)$, is discontinuous is called a *singular set*. Moreover, if this set formulates a surface, this surface is called a *singular surface*.

The next section will discuss approaches that allow the existence of solutions in the presence of discontinuity.

7.2 DIFFERENTIAL EQUATIONS WITH A DISCONTINUOUS RIGHT-HAND SIDE

An approach to finding the solutions of relation (7.1.5), which has a discontinuous right-hand side, amounts to a convexation of this side and then to considering the differential inclusion of this relation, i.e., $\dot{x} \in F(x)$. First, relation (7.1.5) is expressed in the form

$$x(t) = x_0 + \int_{t_0}^{t} F(x(t))\, dt. \tag{7.2.1}$$

It should be obvious that if $x(t)$ is a solution of (7.1.5), then it is a solution of (7.2.1).

In Section 3.1, a Lebesgue measure v_L is defined in a one-dimensional space. Additionally, the integral of v_L is expressed as $\int_a^b f\, dt$ instead of $\int_{[a,b]} f\, dv_L$. Therefore, the integral part of (7.2.1) will be understood as a Lebesgue integral. The measure v_L has also been extended for any arbitrary n-dimensional space. The extension can be made as follows. Let us consider a multimensional rectangle

$$A = \{x = (x_1, x_2, \ldots, x_n) : a_i \le x_i \le b_i,\ i = 1, 2, \ldots, n\},$$

where a_i and b_i are finite numbers, and define $v_L(A) = \prod_{i=1}^{n} (b_i - a_i)$. Obviously, $v_L(A)$ is a generalization of a three-dimensional volume. Therefore, the process of extension of v_L starts from the algebra of all closed rectangles. The measure $v_L(A)$ is extended for the largest σ-algebra, which includes, of course, a Borel σ-algebra in R^n since it contains all the algebra for all closed rectangles. Furthermore, as in Section 3.1, if a function $f(x)$ is nonnegative and Lebesgue measurable (i.e., for any arbitrary L, the set $\{x : f(x) \le L\}$ belongs to the σ-algebra defined above), then there is a sequence of monotone increasing step functions, $\{f_n\}$, such that $f_n(x)$ converges to $f(x)$ for all x, excluding the set of (Lebesgue) measure zero. Generally, the sequence of integrals of $f_n(x)$ converges to a finite number or to $+\infty$. If the limit is a finite number, then f is called integrable. The limit, which does not depend on a specific $\{f_n\}$, is called Lebesgue integral and is denoted as $\int_\Omega f\, dv_L$ or $\int_\Omega f\, dx_1, \ldots, dx_n$. Note that nearly all bounded functions that are defined on a bounded set $\Omega \in R^n$ are Lebesgue integrable. Construction of an example of a Lebesgue nonintegrable function that is bounded in R and defined on a bounded interval requires the application of the "optimal choice" axiom (Schwartz, 1967).

Any set $A \in R^n$ is called *negligible* if its Lebesgue measure is zero. Then a property $P(x)$, where $x \in R^n$, is valid *almost everywhere* (a.e.) if the set A at which $P(x)$ is violated is negligable. It can be shown that any solution of (7.2.1) is continuous and a.e. differentiable. The derivative of this solution satisfies (7.1.5) at any point at which the solution is differentiable, i.e., a solution of (7.2.1) satisfies (7.1.5) a.e. This notion will help to cope with the discontinuity of $F(x)$ in relation (7.1.5) or (7.2.1) as is illustrated in the following example.

Example 7.2.1 Suppose that

$$F(x) = \begin{cases} +1 & \text{if } \; x(t) < 0, \\ +3 & \text{if } \; x(t) \geq 0. \end{cases}$$

Then the solution of (7.1.5), making use of this example when $x(t_0) = x_0 < 0$, is

$$x(t) = \begin{cases} x_0 + (t - t_0) & \text{if } \; x(t) < 0, \\ 3(x_0 + (t - t_0)) & \text{if } \; x(t) \geq 0. \end{cases}$$

This solution is depicted in Figure 7.2.1.

If the function $F(x)$ in (7.1.5) satisfies the conditions of Theorem 7.1.1, then a solution of (7.1.5) is called a *classical solution*, which is different from a *solution*, defined earlier in this section as satisfying (7.1.5) a.e. An analogy of Theorem 7.1.1 can be formulated for the existence of solutions of (7.2.1). However, for convenience in referring to it later, the theorem will be formulated for relation (7.1.4) in which the variable t is explicitly included.

Theorem 7.2.1 Let t be in the interval $[\alpha, \beta]$ and let the function $F(t, x)$ satisfy the conditions

(i) $\|F(t, x)\| \leq k_0(t)(1 + \|x\|)$,
(ii) $\|F(t, x_1) - F(t, x_2)\| \leq k_R(t)\|x_1 - x_2\|$,

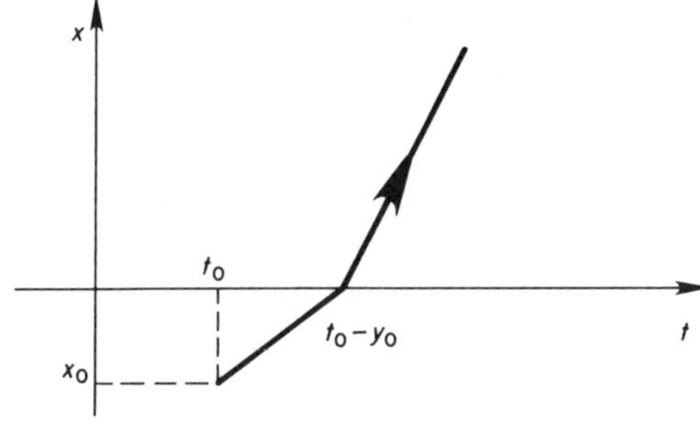

Figure 7.2.1

where $\|x\| < R$, R is a positive constant, and $k_0(t)$ and $k_R(t)$ are Lebesgue integrable functions such that

$$\int_\alpha^\beta k_0(t) < +\infty \qquad \text{and} \qquad \int_\alpha^\beta k_R(t)\, dt < +\infty.$$

Then there exists a unique solution $x(t)$ of (7.1.4), starting from the point

$$x_0 \quad \text{at} \quad t = t_0 \qquad \text{for} \quad t_0 \in [\alpha, \beta].$$

However, even with the above notion of solutions, relation (7.1.5) with a right-hand side as in (7.1.6) cannot have a solution for all t, and if $x_0 = 0$ no solution can be found for any $t \neq t_0$. Therefore, a more general definition of a solution of (7.1.5) should be provided. First, however, it is necessary to recall the following definition. If $A \subset R^n$, then the *convex hull* of A, denoted as $\mathrm{CO}(A)$, is the smallest convex set containing A.

Let $F(x)$ be a function of R^n into R^m, and $x_0 \in R^n$. Then, making use of an ε neighborhood of the point x_0, we can define the set

$$F_\varepsilon(x_0) = \{f : f = F(x) \text{ and } |x - x_0| < \varepsilon\}.$$

Convexation of the function $F(x)$ is defined as a multivalued mapping

$$\bar{F}(x) = \bigcap_{\varepsilon > 0} \overline{\mathrm{CO}}(F_\varepsilon(x))$$

(where the bar sign denotes closure). In the case of (7.1.3), the convexation of $\phi(x, u, w)$ is the multivalued mapping

$$\bar{\phi}(x, u, w) = \bigcap_{\varepsilon > 0} \overline{\mathrm{CO}}(\phi_\varepsilon(x, u, w)),$$

where

$$\phi_\varepsilon(x, u, w) = \{\phi : \phi = \phi(x, u, w), |x - \hat{x}| < \varepsilon,$$
$$|u - \hat{u}| < \varepsilon \text{ and } |w - \hat{w}| < \varepsilon\}.$$

It follows from the definition of continuity that if $F(x)$ is continuous at the point x_0, then $F(x_0) = \{F(x_0)\}$. Additionally, the image set of $\bar{F}$ is closed and convex valued. Figure 7.2.2 shows a discontinuous function on panel (a) and its convexation on panel (b).

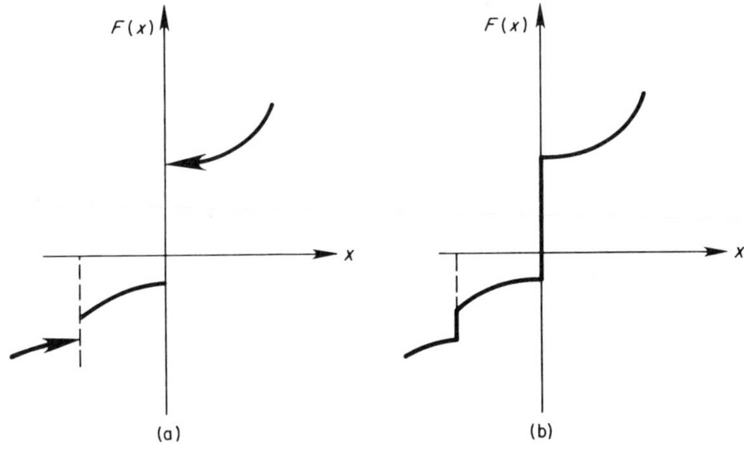

Figure 7.2.2

Now, we shall consider the differential inclusion of (7.1.5), i.e.,

$$\dot{x} \in F(x), \qquad x(t_0) = x_0. \tag{7.2.2}$$

A function $x(t)$ is considered a solution of (7.2.2) if it is continuous and differentiable a.e. on the set $[t_0, T]$ and satisfies $x(t_0) = x_0$ and $\dot{x}(t) \in \bar{F}(x(t))$ at all points, where $x(t)$ is differentiable. Such a solution will be called a *general solution* of (7.1.5).

This notion enables us to seek solutions of a differential equation with a right-hand side such as the one depicted in Figure 7.2.3. The general solutions are shown on parts a, b, and c of Figure 7.2.3, when the initial state $x_0 < 0$, $x_0 > 0$, and $x_0 = 0$, respectively.

This notion of general solutions is not only useful from a mathematical point of view in providing tools for seeking solutions in a wide variety of cases, but it is also useful on practical grounds. It allows smooth change of behavioral strategies. As pointed out before, the difference between (7.1.5) and (7.2.2) appears only in states of the system $\dot{x} = F(x)$, where $F(x)$ is discontinuous. But if we look at the initial problem as defined by (7.1.2), the reason for the discontinuity (when $\phi(x, u, w)$ is continuous) is the discontinuity of controls or behavioral strategies $u(x)$ and/or $w(x)$. Discontinuity of these functions suggests their instantaneous change. This is obviously impossible in real life when the physical object is a machine, such as a bomber. In reality, any change of control takes time and jumps are only an abstraction. Therefore, smooth change of the control function is reasonably approximated by convexation of the right-hand side.

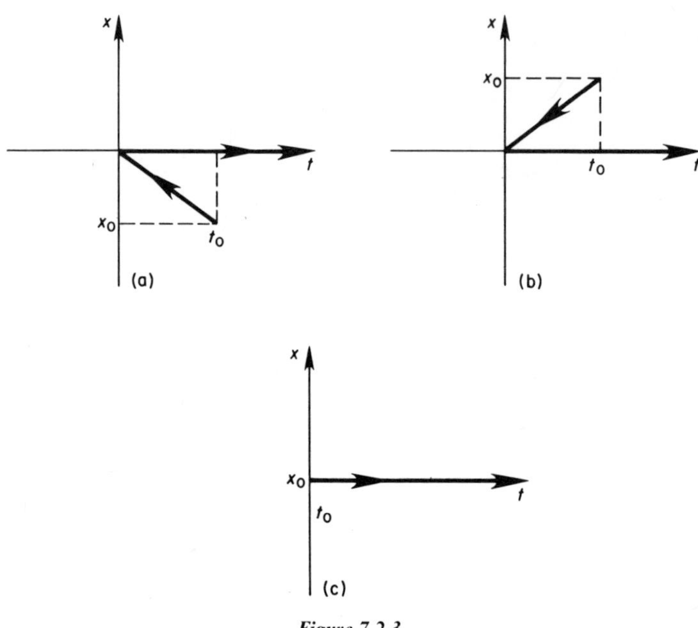

Figure 7.2.3

From the mathematical point of view, the existence of a general solution can be accounted for in the following theorem (Filippov, 1962).

Theorem 7.2.2 Let $F(x)$ be measurable and let it satisfy part (i) of Theorem 7.2.1. Then system (7.2.2) has a general solution for any initial state x_0.

This theorem says that a general solution of (7.2.2) can continue and be sustained for any time interval, starting from the initial time t_0.

7.3 STRATEGIES, OBJECTIVE FUNCTIONS, AND BELLMAN'S FUNCTION

The results of Section 7.2 lay the groundwork for a more rigorous definition of behavioral strategies. A *pure behavioral strategy* of the first (second) player in the differential game governed by relation (7.1.2) is a Lebesgue measurable function u of $R \times R^n$ into R^l (R^m) such that $u(t, x) \in U_1(t, x)$ ($w(t, x) \in U_2(t, x)$) a.e.

Let us assume that the multivalued mappings $U_i(t, x)$, $i = 1, 2$ are bounded [i.e., there is a ball with radius R_i, denoted as $B_i(R_i)$, such that $U_i(t, x) \subset B_i(R_i)$]. Also, there is a positive measurable bounded function $c(t)$ and a constant c_1 such that

$$\|f(t, x, u, w)\| < c(t)(\|x\| + c_1)$$

for all $u \in B_1(R_1)$ and $w \in B_2(R_2)$. By Theorem 7.2.2 it follows that these assumptions are sufficient for the existence of a general solution $x(t)$ of (7.1.2) for any arbitrary choice of pure behavioral strategies u and w.

Thus far in this chapter, the objective functions (i.e., the payoffs) of the players have not been considered. In differential games, each of these functionals is usually comprised of two parts: terminal and integral. The terminal part will be explained first.

It is assumed that given any feasible control (i.e., any pure behavioral strategy) of both players, any feasible trajectory or any general solution of (7.1.2) belongs to a bounded region in $R \times R^n$. In other words, there is a boundary in the space of time and states that no feasible trajectory can pass. In the case of war between two models, for example, it is possible to set the problem such that both players must terminate the game before T.

To simplify exposition of the analysis, an additional variable x_{n+1} is introduced such that $x_{n+1} = t$ and $x_{n+1}(t_0) = t_0$. Then the additional differential equation associated with this variable is $\dot{x}_{n+1} = 1$. Consequently (7.1.2) can be expressed as

$$\dot{x} = \phi(x, u, w), \qquad x(t_0) = x_0, \tag{7.3.1}$$

where $u \in U_1(x)$, $w \in U_2(x)$, and $x \in R^{n+1}$.

As explained above, it is always assumed that there is a terminal surface F in R^{n+1} that constitutes a boundary for the restricted region of feasible trajectories. This region, which has a nonempty interior, is called the *region of the game* and is denoted by D. Let us also assume that $x_0 \in D$ and given any pure behavioral strategies of both players $u(x)$ and $w(x)$, any general solution starting from x_0 reaches the surface F in a finite length of time. As a rule, the terminal surface F is defined by a function Φ of R^{n+1} into R. Specifically,

$$F = \{x = (x_1, x_2, \ldots, x_{n+1}) : \Phi(x_1, x_2, \ldots, x_{n+1}) = 0\}.$$

The set D consists of x such that

$$\Phi(x) = \Phi(x_1, x_2, \ldots, x_{n+1}) > 0.$$

Given feasible strategies $u(x)$ and $w(x)$ and the corresponding trajectory, or general solution $x(t)$ starting from $x(t_0) = x_0$, there exist moments $t_{\bar{F}}$ such that $x(t_{\bar{F}}) \in F$. Since F is closed, the smallest or the first moment $t_F \in F$ exists. This moment is sometimes called the *capture time* of the trajectory $x(t)$, or the capture time corresponding to the strategies $u(x)$ and $w(x)$ (Friedman, 1971). It is assumed that there exists a function f_1 of F into R on the surface F. If the game terminates at t_F when the trajectory reaches the surface F, the first player's payoff function is $f_1(x(t_F))$. This function is called the *terminal part* of the payoff function of the first player. The terminal part $f_1^2(x(t_T))$ of the second player's payoff is defined similarly. However, if the game is antagonistic, then $f_1^2 = -f_1$.

In the case of war between two countries or in the case of games of quality, the function $f_1(x(t_F)$ can take only three values: $+1$, victory; 0, draw; or -1, defeat.

The second part of the payoff function is called the *integral part*. It evaluates the quality of strategies during the playing of the game and is defined as

$$\int_{t_0}^{t_F} f_2(x(t), u(x(t)), w(x(t)))\, dt,$$

where f_2 is a mapping of $R^{n+1} \times R^l \times R^m$ into R. This part is especially important in the case of games of controlled machines (e.g., fighters, tanks, etc.). Also, it is sometimes possible to use this part in choosing optimal methods of economic control in games.

Finally, if $u(x)$ and $w(x)$ are feasible behavioral strategies and $\bar{x} = x(t)$ is the corresponding trajectory starting from $x_0 \in D$, then the payoff function of the first player is defined as

$$P_1(\bar{x}, u, w) = f_1(x(t_F)) + \int_{t_0}^{t_F} f_2(x(t), u(x(t)), w(x(t)))\, dt. \tag{7.3.2}$$

Similarly, the payoff of the second player can be defined.

It can be shown that with the addition of another variable, say x_{n+2}, and of its corresponding differential equation $\dot{x}_{n+2} = f_2(x, u, w)$ with the initial value $x_{n+2}(t_0) = 0$, the integral part of the payoff can be eliminated. Furthermore, under certain restrictions, the terminal payoff of the game, $f_1(x(t_F))$, can be rewritten in an integral form (Volokitin, 1978). This is done by constructing a function $f_\varepsilon(x)$ on the region of game D (i.e., similar to a penalty function) such that the domain of this function is concentrated around the terminal set F (the boundary of D). If for any pair of behavioral strategies

$(u(x), w(x))$, t_F is the moment of capture for the system $\dot{x}(t) = f(x(t), u(x), w(x))$ whose corresponding trajectory begins from $x(t_0) = x_0$, then

$$\left| f_1(x(t_F)) - \int_{t_0}^{t_F} f_\varepsilon(x(t))\, dt \right| < \varepsilon,$$

where $\varepsilon > 0$ is given.

Unfortunately, in differential games the chosen behavioral strategies of both players generally give rise to nonunique trajectories beginning from x_0. This set of all these trajectories is called a jet starting from x_0. Therefore, the payoff of each player as defined in (7.3.2) is nonunique. This is due to the imperfect nature of descriptions of real-life situations by the use of infinitesimal differential equations, as in (7.3.1). This problem will be treated next.

Let $X(x_0, u, w)$ be the jet of all general solutions starting from x_0 and corresponding to a particular choice of strategies u and w. Then the payoff of the first player is defined as

$$P(x_0, u, w) = \inf_{x \in X(x_0, u, w)} P_1(x, u, w). \tag{7.3.3}$$

In fact, it can be shown that infimum in (7.3.3) can be replaced by minimum. The reason for taking infimum (minimum) of the payoff over the jet $X(x_0, u, w)$ is the indeterminacy on the part of the first player in choosing a specific trajectory from that jet.

It is now possible to define a solution of an antagonistic differential game as a pair of optimal strategies $(\bar{u}, \bar{w})$, such that

$$P(x_0, \bar{u}, w) \geq P(x_0, \bar{u}, \bar{w}) \geq P(x_0, u, \bar{w}).$$

That is the solution of an antagonistic differential game governed by (7.3.1) is a saddle point $(\bar{u}, \bar{w})$ with the payoff (7.3.3). Then, as shown in Theorem 2.1.1 of Section 2.1, if an antogonistic game has a solution, the value of the game, here $P(x_0, \bar{u}, \bar{w})$, does not depend on a specific pair of optimal strategies of both players. Thus, even if there exist multiple optimal strategies, the payoff can still be expressed as

$$W(x_0) = P(x_0, \bar{u}, \bar{w}),$$

which is called Bellman's function.[2] This function represents the magnitude of the payoff of the first player under optimal strategies beginning from the

[2] Perhaps, in game theory, this functions should be called Isaacs' function. However, it is better known in control theory, in which it is referred to as Bellman's function.

initial state x_0 and proceeding to the terminal state $x_T = x(t_F)$. Indeed, this function was implicitly used in the proof of a theorem of existence of solutions for difference games in Chapter 6. A general difference game of fixed duration was discussed, and the state of the game was completely described by a pair (τ, x), where x is an intermediate state of the game and τ is the number of moves that are left in the game to attain the terminal position. At the initial period, the state of the game is described by (T, x_0), where x_0 is the initial state and at the terminal moment, the state of the game is described as $(0, x_T)$, where x_T is the terminal state. Let $W(\tau, x)$ stand for the payoff of the first player in the continuous difference game governed by relation (5.2.1) of Section 5.2, which begins with the initial state x_0 and proceeds τ stages, given the optimal mixed strategies of both players. Then from the proof of Theorem 5.2.1 of Section 5.2, it can be concluded that

$$W(\tau, x) = \min_{\nu \in \Pi(U_1(x))} \max_{\mu \in \Pi(U_2(x))} \int W(\tau - 1, f_{T-\tau+1}(x, u, w))\, d\nu\, d\mu, \quad (7.3.4)$$

where $W(0, x) = H(x)$ is the given payoff function in the state x, as in Section 5.2, and $\Pi(U_1(x))$ and $\Pi(U_2(x))$ are the sets of mixed strategies of the first and second players, respectively. As in Chapter 5, Eq. (7.3.4) again emphasizes the "movement" backward in time from the terminal states to the initial states in order to define the value of the difference game in the given initial state. Note that this equation is well known in discrete dynamic control theory when there is one player.

In the previous chapters, the focus of the analysis is centered on the existence of solutions of difference games. In the coming chapter the approach differs. After discussing Isaacs' theory in conjunction with Bellman's function, an approach which provides a tool for finding the solution of some differential games, we shall consider the problem of existence of solutions of these games.

CHAPTER

8

Isaacs' Approach to Differential Games

The study of differential games was pioneered in the early 1950s by Rufus Isaacs. His work played a fundamental role in the establishment of the theory of differential games, as Hamilton's and Pontryagin's theories did with control theory.

Isaacs considered many illustrative examples and formulated theorems on methods of solving differential games. Some of the theorems were heuristically stated and others were established under very restrictive assumptions. Considering the Bellman function instead of the Hamiltonian, Isaacs defined the basic equations of motion that determine the trajectories and optimal behavioral strategies, if they exist. Then he constructed a closed system of differential equations by which, with skillfulness and endurance, optimal strategies and the optimal trajectory of a game can be defined. Owing to these characteristics, many mathematicians tried to improve this approach by putting it on a more strict mathematical basis (Berkovitz, 1967). In a further attempt to do so, this chapter presents rigorous proofs of Isaacs' major results. The proofs are based on exploring the surfaces of switching and reswitching of controls.

The chapter will be structured as follows. Based on the assumption of the smoothness of Bellman's function, which will be shown in Section 8.3, Section 8.1 presents the basic definitions and conditions that are then used in formulating Isaacs' equations. We have chosen to make use of the smoothness of Bellman's function before proving it, to emphasize the attractive features of Isaacs' approach through which solutions can be found, and to illustrate the properties of Isaacs' equations, which define optimal strategies. In

Section 8.2 we shall develop a complete Isaacs' system, which allows many examples of differential games to be solved. This system is applied to war between two one-commodity economies with constant supply. In Section 8.3 we shall prove that Bellman's function is smooth, given some restrictions on the optimal strategies and on the parameters of the game.

Finally, in the last section we shall prove the existence of a saddle point for the game based on the assumption of the existence of a solution of Isaacs' system.

8.1 ISAACS' EQUATIONS

In this section we shall define the main notions that will be used in obtaining Isaacs' equations that govern the game, given the optimal strategies. Additionally, since Isaacs' theory is based primarily on the assumption of sufficient smoothness of Bellman's function, it will be shown in Section 8.3 that if the control functions satisfy certain regularity conditions and smoothness conditions, then Bellman's function is also smooth (i.e., once or twice differentiable as needed in the theory). These control functions, however, will be considered in this section after the introduction of some mathematical definitions. Note that states of a game have been considered to belong to R^{n+1}. For convenience, we shall write R^n instead of R^{n+1}, meaning the latter.

A set $\Phi \subset R^n$ is called an *elementary* $(n-1)$*-dimensional surface* if there is a continuous function Φ of R^n into R, such that[1]

$$\Phi = \{x : \Phi(x) = 0\}.$$

The simplest example of an elementary $(n-1)$-dimensional surface is a hyperplane such that $\Phi(x) = px$, where $p \in R^n$ and $x \in R^n$. The set Φ is called an $(n-1)$*-dimensional surface* if it consists of a finite number of elementary surfaces. Examples of elementary one-dimensional surfaces are shown on panels (a) and (b) of Figure 8.1.1. On panel (a) the set Φ has one elementary surface whereas on panel (b) this set has three elementary surfaces.

An elementary $(n-1)$-dimensional surface is called *regular* if for every point $x_0 \in R^n$ the gradient vector is

$$(\text{grad } \Phi(x_0)) = \left(\frac{\partial\Phi(x_0)}{\partial x_1}, \ldots, \frac{\partial\Phi(x_0)}{\partial x_n}\right) \neq 0.$$

[1] We represent the set and its function by the same notation, Φ.

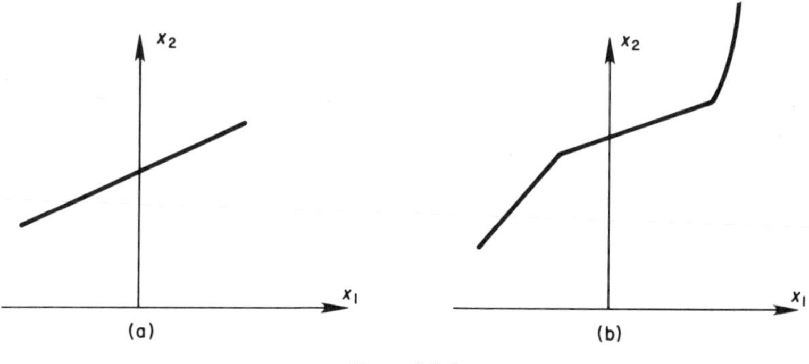

Figure 8.1.1

Let $x_0 \in \Phi$, where Φ is a regular elementary $(n-1)$-dimensional surface. Then the vector $v(x_0) = \text{grad } \Phi(x_0)/\|\text{grad } \Phi(x_0)\|$ is called *a normal vector* to surface Φ at point x_0. This definition has the following interpretation. Let the set Z be a *curve* in R^n such that

$$Z = \{x : x = \phi(t) \text{ and } t \in R\},$$

where $\phi(t)$ is a function of R into R^n. Then the vector $\tau(t_0) = ((\partial\phi_1/\partial t)(t_0), \ldots, (\partial\phi_n/\partial t)(t_0))$ is called a *tangent vector* to the curve Z at point t_0. The curve Z is said to *lie on the surface* Φ and to go through the point $x_0 \in \Phi$ if, for all t, $\phi(t) \in \Phi$ (i.e., $\Phi(\phi(t)) = 0$) and there exists t_0 such that $\phi(t_0) = x_0$. It turns out that for any curve Z lying on the surface Φ and passing through $x_0 \in \Phi$, the vector $v(x_0)$, normal to the surface at point x_0, is orthogonal to the tangent vector $\tau(t)$ at point t_0 such that $x_0 = \phi(x_0)$. That is,

$$(\text{grad } \Phi(x_0), \tau(t_0)) = \sum_{i=1}^{n} \frac{\partial \Phi}{\partial x_i}(x_0) \frac{d\phi_i}{dt}(t_0) = 0.$$

Figure 8.1.2 illustrates this when $n = 3$. In this figure, the curves Z_1 and Z_2 lie on the surface Φ and go through x_0. The normal vector $v(x_0)$ is orthogonal to the tangents of these curves at x_0.

If Φ is an elementary $(n-1)$-dimensional surface, the set $\Phi^+ = \{x: \Phi(x) > 0\}$ is called a *positive halfspace* defined by Φ and the set $\Phi^- = \{x: \Phi(x) < 0\}$ is called a *negative halfspace* defined by Φ. These sets are shown in Figure 8.1.2. The vector $v(x_0)$, which is normal to the surface Φ at point x_0, is said to be *directed in positive halfspace* if the point x_1 deviates from the point x_0 in the direction defined by vector $v(x_0)$ belongs to Φ^+. Formally, if $x_1 = x_0 + v(x_0)t$, where $t \geq 0$, then there exists $t_0 > 0$, such that $x_1 \in \Phi^+$

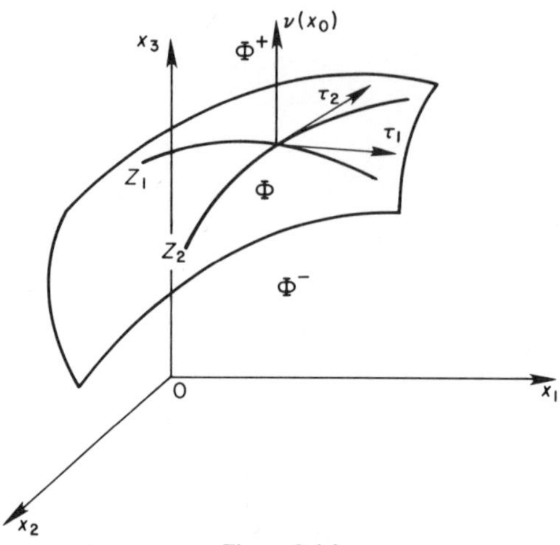

Figure 8.1.2

for all $t \in [0, t_0]$. In Figure 8.1.2, the normal vector $\nu(x_0)$ is shown directed in the positive halfspace of the surface Φ.

The following definitions will help explain the possible sets of the control functions of the players, which cause the discontinuity of the right-hand side of system (7.1.5). The set of all points causing the discontinuity of function F is called a *singular set*. If this set is an $(n-1)$-dimensional surface Φ, then Φ is called a *singular surface*. Furthermore, if F has only one singular surface Φ, then due to the definition, F is continuous in the set $\Phi^- \cup \Phi^+$. The surface Φ is said to be *ε-penetrated from its negative side* if the set

$$\bar{F}(x) \in \{\tilde{x}: (\tilde{x}, \nu(x)) > \varepsilon\} \tag{8.1.1}$$

for any $x \in \Phi$, where $\bar{F}$ is the convex hull of F and $\nu(x)$ is a normal vector directed in the positive halfspace of Φ. By the same token, Φ can be defined to be *ε-penetrated from its positive side.* Note that if $\nu_1(x)$ is normal to the surface Φ and is directed in the positive halfspace of Φ, and $\nu_2(x)$ is a normal to Φ and is directed in the negative halfspace of Φ, then $\nu_2(x) = -\nu_1(x)$. Then it can be concluded that the surface Φ is *ε-penetrated from its positive side if*

$$\bar{F}(x) \subset \{\tilde{x}: (\tilde{x}, \nu(x)) < -\varepsilon\}$$

for all $x \in \Phi$, where $\bar{F}(x)$ is a convex hull of F and $\nu(x)$ is a normal vector directed to the positive side of Φ. When Φ is ε penetrated from the positive side, it is sometimes said, instead, that Φ is ε-nonpenetrated from the negative side. Moreover, Φ is said to be ε-penetrated if it is ε-penetrated from either the negative side or the positive side.

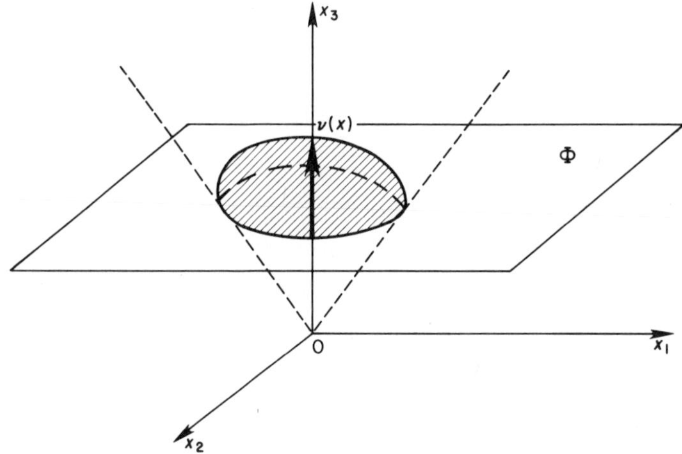

Figure 8.1.3

In order to understand the meaning of (8.1.1), we note that the set $\{\tilde{x}: (\tilde{x}, \nu(x)) > \varepsilon\}$ is the positive halfspace of surface $\{\tilde{x}: (\tilde{x}, \nu(x)) - \varepsilon = 0\}$. System (7.1.5) will be considered only for $x \in D$, where D is the compact region of the game in system (7.1.2). Note that in this region, $\|F(x)\| < R$, where R is a given positive constant. Therefore, instead of (8.1.1), we can consider

$$\bar{F}(x) \subset G = \{\tilde{x}: (\tilde{x}, \nu(x)) > \varepsilon \text{ and } \|\tilde{x}\| < R\}. \tag{8.1.2}$$

Set G is the shaded area in Figure 8.1.3. The normal vector $\nu(x)$ is the unit vector of the x_3 axis in the case of $n = 3$.

It is convenient to approximate G as a convex cone by taking its convex hull. In Figure 8.1.3 the cone hull has its vertex at the origin and is marked by the dotted lines and the x_3 axis. The distance between the origin and the cone hull of G is ε. Then the interpretation of (8.1.1) is that the set $\bar{F}(x)$ belongs to the cone and has a distance not less than ε from the vertex of the cone.

The case when Φ is ε-penetrated from the negative side is shown in Figure 8.1.4, again for $n = 3$.

It is clear that if Φ is ε-penetrated from the negative side to the positive side, then any trajectory of (7.1.5) that begins in the negative halfspace of Φ and passes through to the positive halfspace cannot turn back. Furthermore, it can be shown that if a trajectory begins in the positive halfspace of Φ, it cannot pass through Φ to the negative halfspace. (For a proof, see Filippov, 1962.)

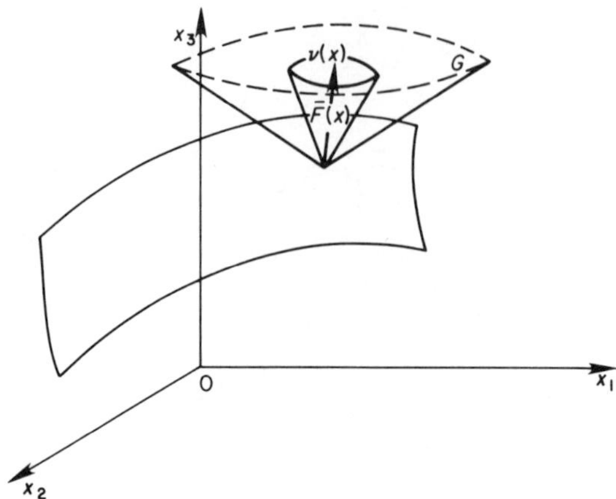

Figure 8.1.4

The next definition will characterize the set of elements that cause discontinuity or switching of behavioral strategies of the players. Let the control function of the first player, $u(x)$, be a mapping of R^n into R^m such that $u(x) \in U_1(x)$. Then u is said to be *regular* if the set of its discontinuity consists of a finite number k_u of disjoint, regular elementary $(n - 1)$-dimensional surfaces Φ_i. If Ξ_u is the surface set of discontinuity of control function u, then $\Xi_u = \bigcup_{i=1}^{k_u} \Phi_i$, where Φ_i, $i = 1, 2, \ldots, k_u$, are the elementary surfaces of discontinuity of u and k_u is the number of these surfaces. It is assumed, however, that u is continuous on every set

$$((\Phi_i \cup \Phi_i^+) \cap D)\backslash((\Phi_{i+1} \cup \Phi_{i+1}^+) \cap D), \tag{8.1.3}$$

where Φ_i and Φ_{i+1} are any two adjacent surfaces of discontinuity of u, $i = 1, 2, \ldots, k_u - 1$, and

$$D = \{(x_1, x_2, \ldots, x_n) = \Phi(x_1, x_2, \ldots, x_n) > 0\}.$$

The control function u can continuously be extended on some closed ε-neighborhood of every set defined by (8.1.3).

Figure 8.1.5 shows the set of discontinuity of a regular control function u and the zero-dimensional surfaces Φ_i for $n = 1$. In this case $\Xi_u = \{x_0, x_1, \ldots, x_n\}$, $\Phi_i = \{x_i\}$, $\Phi_i^+ = \{x : x > x_i\}$, $\Phi_i^- = \{x : x < x_i\}$, and $k_u = n$. In this figure, since u is a function in R, the definition of regularity coincides with that of continuity from the right. As illustrated in the figure, u can be continuously extended on a closed ε-neighborhood of every set

$$((\Phi_i \cup \Phi_i^+) \cap D)\backslash((\Phi_{i+1} \cup \Phi_{i+1}^+ \cap D\} = [x_i, x_{i+1}),$$

where $i = 0, 1, \ldots, n - 1$.

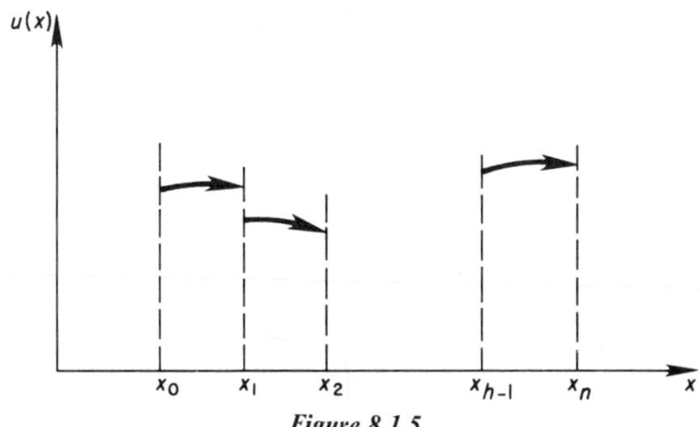

Figure 8.1.5

The control function u is said to have kth-*order smoothness* if it is k times continuously differentiable on every set defined by (8.1.3). The derivatives can be extended continuously on closed ε-neighborhoods of these sets such that the control function u will have k-continuous derivatives (i.e., u is of class C^k in this ε-neighborhood).

By analogy, regularity and smoothness of the control function of the second player can also be defined.

Any pair of control functions (u, w), is said to satisfy the assumption of *ε-penetrability* if every surface Φ_i belonging to the set of discontinuity of (u, w) is ε-penetrated by the function $\phi(x, u(x), w(x))$ as in (7.2.2). As already explained, the condition of ε-penetrability with respect to ϕ makes it impossible for any trajectory of system (7.2.2) to intersect the surface Φ_i more than one time. This condition can be interpreted as follows: The surfaces causing the discontinuity of u and w are "switching" surfaces on which control functions change, by jumping, from one regime to another. Then the assumption of ε-penetrability says that in order to reswitch surfaces, the control functions should be changed so that the state of the game (at least for one player) changes substantially.

No player knows a priori whether a particular choice of strategies by both players will ε-penetrate the same singular surface (i.e., the set of discontinuity of u and w). If the first player, for example, wants to choose his/her strategy so as to ε-penetrate the same singular set, the other player may change his/her choice of strategies to ε-penetrate a different singular set. The results of their choices, therefore, can only be known a posteriori. A restriction will be imposed on the strategies of the player, so that each player can make his/her wish independently of his/her opponent's wish, therefore, additional definitions must be introduced.

Let Φ be a surface of discontinuity of the control function u such that at every point $x \in \Phi$,

$$\min_{w \in U_2(x)} (\phi(x, u, w), v(x)) > \varepsilon, \tag{8.1.4}$$

where $v(x)$ is a vector normal to Φ and is directed in the positive halfspace of Φ. Then Φ is said to be *strongly ε-penetrated from the negative side, given the control function u.* A similar definition can be formed for Φ when it is *strongly ε-penetrated from the positive side* (or strongly ε-nonpenetrated from the negative side) *given the control function u.* Relation (8.1.4) says that the first player can always choose his/her control function u and have the state of the game [i.e., the trajectory of system (7.2.2)] to intersect his/her singular surface Φ, regardless of the opponent's wish. If all singular surfaces of control function u are strongly ε-penetrated (from any side), then u is said to be *strongly ε-penetrating.* By the same token, the control function of the second player, w, can be defined to be *strongly ε-penetrating.*

Finally, we need to have a less restrictive property than the ε-penetrating of the pair of control functions (u, w) or the strongly ε-penetrating of the separate control functions u or w. This property is usually connected with the terminal surface. An elementary surface is *ε-penetrated in the game* if for every point $x \in \Phi$,

$$\max_{u \in U_1(x)} \min_{w \in U_2(x)} \phi(x, u, w)v(x) > \varepsilon,$$

$$\max_{w \in U_2(x)} \min_{u \in U_1(x)} \phi(x, u, w)v(x) > \varepsilon.$$

The meaning of these relations will be provided later. Now, it can be said that these relations make it possible for one player to terminate the game provided that the trajectory of the game is very close to the terminal surface.

The following restrictions on the functions ϕ, f_1, f_2, U_1 and U_2, which are defined in the differential game described by (7.2.2) and (7.3.1) of Chapter 7, will be used in establishing the forthcoming theorems:

(R1) The functions f_1, a mapping of R^n into R, f_2, a mapping of R^{n+m+l} into R, and ϕ, a mapping of R^{n+m+l} into R^n, are twice continuously differentiable. Furthermore, f_2 satisfies the Lipschitz conditions by x [i.e., there exists a positive constant k such that

$$|f_2(x_1, u, w) - f_2(x_2, u, w)| < k\|x_1 - x_2\|$$

for all $u \in U_1(x)$ and $w \in U_2(x)$]. Additionally, the mapping U_1 of R^n into 2^{R^m} and the mapping U_2 of R^n into 2^{R^l} are continuous and their image sets $U_1(x)$ and $U_2(x)$, respectively, are closed and convex valued and nonempty for any $x \in D$.

By (7.2.2) and (7.3.1) of Chapter 7, the above functions and mappings define the game and the player's payoff, which can be expressed as

$$\dot{x} = \phi(x, u, w), \qquad u \in U_1(x), \qquad w \in U_2(x), \qquad x(t_0) = x_0$$

and

$$P(x_0, u, w) = f_1(x(t_F)) + \int_{t_0}^{t_F} f_2(x(\tau), u(x(\tau)), w(x(\tau)))\, dt, \qquad (8.1.5)$$

where t_F is the first moment at which the trajectory t_F captures the terminal surface F, which consists of a finite number of regular $(n - 1)$-dimensional surfaces.

(R2) Let the set that contains the initial points of any trajectory of the game, $x_0 \in D$, be compact and its boundary F consist of a finite number of ε-penetrated surfaces.

Compactness of set D implies that the trajectory under consideration cannot continue to infinity. Then there exists a finite period T such that the game terminates at the moment $t_F < T$. The condition of ε-penetrability can be relaxed by requiring that ε-penetrating of the terminal surface takes place only on those parts to which the trajectory of the game can proceed. It will also be assumed that the initial point x_0 belongs to the negative halfspaces of all singular sets of the control functions u and w, and that the region of game D lies in the negative halfspaces of all terminal surfaces. These definitions and conditions pave the way for formulating and proving the following theorem from Isaacs' theory.

Theorem 8.1.1 Suppose the game Γ satisfies conditions R1 and R2 and has a solution. Moreover, let the optimal control functions $\bar{u}$ and $\bar{w}$ have first-order smoothness and let it satisfy the conditions of ε-penetrability, then Bellman's function $W(x)$ is differentiable and

$$\begin{aligned} 0 &= \sum_{i=1}^{n} \frac{\partial W}{\partial x_i} \phi_i(x, \bar{u}, \bar{w}) + f_2(x, \bar{u}, \bar{w}) \\ &= \max_{u \in U_1(x)} \min_{w \in U_2(x)} \left(\sum_{i=1}^{n} \frac{\partial W}{\partial x_i} \phi_i(x, u, w) + f_2(x, u, w) \right). \end{aligned} \qquad (8.1.6)$$

Proof The proof of the continuity and differentiability will be deferred to Section 8.3.

Suppose first that $x_0 \notin \bigcup_{i=1}^{k} \Phi_i$, where Φ_i and $i = 1, \ldots, k$ are singular surfaces of the control functions $\bar{u}(x)$ and $\bar{w}(x)$. Then there exists an open ball

$S(x_0, \varepsilon)$ with a center x_0 and radius $\varepsilon > 0$, which does not intersect either any Φ_i, $i = 1, 2, \ldots, k$, or the terminal surface F. Since one of the variables in (7.1.2) of Section 7.1 is time (i.e., t) then there exists a constant $h < \varepsilon$ such that at time $t_0 + h$, the trajectory $x(t)$, which starts from x_0 at t_0 [i.e., $x(t_0) = x_0$] and is determined by the strategies $\bar{u}$ and $\bar{w}$, will leave the ball $S(x_0, \varepsilon)$. Then by the definition of Bellman's function and the payoff function, one will have

$$P(x_0, \bar{u}, \bar{w}) = W(x_0) = \int_{t_0}^{t_0+h} f_2(x(t), \bar{u}(x(t)), \bar{w}(x(t)))\, dt + W(x_h), \quad (8.1.7)$$

where $x_h = x(t_0 + h)$, i.e., a shift of the state along the optimal trajectory. Furthermore, since Bellman's function is continuously differentiable in the ball $S(x_0, \varepsilon)$, by applying the Taylor's series expansion one will obtain

$$W(x_h) = W(x_0) + \sum_{i=1}^{n} \frac{\partial W}{\partial x_i}(x_0)\, \Delta x_i + o(\Delta x), \quad (8.1.8)$$

where Δx_i is the ith component of the vector $\Delta x = x(t_0 + h) - x(t_0)$ and the remainder $o(\Delta x)$ satisfies the condition $o(\Delta x)/\|\Delta x\| \to 0$ when $\|\Delta x\| \to 0$. Additionally, since $\phi(x, \bar{u}(x), \bar{w}(x))$ is continuous at $\bar{x}$, then

$$\Delta x_i = \phi_i(x_0, \bar{u}(x_0), \bar{w}(x_0))h + o_i(h), \quad (8.1.9)$$

where $o_i(h)/h \to 0$ if $h \to o$. Similarly,

$$\int_{t_0}^{t_0+h} f_2(x(t), \bar{u}(x(t)), \bar{w}(x(t)))\, dt = f_2(x_0, \bar{u}(x_0), \bar{w}(x_0))h + \alpha(h), \quad (8.1.10)$$

where $\alpha(h)/h \to 0$ if $h \to 0$. Substituting (8.1.9) in (8.1.8) and then the latter in (8.1.7), making use of (8.1.10), yields

$$W(x_0) = W(x_0) + \sum_{i=1}^{n} \frac{\partial W}{\partial x_i}(x_0)\phi_i(x_0, \bar{u}(x_0), \bar{w}(x_0))h + f_2(x_0, \bar{u}(x_0), \bar{w}(x_0))h + o^*(h), \quad (8.1.11)$$

where $o^*(h)/h \to 0$ if $h \to 0$. Dividing (8.1.11) by h and taking the limit when $h \to 0$ yield the left-hand side of (8.1.6) as required.

Now let $\tilde{u}$ be an arbitrary value of $U_1(x_0)$. Then there exists a function $\tilde{u}(x)$ that is continuous at the point x_0 such that $\tilde{u}(x_0) = \tilde{u}$ and $\tilde{u}(x) = \bar{u}(x)$ for $x \in S(x_0, \varepsilon)$. The existence of this function follows from the theorem of existence of a continuous selector for a continuous point to set mapping (Kuratowski, 1966) and from the theorem of extension of continuous functions. Then by the definition of a saddle point, $\bar{u}$ and $\bar{w}$, for the strategy $\tilde{u}(x)$, one will have

$$P(x_0, \tilde{u}, \bar{w}) \leq P(x_0, \bar{u}, \bar{w}) = W(x_0). \tag{8.1.12}$$

If $\tilde{x}(t)$ represents the trajectory that starts from x_0 at time t_0 and is governed by the strategies $\tilde{u}$ and $\bar{w}$, the payoff function can be expressed as

$$P(x_0, \tilde{u}(\tilde{x}), \bar{w}(\tilde{x})) = \int_{t_0}^{t_0+\tilde{h}} f_2(\tilde{x}(t), \tilde{u}(\tilde{x}(t)), \bar{w}(\tilde{x}(t)) \, dt + W(\tilde{x}_h), \tag{8.1.13}$$

where $\tilde{x}_h = \tilde{x}(t_0 + h)$ and $\tilde{h}$ is the moment at which the trajectory $\tilde{x}(t)$ leaves the ball $S(x_0, \varepsilon)$. Applying the same reasoning used above and making use of (8.1.12) yields

$$\sum_{i=1}^{n} \frac{\partial W}{\partial x_i}(x_0)\phi_i(x_0, \tilde{u}, \bar{w}(x_0)) + f_2(x_0, \tilde{u}, \bar{w}(x_0)) \leq 0,$$

which proves the right-hand side of (8.1.6).

By the same token, $\tilde{w}$ can be chosen from $U_2(x_0)$ and the right-hand side of (8.1.6) can be established.

Finally, let $x_0 \in \Phi_i$. Then (8.1.6) can be established on all points of the set

$$(\Phi_i^+ \cap D) \backslash (\Phi_{i+1}^+ \cup \Phi_i) \cap D \tag{8.1.14}$$

by using the same method employed earlier in this proof (i.e., by taking advantage of smoothness of functions $\bar{u}$, $\bar{w}$, W, and $\partial W/\partial x_i$, $i = 1, \ldots, n$ in the sets defined by (8.1.14), which can also be considered smooth in every ε-neighborhood that covers every one of these sets). And then, by taking the limit when $x_k \to x_0$, where x_k is an element of the set defined by (8.1.14), we get (8.1.6) for $x_0 \in \Phi_i$. Q.E.D.

Corollary If system (8.1.5) does not incorporate t as an explicit variable, then in the formula

$$W(x_h) = W(x_0) + \sum_{i=1}^{n} \frac{\partial W}{\partial x_i}(x_0) \cdot \Delta x_i + o(\Delta x)$$

the summation takes place with respect to the vector x excluding t and Bellman's function does not depend on t (i.e., $\partial W/\partial t = 0$).

Theorem 8.1.1 and its corollary make it possible to distinguish between optimal control functions in game theory and in control theory. Suppose there is only one player, the first player, and he/she wants to maximize the payoff $P(x, u)$ subject to

$$\dot{x} = \phi(x, u), \qquad u \in U(x).$$

Then the functions ϕ and f_2 do not depend on strategy w, and by (8.1.6) one will have

$$0 = \sum_{i=1}^{n} \frac{\partial W}{\partial x_i} \phi_i(x, \bar{u}) + f_2(x, \bar{u}) = \max_{u \in U(x)} \left(\sum_{i=1}^{n} \frac{\partial W}{\partial x_i} \phi_i(x, u) + f_2(x, u) \right). \tag{8.1.15}$$

Let $\partial W(x)/\partial x_i = H_i(x)$. Then

$$H(x, u) = \sum_{i=1}^{n} H_i(x)\phi_i(x, u) + f_2(x, u(x)),$$

which is known as the Hamiltonian function (or simply the Hamiltonian) in control theory. Therefore, Eq. (8.1.15) can be expressed as

$$H(x, \bar{u}) = \max_{u \in U(x)} H(x, u),$$

which is known in control theory as Pontryagin's maximum principle. Thus Theorem 8.1.1 establishes the maximum principle. In control theory the theorem that establishes this principle does not usually require assumptions on optimal control functions that are as restrictive as those of Theorem 8.1.1. The restrictions stem from the specifications of these functions in game theory. In control theory, optimal control functions depend on t, whereas in game theory these functions (i.e., behavioral strategies) depend on x. This kind of control function is called a synthetic control function in control theory. Theorem 8.1.1, therefore, establishes the maximum principle for synthetic control functions. Other useful relations can be derived from Isaacs' theory. Before doing that, however, more assumptions concerning the control sets $U_1(x)$ and $U_2(x)$ will be introduced.

It is assumed that the set $U_1(x)$ can be described by a system of inequalities

$$g_i(x, u) \geq 0, \tag{8.1.16}$$

where g_i are continuously differentiable functions of $R^n \times R^m$ into R. Moreover, the Jacobian matrix $[\partial g_i(x, \bar{u}(x))/\partial u_k]$, $i = 1, 2, \ldots, n_1$, and $k = 1$,

$2, \ldots, m$, is assumed to have full rank at every $x \in D$ [i.e., the rank of the matrix is $\min(m, n_1)$]. Similarly, the set $U_2(x)$ can be described by a system of inequalities

$$q_j(x, w) \geq 0, \qquad j = 1, 2, \ldots, n_2. \tag{8.1.17}$$

The Jacobian matrix $[\partial q_j(x, \bar{w}(x))/\partial w_k]$, $j = 1, 2, \ldots, n_2$, and $k = 1, 2, \ldots, l$, associated with this system is also assumed to have full rank. These assumptions will be referred to as (R3).

Finally, (R4) stipulates that the terminal surface is an elementary surface which is twice continuously differentiable.

Theorem 8.1.2 Under the conditions of Theorem 8.1.1, assumptions (R3) and (R4), and the assumption that the control functions have second-order smoothness,

$$\dot{W}_k = -\sum_{i=1}^{n} W_i \phi_{ik}(x, \bar{u}, \bar{w}) - f_2^k(x, \bar{u}, \bar{w}) \tag{8.1.18}$$

holds a.e., where

$$\dot{W}_k = \frac{d}{dt} W_k(x(t)), \qquad W_k = \frac{\partial W}{\partial x_k},$$

$$\phi_{ik} = \frac{\partial \phi_i}{\partial x_k} \qquad \text{and} \qquad f_2^k = \frac{\partial f_2}{\partial x_k}.$$

Proof Let $x \notin \bigcup_{i=1}^{n} \Phi_i$, where Φ_i is a singular surface of u and w. Then Bellman's function W and the functions $\bar{u}$ and $\bar{w}$ are differentiable at x. Therefore, differentiating (8.1.8) with respect to x_k yields

$$\sum_{i=1}^{n} \left(\frac{\partial^2 W}{\partial x_i \, \partial x_k} \phi_i(x, \bar{u}, \bar{w}) + \sum_{j=1}^{m} \frac{\partial W}{\partial x_i} \frac{\partial \phi_i}{\partial u_j}(x, \bar{u}, \bar{w}) \frac{\partial \bar{u}_j}{\partial x_k} \right.$$
$$\left. + \sum_{j=1}^{m} \frac{\partial W}{\partial x_i} \frac{\partial \phi_i}{\partial w_j}(x, \bar{u}, \bar{w}) \frac{\partial \bar{w}_j}{\partial x_k} \right) + \sum_{j=1}^{m} \frac{\partial f_2}{\partial u_j}(x, \bar{u}, \bar{w}) \frac{\partial \bar{u}_j}{\partial x_k}$$
$$+ \sum_{j=1}^{m} \frac{\partial f_2}{\partial w_j}(x, \bar{u}, \bar{w}) \frac{\partial \bar{w}_j}{\partial x_k} + \frac{\partial f_2}{\partial x_k}(x, \bar{u}, \bar{w}) = 0. \tag{8.1.19}$$

Let us consider the expression

$$\sum_{i=1}^{n} \frac{\partial W}{\partial x_i} \phi_i(x, \bar{u}(x), w(x)) + f_2(x, \bar{u}(x), w(x)). \tag{8.1.20}$$

Then by Theorem 8.1.1 this expression will attain its minimum over all $w \in U_2(x)$ at $w = \bar{w}(x)$. Differentiating $w(x)$ in (8.1.20) with respect to x_k, while keeping $\bar{u}$ fixed and making use of assumption R3 concerning $U_2(x)$ for every $x \in D$, gives rise to

$$\sum_{j=1}^{m} \frac{\partial w_j}{\partial x_k} \left(\sum_{i=1}^{n} \frac{\partial W}{\partial x_i} \frac{\partial \phi}{\partial w_j} (x, \bar{u}(x), \bar{w}(x)) + \frac{\partial f_2}{\partial w_j} (x, \bar{u}(x), \bar{w}(x)) \right) = 0 \tag{8.1.21}$$

(Bliss, 1946).

Analogously, consider the expression

$$\sum_{i=1}^{n} \frac{\partial W}{\partial x_i} \phi_i(x, u(x), \bar{w}(x)) + f_2(x, u(x), \bar{w}(x)). \tag{8.1.22}$$

This expression reaches the maximum at $\bar{u}(x)$ for all $u \in U_1(x)$. Differentiating $u(x)$ in (8.1.22) with respect to x_k, while keeping $\bar{w}$ fixed, yields

$$\sum_{j=1}^{m} \frac{\partial u_j}{\partial x_k} \left(\sum_{i=1}^{n} \frac{\partial W}{\partial x_i} \frac{\partial \phi_i}{\partial u_j} (x, \bar{u}(x), \bar{w}(x)) + \frac{\partial f_2}{\partial u_j} (x, \bar{u}(x), \bar{w}(x)) \right) = 0. \tag{8.1.23}$$

Moreover, we have on the trajectory of system (7.1.2)

$$\sum_{i=1}^{n} \frac{\partial^2 W}{\partial x_i \, \partial x_k} \phi_i(x, \bar{u}, \bar{w}) = \sum_{i=1}^{n} \frac{\partial^2 W}{\partial x_k \, \partial x_i} \phi_i(x, \bar{u}, \bar{w}) = \frac{d}{dt} \frac{\partial W}{\partial x_k} = \dot{W}_k. \tag{8.1.24}$$

Hence, substituting (8.1.24), (8.1.23), and (8.1.21) in (8.1.19) establishes (8.1.18) at all points at which Bellman's function is twice continuously differentiable.[2] Note that the condition of ε-penetration of any trajectory under control functions $\bar{u}(x)$ and $\bar{w}(x)$ starting from the interior of region D can intersect the singular surfaces for only a finite period of time. That is, (8.1.18) can be violated only in the set with a zero measure. Q.E.D.

[2] We shall show later that the points at which Bellman's function is not twice continuously differentiable belong to the singular set of control functions $\bar{u}(x)$ and $\bar{w}(x)$.

To conclude this section, two remarks on Theorems 8.1.1 and 8.1.2 will be presented. Consider the system

$$\begin{aligned} \dot{x} &= \phi(x, \bar{u}, \bar{w}), \qquad x(t_0) = x_0, \\ \dot{W}_k &= -\sum_{i=1}^{n} W_i \phi_{ik}(x, \bar{u}, \bar{w}) - f_2^k(x, \bar{u}, \bar{w}), \\ 0 &= \sum_{i=1}^{n} W_i \phi_i(x, \bar{u}, \bar{w}) + f_2(x, \bar{u}, \bar{w}) \\ &= \max_{u \in U_1(x)} \min_{w \in U_2(x)} \left(\sum_{i=1}^{n} W_i \phi_i(x, u, w) + f_2(x, u, w) \right). \end{aligned} \tag{8.1.25}$$

System (8.1.25) gives us additional assumptions for defining $\bar{u}$, $\bar{w}$, and W. In fact, the last equality defines $\bar{u}$ and $\bar{w}$ as functions at which the expression

$$\sum_{i=1}^{n} W_i \phi_i(x, u, w) + f_2(x, u, w)$$

attains its maximin. The second differential equation of (8.1.25) makes it possible to define the value of the change in Bellman's function with respect to time, i.e., $\dot{W}_k$. Additionally, knowing the value of $\dot{W}_k$ on the boundary of the region D, it is possible to calculate this value everywhere in this region. Finally, the first differential equation makes it possible to define optimal trajectory $x(t)$.

The last equality of (8.1.25) also has an interesting interpretation. If $f_2 = 0$ (recall that this is possible by introducing an additional variable), then on the optimal trajectories

$$\frac{dW}{dt}(x(t)) = \sum_{i=1}^{n} \frac{\partial W}{\partial x_i} \dot{x}_i = \sum_{i=1}^{n} W_i \phi_i(x, \bar{u}, \bar{w}) = 0.$$

In other words, the value of Bellman's function on the optimal trajectories given $\bar{u}$ and $\bar{w}$ does not change, i.e., these trajectories "transfer" the value of Bellman's function from the boundary to the interior of the region of the game D, while keeping it constant. Moreover, if $u = \bar{u}$ and $w \neq \bar{w}$, then

$$\frac{dW}{d}(x(t)) \geq \sum_{i=1}^{n} W_i \phi_{ik}(x, \bar{u}, \bar{w}) = 0.$$

That is, any change in the control function of the second player, away from $\bar{w}$, gives the first player the possibility of increasing his/her payoff. In the case

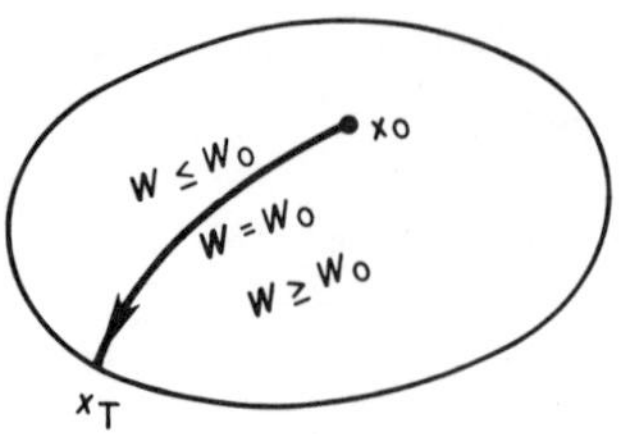

Figure 8.1.6

of $n = 2$, for example, the optimal trajectory divides the region of the game D into two parts, one to the left of the trajectory, in which the value of Bellman's function is equal or less than its value on the optimal trajectory, and the other to the right of the trajectory, in which the value of W is equal to or greater than its value on the optimal trajectory (see Figure 8.1.6).

Note that in the case of one player, system (8.1.25) can be expressed as

$$\begin{aligned} \dot{x} &= \phi(x, \bar{u}), \qquad x(t_0) = x_0, \\ \dot{H}_k &= -\sum_{i=1}^{n} H_i \phi_{ik}(x, \bar{u}) - f_2^k(x, \bar{u}), \qquad k = 1, \ldots, n, \\ 0 &= \sum_{i=1}^{n} H_i \phi_i(x, \bar{u}) + f_2(x, \bar{u}) \\ &= \max_{u \in U(x)} \left(\sum_{i=1}^{n} H_i \phi_i(x, u) + f_2(x, u) \right). \end{aligned} \tag{8.1.26}$$

The second system of (8.1.26) is called the dual equality. If the matrix $[H_{ij}]$, where $H_{ij} = \partial H_i/\partial x_j$, $i = 1, \ldots, n$ and $j = 1, \ldots, n$, is nondegenerate, then system (8.1.26) has a solution. Consequently, the optimal control function of this system can be defined.

8.2 APPLICATION OF THE REGRESSION EQUATIONS TO WAR BETWEEN ONE-COMMODITY MODELS

There are numerous examples of differential games in which solutions are obtained by using Isaacs' method. In this section, Isaacs' theory will be applied to war between one-commodity models (i.e., economies). First, Isaacs' system of equations as defined by (8.1.25) will be expressed in regression form. The idea of this method is rather simple. The value of Bellman's function is not known in the interior region of D, however, it is known at the boundary of that region. If time is reversed such that the terminal state x_T is at the initial time t_0, where $t_0 = 0$, then the trajectory of system (8.1.25) starts from the boundary of region D and proceeds to the initial state x_0 at the terminal moment T. In Figure 8.1.6 the optimal trajectory starts from the point x_T and moves backward with time. Substituting $-\tau$, where $\tau \in [0, +\infty)$, for t in system (8.1.25) and letting $\dot{x}$ stand for the derivative of x with respect to τ yields

$$\begin{aligned}
\dot{x} &= -\phi(x, \bar{u}, \bar{w}), \\
\dot{W}_k &= \sum_{i=1}^{n} W_i \phi_{ik}(x, \bar{u}, \bar{w}) + f_2^k(x, \bar{u}, \bar{w}), \qquad k = 1, \ldots, n \\
0 &= \sum_{i=1}^{n} W_i \phi_i(x, \bar{u}, \bar{w}) \\
&= \min_{w \in U_2(x)} \max_{u \in U_1(x)} \left(\sum_{i=1}^{n} W_i \phi_i(x, u, w) + f_2(x, u, w) \right).
\end{aligned} \tag{8.2.1}$$

This system is called *Isaacs' system in regression form.* Since $x(0) = x_T$, the question is how to define $W_i(0)$, $i = 1, \ldots, n$, which are required in (8.2.1). To answer this question, the following definition is needed. A surface F can be *parameterized* if there exists a one-to-one differential function F of R^{n-1} into R^n such that $F = F(Q)$, where Q is an open ball in R^{n-1}, or if for any $x \in F$, then $x = F(\sigma_1, \ldots, \sigma_{n-1})$, where $\sigma = (\sigma_1, \ldots, \sigma_{n-1}) \in Q$. The variables σ_i, $i = 1, \ldots, n-1$ are called *parameters.* Then any parameterized surface can be presented as an elementary surface with the use of a differentiable function Φ of R^n into R [i.e., $\Phi = \Phi^{-1}(0)$] (Spivak, 1965). Locally, that is, in an open neighborhood of any point, any elementary surface can be parameterized, and vice versa. Therefore, since the boundary of the region D is an $(n-1)$-dimensional surface in R^n, then if that boundary is a parameterized $(n-1)$-dimensional surface in a neighborhood of the terminal state x_T, one will have $x = x(\sigma_1, \ldots, \sigma_{n-1})$ [or more strictly $x = F(\sigma_1, \ldots, \sigma_{n-1})$]. As a consequence, Bellman's function can be expressed as

$$W(x) = W(x(\sigma_1, \ldots, \sigma_{n-1})).$$

Differentiating this function with respect to σ_i yields

$$\frac{\partial W}{\partial \sigma_i} = \sum_{k=1}^{n} \frac{\partial W}{\partial x_k} \frac{\partial x_k}{\partial \sigma_i} = \sum_{k=1}^{n} W_k \frac{\partial x_k}{\partial \sigma_i}, \qquad i = 1, \ldots, n-1. \tag{8.2.2}$$

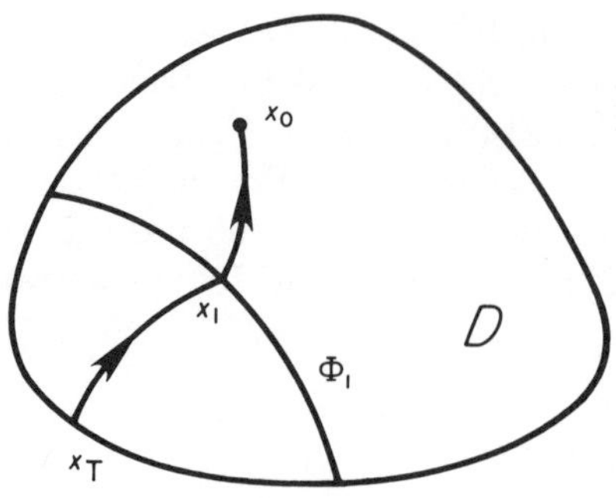

Figure 8.2.1

System (8.2.2) evaluated at $\sigma_T = (\sigma_1^T, \ldots, \sigma_{n-1}^T)$ such that $x_T = x(\sigma_T)$ gives rise to $(n - 1)$ equations. But at this point there are n unknowns, namely, $W_1, \ldots, W_n$. However, as usual, the nth equation of system (8.2.2) is the third equation in (8.2.1), which is also known on the boundary of region D. Therefore, system (8.2.2) becomes a system of n differential equations with n knowns, in addition to the initial conditions. This system should be solved, beginning from the boundary of region D and proceeding to the interior of that region. Any singular surface that is met by the trajectory of the system is considered a new boundary from which the trajectory will start and proceed until the state x_0 is attained. These surfaces are surfaces of switching and reswitching of control functions. This process is schematically shown in Figure 8.2.1. The trajectory starts from x_T on the boundary of region D and proceeds until it meets the singular surface Φ_1 which has x_1 as a point of switching of control. Then the trajectory continues inside D, starting from x_1 as the initial state and so on until x_0 is attained.

The following example is a continuous version of Example 5.2.2 of a war between two one-commodity models with fixed supply.

Example 8.2.1 Consider the system

$$\dot{x}_1 = m_1 - s_2 \psi x_2,$$

$$\dot{x}_2 = m_2 - s_1 \phi x_1,$$

where $x_i(t)$ is the amount of resource stock available to model i, $i = 1, 2$, at time t, m_i is the fixed productive capacity of model i and is measured as units per hour, s_i is the interaction coefficient of model i, ϕ is the intensity level of allocating the resource to the military industry by the first model to inflict damages on the second model, and ψ is the intensity level of allocating the resource to the military industry by the second model to inflict damages on the first model. The coefficient s_i has the same interpretation as the interaction *matrix* S_i has in the difference games. It represents the efficiency of the military industry of model i by allowing a comparison between the amount of damage model i can inflict on its opponent and the amount of the resource stock of the latter, which it spares by choosing not to attack model i. The intensities ϕ and ψ assume values in the interval [0, 1]. The region of the game is $D = R_+^2$ and the boundary is the axes of the positive orthant, i.e.,

$$\partial D = \{(x_1, x_2): x_1 \geq 0 \text{ and } x_2 = 0\} \cup \{(x_1, x_2): x_1 = 0 \text{ and } x_2 \geq 0\}.$$

The region of the game, therefore, is not compact. An additional assumption is needed to make this region compact. One way is to restrict the duration of the game to a finite period (i.e., the duration is $t \leq T$). Another way is to introduce a special payoff function that forces all optimal trajectories to be in a compact set which includes the initial state. Here we shall use the second way. The payoff will be considered to be comprised of two parts: the terminal part and the integral part. The terminal part is defined as

$$f_1(x_1, x_2) = \begin{cases} \alpha x_1 & \text{if } x_2 = 0, \\ -\beta x_2 & \text{if } x_1 = 0, \end{cases}$$

where $\alpha > 0$ and $\beta > 0$. The interpretation of this function is that if model 1 wins, then the larger the amount of the resource stock remaining after victory, the better off that model is. If it loses, the smaller the amount left for its opponent at the end of the war, the better off model 1 is. If the payoff is composed of the terminal part, only then is it possible that optimal trajectories continue infinitely because that model will be better off if it does not terminate the game. This can be called a "paradox of infinity." To take advantage of this possibility, an integral part of the payoff function is required. This part can be defined in the form

$$-\int_{t_0}^{t} d\tau.$$

That is, model 1 is interested in terminating the game as soon as possible. Therefore, the payoff function takes the form

$$P(x_0, \phi, \psi) = f_1(x(t_F)) - \int_{t_0}^{t_F} dt,$$

where $f_2 = -1$.

At first, consider the case when the terminal surface is the x_1 axis. The parametric representation of this surface is $x_1 = \sigma_1$ and $x_2 = 0$. In terms of regression system (8.2.1), this case can be represented as

$$\begin{aligned}
\dot{x}_1 &= -m_1 + s_2 \psi x_2, \\
\dot{x}_2 &= -m_2 + s_1 \phi x_1, \\
\dot{W}_1 &= -s_1 \phi W_2, \\
\dot{W}_2 &= -s_2 \psi W_1, \\
0 &= W_1 \cdot (m_1 - s_2 \psi x_2) + W_2 \cdot (m_2 - s_1 \phi x_1) - 1 \\
&= \min_{\psi} \max_{\phi} [W_1(m_1 - s_2 \psi x_2) + W_2(m_2 - s_1 \phi x_1) - 1].
\end{aligned} \tag{8.2.3}$$

From the last equation,

$$\bar{\phi} = \begin{cases} 0 & \text{if } W_2 > 0, \\ 1 & \text{if } W_2 < 0, \\ \text{not defined} & \text{if } W_2 = 0. \end{cases}$$

Similarly,

$$\bar{\psi} = \begin{cases} 1 & \text{if } W_1 > 0, \\ 0 & \text{if } W_1 < 0, \\ \text{not defined} & \text{if } W_1 = 0. \end{cases}$$

The initial conditions are $x_1(0) = x_{10}$, and $x_2(0) = 0$ and $W(0) = \alpha x_{10}$. Then W_1 evaluated at the initial state is

$$\frac{\partial W}{\partial \sigma_1} = \frac{\partial W}{\partial x_1} = W_1(0) = \alpha > 0.$$

Therefore, $\bar{\psi}(x_1(0), x_2(0)) = 1$. That is, if at the initial period the payoff function is an increasing function of that model's state, then the model's optimal strategy is to allocate all its resources to its military industry. Moreover, it can be seen from (8.2.3) that if $\phi = 0$, then the trajectory will leave region D since $x_2(0) = 0$ and $\dot{x}_2 = -m_2 < 0$. That is, if $\phi = 0$, then $x_2(\tau) < 0$ for $\tau > 0$. Therefore, it is assumed that $\phi > 0$. Then it is necessary that $W_2(0) < 0$, which, in turn, yields that $\phi(x_1(0), x_2(0)) = 1$. In fact,

$$W_2(0) = -\frac{1 - m_1 \alpha}{m_2 - s_1 x_{10}}.$$

Note that it should be that $m_1\alpha < 1$, otherwise the loss in the payoff function caused by a longer duration of the game can be more than offset by gains in the terminal payoff. Therefore it is possible that the game can proceed infinitely. Furthermore, one should only consider the initial state $x_1(0)$, which satisfies $m_2 < s_1x_1(0)$ because the segment $0 \le x_1(0) \le m_2/s_1$ is not ε-penetrated by the first model. That is, model 2 may drive the trajectory off the terminal surface. In addition, if $0 \le x_1 \le m_2/s_1$, the normal to the terminal surface that is directed from region D is $v_F = (0, -1)$ and

$$\bar{\phi}(x_1(0), x_2(0), \phi, \psi) \cdot v_F = -m_2 + s_1\phi x_1(0) \le 0,$$

where $\bar{\phi}(x_1, x_2, \phi, \psi)$ is the kinematic equation of our game system.

Making use of these assumptions and their implication, system (8.2.3) yields

$$\begin{aligned}\dot{x}_1 &= -m_1 + s_2x_2,\\ \dot{x}_2 &= -m_2 + s_1x_1,\\ \dot{W}_1 &= -s_1W_2,\\ \dot{W}_2 &= -s_2W_1,\end{aligned}$$

and $x_1(0) = x_{10}, x_2(0) = 0, W_1(0) = \alpha$, and $W_2(0) = -(1 - m_1\alpha)/(m_2 - s_1x_{10})$. This system has the following solution

$$\begin{aligned}x_1(\tau) &= L_1(s_1s_2)^{1/2}\exp[(s_1s_2)^{1/2}\tau] - L_2(s_1s_2)^{1/2}\exp[-(s_1s_2)^{1/2}\tau] + \frac{m_2}{s_1},\\ x_2(\tau) &= L_1s_1\exp[(s_1s_2)^{1/2}\tau] + L_2s_1\exp[-(s_1s_2)^{1/2}\tau] + \frac{m_1}{s_2},\\ W_1(\tau) &= R_1(s_1s_2)^{1/2}\exp(s_1s_2)^{1/2}\tau + R_2(s_1s_2)^{1/2}\exp[-(s_1s_2)^{1/2}\tau],\\ W_2(\tau) &= -R_1s_2\exp[(s_1s_2)^{1/2}\tau] + R_2s_2\exp[-(s_1s_2)^{1/2}\tau],\end{aligned} \tag{8.2.4}$$

where

$$R_1 = \frac{\alpha Z_1 - s_1^{1/2}}{2s_1s_2^{1/2}(m_2 - s_1x_{10})}, \qquad R_2 = \frac{\alpha Z_2 + s_1^{1/2}}{2s_2s_1^{1/2}(m_2 - s_1x_{10})},$$

$$L_1 = -\frac{Z_1}{2s_1s_2s_1^{1/2}}, \qquad L_2 = \frac{Z_2}{2s_1s_2s_1^{1/2}}$$

are defined by the initial conditions such that

$$Z_1 = s_2^{1/2}(m_2 - s_1 x_{10}) + s_1^{1/2} m_1 \qquad \text{and} \quad Z_2 = s_2^{1/2}(m_2 - s_1 x_{10}) - s_1^{1/2} m_1.$$

From the assumptions discussed above, it follows that $Z_2 < 0$ and $R_1 > 0$. In addition, it follows from (8.2.4) that W_1 and W_2 do not change sign, i.e., there is no reswitching and both models attack with all of their resource (i.e., full attack) all the time.

Solving the first two equations of (8.2.4) yields

$$\tilde{x}_1(\tau) = \frac{-Z_1 Z_2}{(\tilde{x}_2(\tau) - m_1\sqrt{s_1} + m_2\sqrt{s_2})} + m_1\sqrt{s_1} + m_2\sqrt{s_2},$$

where

$$\tilde{x}_1(\tau) = s_1\sqrt{s_2}\,x_1(\tau) + s_2\sqrt{s_1}\,x_2(\tau),$$

$$\tilde{x}_2(\tau) = s_2\sqrt{s_1}\,x_2(\tau) - s_1\sqrt{s_2}\,x_1(\tau).$$

Then the trajectories are parts of hyperboles. The case in which the game finishes on the x_2 axis can be discussed similarly. The trajectories of both cases are shown in Figure 8.2.2. It is assumed in this figure that $m_1 s_1^{1/2} > m_2 s_2^{1/2}$. The heavy line consists of points from which the trajectories deter-

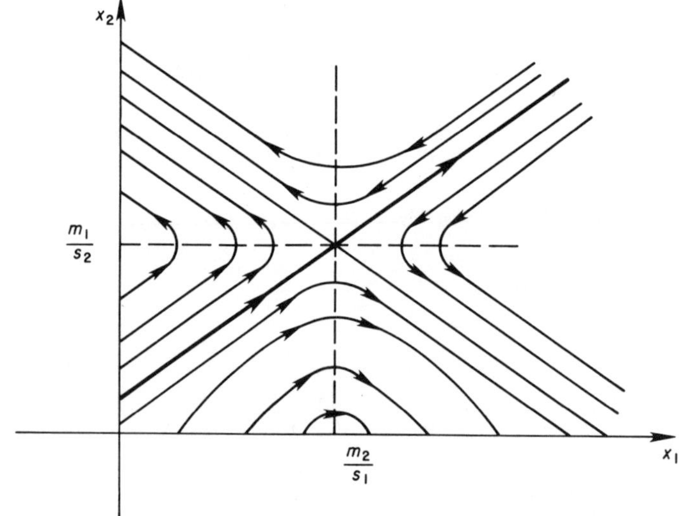

Figure 8.2.2

mined by the optimal strategies will go to the stationary state, i.e., $x_1(\tau) \equiv x_1(0) = m_2/s_1$ and $x_2(\tau) \equiv x_2(0) = m_1/s_2$. This line is called a stationery barrier. Below this line model 1 is the victor and above it model 2 is the victor. For both models to stay on that barrier, they must attack all the time. If model 1, for example, slows down its attack, then the state of the game shifts to the region above the barrier line and model 2 will win. Similarly, if model 2 weakens its attack campaign, the state of the game shifts to the region below the barrier line and model 1 will win.

8.3 CONTINUITY AND DIFFERENTIABILITY OF BELLMAN'S FUNCTION

It will be shown in this section that with some restriction on optimal control functions, including conditions of regularity, smoothness and ε-penetration, and with the assumption of ε-penetration of the terminal surface, Bellman's function is continuous and differentiable. Consider the system of differential equations

$$\dot{x} = F(x), \qquad x(t_0) = x_0, \tag{8.3.1}$$

where $x \in R^n$, with one elementary $(n-1)$-dimensional surface as its singular set.

It is assumed here that F is continuous on the sets Φ^- and $\Phi \cup \Phi^+$ and satisfies the Lipschitz condition on these sets. Moreover, it is assumed that there exists a constant M such that $\|F(x)\| \leq M$ for all $x \in R^n$. Let the set

$$\{x : x \in \Phi^- \text{ and } d(x, \Phi) < \delta\}$$

be denoted by Φ_δ^-. Similarly, the set

$$\{x : x \in \Phi^+ \text{ and } d(x, \Phi) < \delta\}$$

will be denoted by Φ_δ^+.

Lemma 8.3.1 Let Φ be an elementary $(n-1)$-dimensional surface which is the singular set for (8.3.1). Moreover, let Φ be compact and ε-penetrated from the negative side. Then there exists δ_ε such that for any $\delta \leq \delta_\varepsilon$, $\Delta \in (2\delta/\varepsilon, 4\delta/\varepsilon)$ and $x(\bar{t}) \in \Phi_\delta^-$, it follows that $x(\bar{t} + \Delta) \in \Phi_{\delta_1}^+$, where $\delta_1 \leq (2\delta/\varepsilon)M$.

Proof Let $\bar{x}$ be a point on Φ. Without loss of generality, it can be assumed that $\bar{x}$ is the origin of the coordinate system and the normal vector $v(\bar{x})$ to Φ at $\bar{x}$ is a unit vector of the x_n axis. Furthermore, let $Q(\bar{x}, \delta)$ be an n-dimensional rectangle with $\bar{x}$ as its center, and which satisfies

$$Q(x, \delta) = \{x : |x_i| < (2\delta/\varepsilon)M, i = 1, \ldots, n\}.$$

Choose $\delta(\varepsilon, \bar{x}) = \delta_\varepsilon$ such that

(i) $d(\Phi \cap Q(\bar{x}, \delta_\varepsilon), P \cap Q(\bar{x}, \delta_\varepsilon)) < \frac{1}{8}\delta_\varepsilon$ where P is a hyperplane tangent to Φ at $\bar{x}$, which in this case coincides with the coordinate hyperplane $P = \{(x_1, \ldots, x_n): x_n = 0\}$, and
(ii) $|F(x), v(\bar{x})| > \frac{1}{2}\varepsilon$ for all $x \in Q(\bar{x}, \delta_\varepsilon)$.

Note that δ_ε exists because (i) can be satisfied since the surface Φ^- is smooth (Sipvak, 1965) and (ii) can also be satisfied due to the continuity of F on the sets Φ^- and $\Phi \cup \Phi^+$.

Let $Q_1(\bar{x}, \delta_\varepsilon) \subset Q(\bar{x}, \delta_\varepsilon)$ be an n-dimensional rectangle described by

$$Q_1(\bar{x}, \delta_\varepsilon) = \{x: |x_i| < \delta_\varepsilon, i = 1, \ldots, n\}$$

and let $x(\bar{t}) \in \Phi^- \cap Q_1(\bar{x}, \delta_\varepsilon)$. Then $x(\bar{t}) \in \Phi^-_{\delta_\varepsilon}$ and

$$d(x(\bar{t}), P) = (v(\bar{x}), x(\bar{t})) < \delta_\varepsilon.$$

Therefore,

$$\frac{d}{dt}(x(t) \cdot v(\bar{x})) = (\dot{x}(t) \cdot v(\bar{x})) > \tfrac{1}{2}\varepsilon \tag{8.3.2}$$

for all t such that $x(t) \in Q(\bar{x}, \delta_\varepsilon)$.

Choosing $\Delta > 0$, such that $\frac{1}{2}\Delta\varepsilon > \delta_\varepsilon$, then from (8.3.2) one will have

$$d(x(\bar{t} + \Delta), P) = (x(\bar{t} + \Delta), v(\bar{x})) > \tfrac{1}{2}\Delta\varepsilon > \delta_\varepsilon.$$

This is, $x(\bar{t} + \Delta) \in P^+$. On the other hand, if $\Delta\varepsilon < 4\delta_\varepsilon$, then

$$|x_i(\bar{t} + \Delta) - x_i(\bar{t})| \leq \Delta \cdot M \leq (4\delta_\varepsilon/\varepsilon)M.$$

Therefore, $x(\bar{t} + \Delta) \in Q(x, \delta_\varepsilon)$. Then, by condition (i) on δ_ε, this yields that $x(\bar{t} + \Delta) \in \Phi^+_{\delta'_\varepsilon}$, where $\delta'_\varepsilon \leq (2\delta_\varepsilon/\varepsilon)M$. Thus δ_ε is the desired number that satisfies conditions of the lemma, given $\bar{x}$.

Note that in this discussion, δ_ε depends on both ε and $\bar{x}$. Then δ_ε should be written as $\delta_\varepsilon(\varepsilon, \bar{x})$. But as required by the lemma, we must show that there

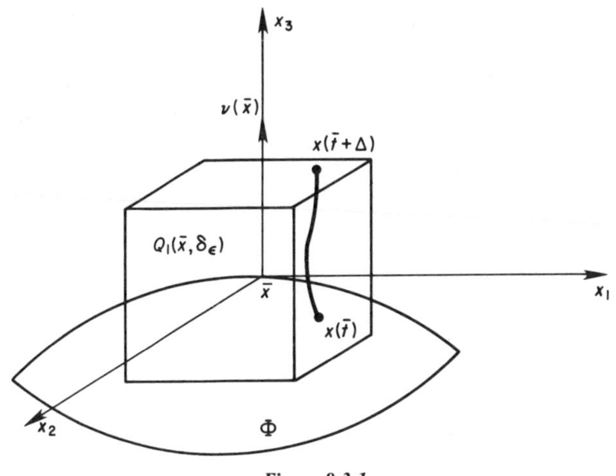

Figure 8.3.1

exists δ_ε that does not depend on x. To do that, let us connect a neighborhood $Q_1(\tilde{x}, \delta(\varepsilon, \tilde{x}))$ with $\tilde{x} \in \Phi$ as described in the reasoning above. Then Φ will be covered with those neighborhoods. Since Φ is compact, then there exist $x_1, \ldots, x_n \in \Phi$ such that

$$\Phi \subset \bigcup_{i=1}^{n} Q(x_i, \delta(\varepsilon, x_i)).$$

Hence the desirable δ_ε is such that $\delta_\varepsilon = \min_{1 \leq i \leq n} \delta(\varepsilon, x_i)$. Q.E.D.

The situation discussed in this lemma is depicted in Figure 8.3.1 for $n = 3$.

Theorem 8.3.1 Let the function F have one singular surface that satisfies the conditions of Lemma 8.3.1. Then the solution of (8.3.1) continuously depends on the initial data x_0.

In other words, if $x(t, x_0)$ is the solution of (8.3.1) starting from x_0 at time t_0, then this solution is continuous in x_0.

Proof Let $x(t, x_0)$ be a solution of (8.3.1) such that $x(t_0, x_0) = x_0$, and let $x_k \to x_0$. If the trajectory $x(t, x_0)$ does not reach the surface Φ, then by the classical theory, the solution of a system of differential equations continuously depends on the initial data, if the right part of the system is continuous. If $x(t, x_0)$ meets the surface Φ, then there exists $\bar{t}$ such that $x(\bar{t}) \in \Phi$. Then by

Lemma 8.3.1 there exists a point t_δ such that $x(t_\delta) \in \Phi^-_{\delta/2}$. Then by the classical definition of continuity there exists $\bar{k}$ such that

$$\|x(t, x_k) - x(t, x_0)\| < \delta/\varepsilon$$

for all $k > \bar{k}$ and $t \in [t_0, \bar{t}]$. But then $x(t, x_k) \in \Phi^-_\delta$, and by Lemma 8.3.1 it intersects Φ in a time not longer than $(t + \Delta)$, where $\Delta \leq 2\delta/\varepsilon \leq 2\delta_\varepsilon/\varepsilon$. Since $\|F\| < M$, then

$$\|x(\bar{t}, x_0) - x(\bar{t}_k, x_k)\| < \Delta \cdot M.$$

Furthermore, due to $\delta < \delta_\varepsilon$, if $x_k \to x_0$, then

$$x(\bar{t}_k, x_k) \to x(\bar{t}, x_0).$$

Hence using $x(\bar{t}_k, x_k)$ and $x(\bar{t}, x_0)$ as the new initial conditions on the surface Φ^+ yields the continuity of F by the classical theory. Q.E.D.

Corollary Under the assumptions of Theorem 8.3.1, the moment $t^k_\Phi \to t_\Phi$ if $x_k \to x_0$, where t^k_Φ and t_Φ are the first moments at which the trajectories $x(t, x_k)$ and $x(t, x_0)$, respectively, capture the singular surface Φ.

The proof of this corollary follows the same reasoning as that of Lemma 8.3.1.

Theorem 8.3.2 Suppose that the differential game Γ satisfies (R1) and (R2) of Section 8.1 and that the optimal control function $\bar{u}$ and $\bar{w}$ are regular and satisfy the assumption of ε-penetrability. Moreover, assume that the terminal surface is also ε-penetrated; then Bellman's function is continuous.

Proof Under condition of Theorem 8.3.1, the system

$$\dot{x} = \phi(x, \bar{u}(x), \bar{w}(x)), \qquad x(t_0) = x_0, \tag{8.3.3}$$

where $\bar{u}(x) \in U_1(x)$ and $\bar{w}(x) \in U_2(x)$ satisfies all the assumptions of Lemma 8.3.1 in the interior of region D. If $t_F(x_0)$ represents the first moment at which the trajectory of system (8.3.3) attains the terminal surface, given the optimal control functions $\bar{u}$ and $\bar{w}$, then for any $\bar{t} < t_F(x_0)$ and $x_k \to x_0$ it follows by Lemma 8.3.1 that

$$\max_{t \in [t_0, \bar{t}]} \|x(t, x_k) - x(t, x_0)\| \to 0 \tag{8.3.4}$$

when $k \to \infty$, where $x(t, x_k)$, $k = 0, 1, 2, \ldots$ is a optimal trajectory that begins from $x(t_0, x_k) = x_k$. If $x(\bar{t}, x_0) \in F^-_\delta$, where

$$F^-_\delta = \{x : x \in F^- \text{ and } d(x, F) < \delta\},$$

then due to ε-penetration of the terminal surface F and the continuity of the mapping $U_1(x)$, the first player can choose the controls $\tilde{u} \in U_1(x(\bar{t}, x_0))$, which provide ε-penetration of the terminal surface regardless of the second player's choice of controls in system (8.3.3). Then since the image set $U_1(x)$ is compact and convexvalued, if $x = x(\bar{t}, x_0)$, there exists a continuous control function $\tilde{u}(x) \in U_1(x)$ such that $\tilde{u}(x) = \tilde{u}$. Then by (8.3.4) there exists a constant $k_0(\delta)$ such that for any $k > k_0(\delta)$ it follows that

$$x(\bar{t}, x_k) \in Q_1(x(\bar{t}, x_0), \delta),$$

where $Q_1(x(\bar{t}, x_0), \delta)$ is a neighborhood constructed on $x(\bar{t}, x_0)$ as described in Lemma 8.3.1. If the first player applies the controls $\tilde{u}(x)$ starting from moment $\bar{t}$, then due to the continuity of $U_1(x)$ that player provides $\frac{1}{2}\varepsilon$-penetration of the terminal surface in the neighborhood $Q_1(\bar{x}(t, x_0), \delta)$ and consequently attains the terminal surface in a time not longer than $\Delta < 4\delta/2$, where $\delta < \delta_\varepsilon/2$. Making use of (8.3.4), it follows that

$$|P(x_0, \bar{u}(x), \bar{w}(x)) - P(x_k, \tilde{\bar{u}}(x), w(x))| \leq \sigma_k \tag{8.3.5}$$

and $\sigma_k \to 0$ as $k \to \infty$, where $\tilde{\bar{u}}(x)$ is a strategy such that $u = \tilde{u}(x)$ if $x \in Q_1(x(\bar{t}, x_0), \delta)$ and $u = \bar{u}(x)$ if $x \notin Q_1(x(\bar{t}, x_0), \delta)$. By (8.3.5), the trajectories $x(t, x_0)$ and $x(t, x_k)$ can become very close right from the initial moments by having k grow as large as possible. Since f_1 and f_2 are continuous, then by imposing the Lipschitz condition on f_2 in x, Eq. (8.3.5) holds.

By the same token, the control function of the second player, $\tilde{\bar{w}}(x)$, can be constructed such that

$$|P(x_0, \bar{u}(x), \bar{w}(x)) - P(x_k, \bar{u}, \tilde{\bar{w}})| \leq \sigma_k^1 \tag{8.3.6}$$

and $\sigma_k^1 \to 0$ as $k \to \infty$.

Hence, by the definition of the optimality of $\bar{u}$ and $\bar{w}$,

$$P(x_k, \bar{u}, \tilde{\bar{w}}) \geq P(x_k, \bar{u}, \bar{w}) \geq P(x_k, \tilde{\bar{u}}, \bar{w}),$$

which together with (8.3.5) and (8.3.6) yields

$$P(x_k, \bar{u}, \bar{w}) \to P(x_0, \bar{u}, \bar{w}). \quad \text{Q.E.D.}$$

Corollary If the condition of ε-penetrability for the pair $(\bar{u}, \bar{w})$ in Theorem 8.3.2 is replaced by that of strong ε-penetrability while other conditions are kept the same, then the theorem also holds.

Theorem 8.3.1 was proved without any assumptions on the extension of $\bar{u}(x)$ and $\bar{w}(x)$ as demanded in the definition of regularity. This assumption will be added now.

Lemma 8.3.2 Suppose in addition to the conditions of Lemma 8.3.1 that the surface Φ is smooth of kth order and the function F of (8.3.1) has at least k-times continuous derivatives on the sets Φ^- and $\Phi^+ \cup \Phi$ and can be extended on some ε-neighborhoods of these sets while preserving these properties. Furthermore, let the function $t_\Phi(x_0)$ be the first moment at which the trajectory $x(t)$, which starts from x_0, captures the surface Φ. Then $t_\Phi(x_0)$ is at least k times differentiable.

Proof The moment $t = t_\Phi(x_0)$ is the moment of capture such that

$$\Phi(x(t, x_0)) = 0, \tag{8.3.7}$$

where $x(t, x_0)$ is the trajectory of (8.3.1), beginning from $x(t_0, x_0) = x_0$. Owing to the assumption of the extension of F, the function $\Phi(x(t, x_0))$ can be considered to be in a neighborhood of the pair $(t_\Phi(x_0), x_0)$. Furthermore, since Φ and F are differentiable, then

$$\left.\frac{\partial \Phi}{\partial t}\right|_{t=t_\Phi(x_0)} = \sum_{i=1}^{n} \frac{\partial \Phi}{\partial x_i}(x(t_\Phi(x_0), x_0)) \frac{dx_i}{dt}$$

and the vector $((\partial\Phi/\partial x_1)(x_\Phi), \ldots, (\partial\Phi/\partial x_n)(x_\Phi))$, letting $x_\Phi = x(t_\Phi(x_0), x_0)$, is equal to $\lambda(x_\Phi) \cdot v(x_\Phi)$, where $\lambda(x_\Phi)$ is a nonzero constant (because of the definition of elementary surfaces) and $v(x_\Phi)$ is a normal to Φ at the point x_Φ. Then by the assumption of ε-penetration of Φ,

$$\left(v(x_\Phi) \frac{dx}{dt}\right) = (v(x_\Phi)F(x_\Phi)) \geq \varepsilon,$$

i.e., $\partial\Phi/\partial t|_{t=t_\Phi(x_0)} \neq 0$. Hence, by the implicit function theorem, (8.3.7) can be solved yielding

$$t_\Phi = t_\Phi(x_0),$$

which has the same number of derivates as Φ and F. Q.E.D.

Theorem 8.3.3 Let the differential game Γ satisfy the conditions (R1) and (R2) and (R4) of Section 8.1, and let the pair of optimal control functions $(\bar{u}, \bar{w})$ satisfy the assumption of ε-penetrability and have smoothness of the kth order. Then Bellman's function is k times differentiable a.e.

Proof As in Theorem 8.3.2, due to the classical definition of continuity of the right-hand side, the solution of (8.3.1) is k times differentiable a.e. in the initial data x_0 for all $t < t_{\Phi_1}(x_0)$, where $t_{\Phi_1}(x_0)$ is the first moment of capture of the first singular surface Φ_1. Then by Lemma 8.3.2 it follows that $t_{\Phi_1}(x_0)$ and, hence, $x(t_{\Phi_1}(x_0), x_0)$ is k times differentiable in x_0. Owing to ε-penetration, once the trajectory attains Φ_1, it intersects this surface and will not turn back.

The same reasoning can be applied from when the trajectory attains the next singular surface until the terminal surface is captured. Therefore, the trajectory $x(t, x_0)$ is differentiable in x_0 a.e., excluding the singular surfaces Φ_i, which consist of sets with a zero (Lebesgue) measure. Q.E.D.

Corollary Under the conditions of the theorem, Bellman's function is differentiable at any interior point of the regions

$$((\Phi_i \cup \Phi_i^+) \cap D) \backslash ((\Phi_{i+1} \cup \Phi_{i+1}^+) \cap D),$$

where $i = 1, \ldots, k$, and the derivatives have limits when the point is on the boundary of these regions.

8.4 EXISTENCE OF SOLUTIONS

The existence of solutions of differential games is a very complicated problem, with its resolution strongly dependent on the assumptions imposed on the game. The assumptions stated below substitute the problem of the existence of a solution of an Isaacs' system for the one of the solution of a differential game (it is assumed without loss of generality that there is no integral part of the payoff).

(A1) Let Isaacs' system be expressed as

$$\dot{x} = (x, \bar{u}, \bar{w}), \qquad \bar{u}(x) \in U_1(x), \qquad \text{and} \quad \bar{w} \in U_2(x),$$

$$\dot{W}_k = \sum_{i=1}^{n} W_i(x)\phi_{ik}(x, \bar{u}, \bar{w}), \qquad k = 1, \ldots, n,$$

$$0 = \sum_{i=1}^{n} W_i(x)\phi_i(x, \bar{u}, \bar{w}) \tag{8.4.1}$$

$$= \max_{u \in U_1(x)} \min_{w \in U_2(x)} \sum_{i=1}^{n} W_i \phi_i(x, u, w),$$

$$W(x_T) = H(x_T), \qquad W_i(x) = \frac{\partial W}{\partial x_i}, \qquad \text{and} \quad x(t_0) = x_0,$$

where the first three equations are defined a.e. on D, the region of the game, where x_T is a boundary point of D, and $H(x_T)$ is the terminal payoff function. It is assumed that this system has a solution for all $x_0 \in D$.

(A2) For all $x \in D$, equation

$$\max_{u \in U_1(x)} \min_{w \in U_2(x)} \sum_{i=1}^{n} W_i(x)\phi_i(x, u, w) = \min_{w \in U_2(x)} \max_{u \in U_1(x)} \sum_{i=1}^{n} W_i(x)\phi_i(x, u, w),$$

holds, where W_i are functions defined in (8.4.1).

(A3) The region D is compact, and any trajectory determined by any feasible pair of control functions is terminated at the boundary of D in a finite period of time. Moreover, the mappings U_i and the functions ϕ_i are continuous.

Recall that $u(x)$ is a feasible control function of R^n into R^m if $u(x) \in U_1(x)$ and $u(x)$ is measurable. Since the mapping U_1 is continuous and the region D is compact, the values of $u(x)$ belong to a compact set in R^m. Similarly, $w(x)$ is a feasible control function of R^n into R^l if $w(x) \in U_2(x)$ and $w(x)$ is measurable. By the same token, the values of $w(x)$ belong to a compact set in R^l.

Theorem 8.4.1 Under assumptions (A1), (A2), and (A3), the differential game Γ has a solution.

Proof The proof will be presented in three stages. The existence of a function $W(\bar{x})$, which will be shown to be Bellman's function, will be presented first. Next, given the second player's control function $\bar{w}$, any choice of control functions by the first player to maximize the payoff will not make him/her better off than would the choice of the control function $\bar{u}$, i.e., $P(\bar{x}, u, \bar{w}) \leq P(\bar{x}, \bar{u}, \bar{w})$. Finally, it will be shown that the pair $(\bar{u}, \bar{w})$ is a saddle point of the game Γ.

First, let $\bar{x}$ be an arbitrary point in D and let $W(\bar{x})$ be any value of the function that exists at this point, by (A1). Then it will be shown that $W(\bar{x}) = P(\bar{x}, \bar{u}(\cdot), \bar{w}(\cdot))$. Let $x(t, \bar{x})$ be a trajectory going from $\bar{x}$ and determined by the controls $\bar{u}$ and $\bar{w}$. Furthermore, let this trajectory attain the boundary of D at the point $x_F = x(t_F, \bar{x})$ at the moment t_F. Then by (A1), $W(x_F) = H(x_F)$, and by the definition of a payoff (here with no integral part), $W(x_F) = P(\bar{x}, \bar{u}, \bar{w})$. But

$$\frac{dW}{dt}(x(t, \bar{x})) = 0 = \sum_{i=1}^{n} W_i(x(t, \bar{x}))\phi_i(x(t, \bar{x}), \bar{u}, \bar{w}).$$

Then

$$W(x_F) = W(x_F) + \int_{t_0}^{t_F} \frac{dW}{dt}\,dt = W(\bar{x}) = P(\bar{x}, \bar{u}, \bar{w}),$$

which establishes the first stage of the proof.

Second, let $\bar{u}_1$ be an arbitrary admissible control function of the first player [i.e., $\bar{u}_1 \in U_1(x)$] and let $x_1(t, \bar{x})$ be a trajectory determined by the control functions $\bar{u}_1$ and $\bar{w}$ and starting from $\bar{x}$. Additionally, let $\bar{u}_1$ satisfy

$$\max_{u \in U_1(x(t,\bar{x}))} \sum_{i=1}^{n} W_i(x_1(t, \bar{x}))\phi_i(x_1(t, \bar{x}), u, \bar{w}(x(t, \bar{x})))$$

$$= \sum_{i=1}^{n} W_i(x_1(t, \bar{x}))\phi_i(x_1(t, \bar{x}), \bar{u}_1(x(t, \bar{x})), \bar{w}(x(t, \bar{x}))).$$

That is, given $\bar{w}$, the function $\bar{u}_1$ maximizes the payoff almost everywhere. Then

$$P(x, \bar{u}_1, \bar{w}) = P(x, \bar{u}, \bar{w}) = W(\bar{x}).$$

Therefore,

$$\sum_{i=1}^{n} W_i(x_1(t, \bar{x}))\phi_i(x_1(t, \bar{x}), \bar{u}_1(x(t, \bar{x})), \bar{w}(x_1(t, \bar{x})))$$

$$= \sum_{i=1}^{n} W_i(x_1(t, \bar{x}))\phi_i(x_1(t, \bar{x}), \bar{u}(x(t, \bar{x})), \bar{w}(x(t, \bar{x}))) = 0$$

since $\bar{u}$ is also a payoff maximizing control. Hence

$$H(x_F^1) = P(\bar{x}, \bar{u}_1, \bar{w}) = W(x_F^1) = W(\bar{x}) = P(x, \bar{u}, \bar{w}),$$

where x_F^1 is the first point at which the trajectory which starts from $\bar{x}$ under the control functions $\bar{u}_1$ and $\bar{w}$ attains the terminal surface. This proves the second stage.

Finally, it will be shown that the pair $(\bar{u}, \bar{w})$ as defined in (A1) is a solution of the game Γ. Suppose it is not. Then there exists $\bar{x} \in D$ and an admissible control u such that

$$P(\bar{x}, u, \bar{w}) > P(\bar{x}, \bar{u}, \bar{w}). \tag{8.4.2}$$

Then the above reasoning shows that u is not a payoff maximizer on the trajectory $x(t, \bar{x})$ determined by the controls u and $\bar{w}$. Therefore, there is a measurable set $E \subset [t_0, t_F]$ such that $\mu(E) \neq 0$, where t_F is the first moment at which the trajectory $x(t, \bar{x})$ captures the terminal surface and $\mu(E)$ is a Lebesgue measure defined on the set E and

$$\sum_{i=1}^{n} W_i(x(t, \bar{x}))\phi_i(x(t, x), u(x(t, \bar{x})), \bar{w}(x(t, \bar{x}))) < 0$$

for all $t \in E$. Then

$$\begin{aligned} W(x_F) &= W(\bar{x}) + \int_{t_0}^{t_F} \frac{dW}{dt}(x(t, \bar{x}))\,dt \\ &= W(\bar{x}) + \int_E \frac{dW}{dt}(x(t, \bar{x}))\,dt < W(\bar{x}), \end{aligned}$$

where $x_F = x(t_F, \bar{x})$. Thus

$$W(x_F) = H(x_F) = P(\bar{x}, u, \bar{w}) < W(\bar{x}) = P(x, \bar{u}, \bar{w}),$$

which contradicts (8.4.2). Therefore,

$$P(\bar{x}, u, \bar{w}) \leq P(\bar{x}, \bar{u}, \bar{w})$$

for any admissible control functions of the first player. Making use of (A2) and following the same reasoning as used above, it can be shown that

$$P(\bar{x}, \bar{u}, w) \geq P(x, \bar{u}, \bar{w})$$

for any admissable control function of the second player. Q.E.D.

CHAPTER

9

Other Approaches to Differential Games

Isaacs' approach to differential games is complete in the sense that it consists of systems of differential equations whose solutions, if they exist, are the optimal strategies of the players. This approach, however, has many drawbacks. First, it can only be applied if all functions in the system of kinematic equations, and in the payoff functions, are smooth and if the functions that define the terminal sets of the game are also smooth. Practical problems, particularly games of survival, do not usually exhibit this smoothness. Second, the problem of existence of solutions of differential games in this approach is seen as the problem of existence of solutions of an Isaacs' system where the solutions have certain qualities (e.g., regularity and kth-order smoothness of behavioral strategies, ε-penetration of surfaces, etc.). In other words, the problem of existence of solutions of games according to this approach is not directly connected with the properties of the functions and surfaces that define the game. Therefore, other approaches which deal directly with solutions of differential games were developed.

In some of these approaches, the existence of a solution of the game can be proved using only the properties of the direct parameters of the game. These approaches include those of Friedman and Krasovsky.

This chapter, however, will start with an approach which relies on the geometric properties of games. This geometric approach is not designed to prove the existence of solutions, but rather to find solutions of some games for which Isaacs' approach cannot, or for which that approach is very difficult to apply. The geometric approach, which will be discussed in Section 9.1, will be applied to war between two Leontief models. This example is different from that of Section 8.4 of Chapter 8 in that in this example the economies are allowed to expand.

Friedman's approach will be discussed in Section 9.2. In this approach, Friedman uses the method of δ-approximation of behavioral strategies, i.e., every player makes decisions based on information on his/her own decisions and his/her opponent's in past moments of time and, in some cases, on additional information concerning the opponent's current decisions. The distance between any two moments of time does not exceed some positive δ. Therefore, the game can be discriminatory in the sense that one of the players has more up-to-date information on the behavior of his/her opponent (i.e., upper and lower δ-games) and the existence of a saddle point can be explored.

Section 9.3 will be a discussion of Krasovsky's approach. To some extent, this is a combination of the geometric approach and Friedman's approach. Krasovsky uses the idea of approximation in defining behavioral strategies and he uses ideas from the geometric approach (e.g., set of desired directions) in defining optimal strategies.

9.1 THE GEOMETRIC APPROACH WITH APPLICATION TO WAR BETWEEN ONE-COMMODITY MODELS

As indicated before, Isaacs' approach, in particular, his regression equations, provides powerful tools in finding optimal strategies. The approach, however, is very difficult to employ when the terminal surface and the payoff functions are not smooth. In fact, when the region of the game is not compact, the approach is often not applicable. Therefore, in such cases it is useful to have other approaches for finding solutions of differential games. In this section, an approach based on the geometric properties of games will be described and then applied to a game of survival. In this case, the terminal surfaces are usually hyperplanes or parts of these (as in the example of war between two models with constant production).

Let the boundary of the region of the game $D \subset R^n$ consist of three types of terminal sets Ω_1, Ω_2, and Ω_3. If at time t the tragectory of the game reaches Ω_1 [i.e., $x(t) \in \Omega_1$], then the first player will be the victor. If the trajectory reaches Ω_2 [i.e., $x(t) \in \Omega_2$], then the second player is the victor. Finally, if $x(t) \in \Omega_3$, the game ends in a draw. In the case of the example of Section 6.2, the terminal sets can be expressed as

$$\Omega_1 = \{(x_1, x_2) : x_1 > 0 \text{ and } x_2 = 0\},$$

$$\Omega_2 = \{(x_1, x_2) : x_1 = 0 \text{ and } x_2 > 0\},$$

and

$$\Omega_3 = \{(0, 0)\}.$$

For simplicity, it is assumed that the sets Ω_i, $i = 1, 2, 3$ are convex. This approach is also applicable when every terminal set Ω_i can be represented as a union of disjoint convex subsets. The boundary of region D consists of a regular $(n - 1)$-dimensional surface.

The following definitions will be used in the proofs of the forthcoming lemmas and theorems, which will be applied to war between models. Let $x_0 \in D \subset R^n$ and $v \in R^n$ such that $\|v\| = 1$. Then the set

$$\Lambda(x_0, v) = \{z : z = x_0 + tv \text{ and } t \geq 0\}$$

is called *a ray in the direction of* v, starting from x_0. Then the *cone of desired directions* of the ith player is defined by the set

$$N_i(x_0) = \left\{v : \Lambda\left(x_0, \frac{v}{\|v\|}\right) \cap \Omega_i \neq \varnothing \text{ and } \Lambda\left(x_0, \frac{v}{\|v\|}\right) \bigcap_{i \neq j} \Omega_j = \varnothing\right\},$$

where $i = 1, 2$. Therefore, at point x_0 the ith player can "see" his/her terminal set Ω_i by looking along the rays that start from x_0 and proceed in the directions defined by the cone $N_i(x_0)$. Figure 9.1.1 shows $N_1(x_0)$ in the case

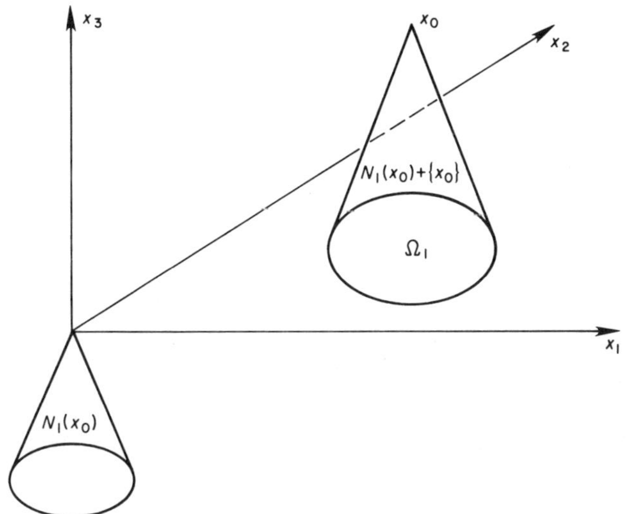

Figure 9.1.1

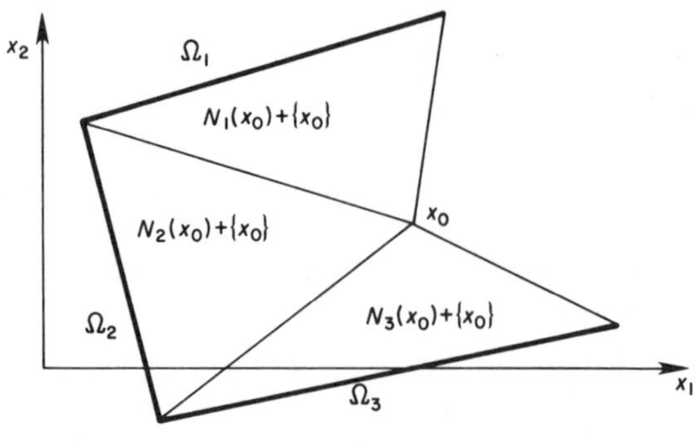

Figure 9.1.2

$n = 3$. In this figure, the cone $N_1(x_0)$ has the origin as its vertex. The set $N_1(x_0) + \{x_0\}$ is constructed by shifting the vertex of the cone from the origin to x_0. This set consists of all rays that start from x_0 and proceed in the direction of the terminal set Ω_1. Therefore, it is the set of rays which are desired by the first player.

In this game, it is assumed that for any $x_0 \in D$, the rays leading to different terminal surfaces do not intersect. That is,

$$N_i(x_0) \bigcap_{i \neq j} N_j(x_0) = \phi.$$

This is shown in Figure 9.1.2 for $n = 2$.

Cones of desired directions have very useful properties.

Lemma 9.1.1 Let $x_1 \in N_i(x_0) + \{x_0\}$. Then $N_i(x_1) \supset N_i(x_0)$.

Proof Let $v \in N_i(x_0)$, and consider the three rays $L_1 = \Lambda(x_1, v)$, $L_2 = \Lambda(x_0, v)$ and $L_3 = \Lambda(x_0, (x_1 - x_0)/\|x_1 - x_0\|)$. Since x_1 belongs to the set

$$x_1 \in N_i(x_0) + \{x_0\}$$

and this set is convex, then $(x_1 - x_0)/\|x_1 - x_0\| \in N_i(x_0)$. Therefore, there exists points z_2 and z_3 at the intersection of the rays L_2 and L_3 with the set Ω_i. The rays L_2 and L_1 are parallel. Thus the rays L_1, L_2, and L_3 lie in a two-dimensional plane. Then, because of the convexity of Ω_i, the rays L_2 and L_3 and the line belonging to Ω_i that connects z_2 and z_3 form a triangle such that x_1 lies on side L_3 and L_1 is parallel to side L_2. Therefore, L_1 intersects the side of the triangle which lies in Ω_i. Hence, by the definition of $N_i(x_1)$, the direction $v \in N_1(x_1)$. Q.E.D.

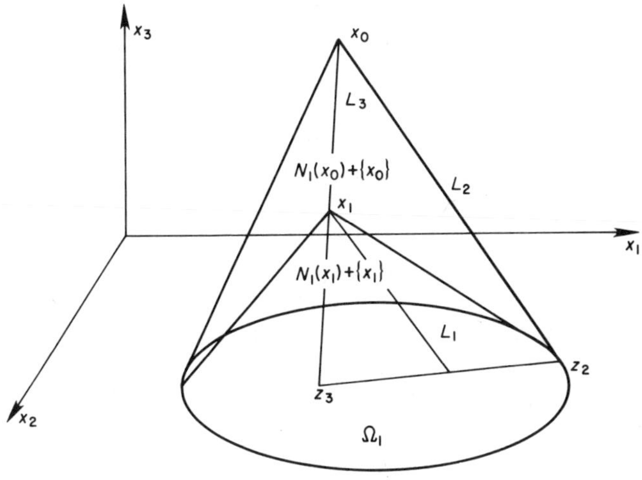

Figure 9.1.3

A schematic drawing of this proof is shown in Figure 9.1.3.

Lemma 9.1.2 If $x_1 \in (N_i(x_0) + \{x_0\}) \cap D$, then $(N_i(x_1) + \{x_1\}) \cap D \subset (N_i(x_0) + \{x_0\}) \cap D$.

Proof Let $v \in N_i(x_1)$. Then there exists $z \in \Lambda(x_1, v/\|v\|) \cap \Omega_i$. Then by the definition of $N_i(x)$, $z \in N_i(x_0) + \{x_0\}$ because the point z is in Ω_i and hence can be seen from $x_0 \in D$. But since the set $N_i(x_0) + \{x_0\}$ is convex,

$$\Lambda(x_1, v/\|v\|) \cap D \subset N_i(x_0) + \{x_0\}.$$

But by definition,

$$(N_i(x_1) + \{x_1\}) \cap D = \bigcup_{v \in N_i(x_1)} \left(\Lambda\left(x, \frac{v}{\|v\|}\right) \cap D\right). \quad \text{Q.E.D.}$$

The next theorem will show the connection between the trajectories of the system of differential equations and the set of desired directions.

Theorem 9.1.1 Let $\dot{x}(t)$ belong to $\mathring{N}_i(x(t))$, where $\dot{x}(t)$ is the time derivative of the trajectory $x(t)$ of system (7.1.3) and where $\mathring{N}_i(x(t))$ is the interior of $N_i(x(t))$. Then $x(t)$ cannot go to sets $\Omega_j, j \neq i$ and

$$X(t) \in (N_i(x(t_0)) + \{x(t_0)\}) \cap D. \tag{9.1.1}$$

for all $t \geq t_0$.

Proof The first part of the theorem, which states that the trajectory $x(t)$ cannot go to the points of the terminal sets Ω_j, where $j \neq i$, follows from the definition of $N_i(x)$. That is, if at time $\bar{t}$ the state $x(\bar{t}) \in \Omega_j$, $j \neq i$, then by the definition, $x(\bar{t}) \notin N_i(x)$.

To show the second part of the theorem, let us assume that (9.1.1) is violated at some $t = t_1$. Then due to the continuity of the trajectory $x(t)$, there is $t = t_2 < t_1$ such that

$$x(t_2) \in \partial(N_i(x(t_0)) + \{x(t_0)\}),$$

where $\partial(N_i(x(t_0)) + \{x(t_0)\})$ is the boundary of the set $N_i(x(t_0)) + \{x(t_0)\}$. Moreover, the moment t_2 can be chosen such that for any $\varepsilon > 0$, there exists $t > t_2$ and $|t - t_2| > \varepsilon$ such that

$$x(t) \notin N_i(x(t_0)) + \{x(t_0)\}. \tag{9.1.2}$$

But also by Lemma 9.1.2,

$$(N_i(x(t_2)) + \{x(t_2)\}) \subset (N_i(x(t_0)) + \{x(t_0)\}). \tag{9.1.3}$$

On the other hand, by the Taylor's series expansion, the trajectory

$$x(t) = x(t_2) + \dot{x}(t_2)(t - t_2) + o(t - t_2),$$

where $o(t - t_2)/(t - t_2) \to 0$ as $t \to t_2$. Then for $t > t_2$, by the definition of a cone,

$$\dot{x}(t_2)(t - t_2) \in \mathring{N}_i(x(t_2)),$$

which implies that

$$x(t_2) + \dot{x}(t_2)(t - t_2) \subset \operatorname{int}(N_i(x(t_2)) + \{x(t_2)\}).$$

Therefore, there exist $\varepsilon > 0$, such that for all $t > t_2$ and $|t - t_2| < \varepsilon$ the trajectory

$$x(t) \in (N_i(x(t_2)) + \{x(t_2)\}),$$

which contradicts (9.1.2) and (9.1.3). Q.E.D.

This theorem says that if $\dot{x}(t) \in \mathring{N}_i(x(t))$, then the trajectory $x(t)$ cannot leave the set $N_i(x_0) + \{x_0\}$. Therefore, in the case of two players, $i = 1, 2$, the

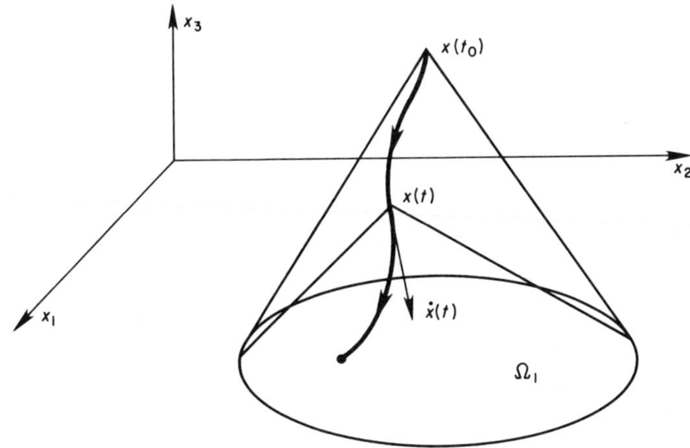

Figure 9.1.4

game can terminate when one of the players wins, or it will continue indefinitely with respect to time. The situation described in this theorem is shown in Figure 9.1.4.

Example 9.1.1 This example describes a war between two one-commodity Leontief models, model i, $i = 1, 2$. Let model i expand continuously in time according to

$$\dot{x}_i(t) = \alpha_i x_i(t), \qquad x_i(t_0) = x_{i0},$$

where $x_i(t)$ is the commodity stock of model i at time t and where α_i is the growth factor of that model. Then as in Section 6.2, the game evolves according to

$$\dot{x}_1 = \alpha_1(1 - \phi)x_1 - s_2\psi x_2, \qquad x_1(t_0) = x_{10},$$

$$\dot{x}_2 = \alpha_2(1 - \psi)x_2 - s_1\phi x_1, \qquad x_2(t_0) = x_{20},$$

where ϕ is the share of model 1's military industry of the commodity stock of that model and ψ is the share of model 2's military industry of that model's commodity stock. As indicated before, the boundary sets are represented by $\Omega_1 = \{(x_1, x_2): x_2 = 0\}$, $\Omega_2 = \{(x_1, x_2): x_1 = 0\}$, and $\Omega_3 = \{(0, 0)\}$. Let $x = (x_1, x_2) \subset \mathring{R}^2_+$, where $\mathring{R}^2_+$ is the positive orthant excluding the boundaries. Then $N_1(x_0)$ consists of vectors v, which satisfy either

(i) $(v, v_2) \geq 0$ and $(v, v_1) < 0$ or
(ii) $(v/\|v\|, v_1) < \cos\sigma(x)$,

where $\cos\sigma(x) = -x_2/\sqrt{x_1^2 + x_2^2}$ and $(v, v_1) < 0$.

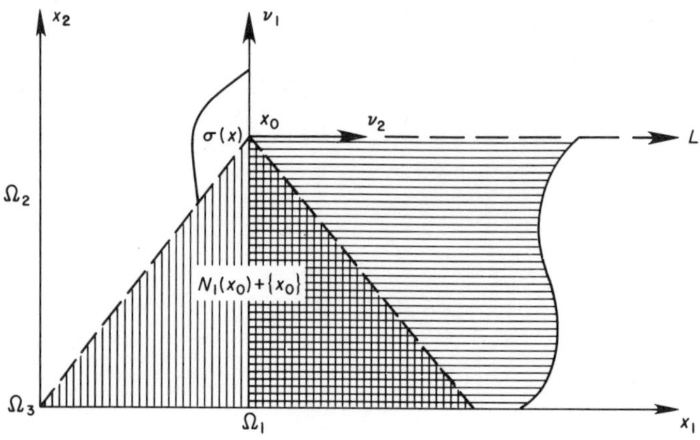

Figure 9.1.5

In this example, $v_1 = (0, 1)$ is normal to the set Ω_1 and $v_2 = (1, 0)$ is normal to the set Ω_2.

In Figure 9.1.5, the set $N_1(x_0) + \{x_0\}$ is delineated by $0x_0L$ (not including the boundary from the origin to x_0). The horizontally shaded part of this set includes all the vectors which satisfy (i). The vertically shaded part is composed of the vectors which satisfy (ii).

By applying Theorem 9.1.1 to this example [i.e., $\dot{x} \in N_i(x_0)$], it can be seen that the condition $(\dot{x}, v_1) < 0$, which is common to both conditions (i) and (ii), yields

$$\alpha_2(1 - \psi)x_2 - s_1\phi x_1 < 0.$$

Model 1 is interested in preserving the sign of this inequality for the maximum range of possible controls of model 2. Therefore, model 1 must choose $\bar{\phi} = 1$. Then it can be seen from (i) [i.e., (x, v_2)] that $-s_2x_2 \geq 0$. This inequality should be satisfied for all $\psi \in [0, 1]$, which is impossible if $x_2 \neq 0$. Hence (i) will be eliminated. Then from condition (ii),

$$\left(\frac{\dot{x}}{\|\dot{x}\|}, v_1\right) < -\frac{x_2}{\sqrt{x_1^2 + x_2^2}},$$

which after substitution yields

$$\frac{\alpha_2(1 - \psi)x_2 - s_1x_1}{\sqrt{(s_2\psi x_2)^2 + (\alpha_2(1 - \psi)x_2 - s_1x_1)^2}} < -\frac{x_2}{\sqrt{x_1^2 + x_1^2}}.$$

If the left-hand side of this inequality is denoted by $F(\psi)$, then

$$\max_{\psi \in [0,1]} F(\psi) < -\frac{x_2}{\sqrt{x_1^2 + x_2^2}}. \tag{9.1.4}$$

But max $F(\psi)$ occurs on the end points 0 or 1. If $\psi = 0$, then (9.1.4) becomes

$$F(0) = \frac{\alpha_2 x_2 - s_1 x_1}{|\alpha_2 x_2 - s_1 x_1|} = 1 \tag{9.1.5}$$

provided that $\alpha_2 x_2 - s_1 x_1 > 0$, which contradicts (9.1.4) if $\alpha_2 x_2 - s_1 x_1 < 0$. Then (9.1.4) holds if

$$F(1) = \frac{-s_1 x_1}{\sqrt{s_1^2 x_1^2 + s_2^2 x_2^2}} < -\frac{x_2}{\sqrt{x_1^2 + x_2^2}}.$$

Dividing the left-hand side of this inequality by $s_1 x_1$ and the right-hand side by x_2 gives rise to a monotone decreasing function in the denominator and then

$$s_2^{1/2} x_2 < s_1^{1/2} x_1.$$

Therefore, due to Theorem 9.1.1, if $x_0 = (x_1^0, x_2^0)$ belongs to the set

$$O_1 = \{(x_1, x_2) : \alpha_2 x_2 - s_1 x_1 < 0 \text{ and } s_2^{1/2} x_2 < s_1^{1/2} x_1\},$$

then the first player can move in the desired direction to reach the terminal set Ω_1. This is so because in this region

$$\dot{x} = (\dot{x}_1, \dot{x}_2) \in \mathring{N}_1(x_0).$$

Thus the solution of this game, according to this approach, depends on the relations among the parameters of that game. Let us suppose that the relations are such that

$$\alpha_1 > \alpha_2 \qquad \text{and} \qquad \alpha_2^2 > s_1 s_2.$$

These relations, together with the relations that define set O_1, when they hold as equalities, give rise to the lines shown in Figure 9.1.6. In this case, the region of victory of the first player is

$$O_1^1 = \{(x_1, x_2) : \alpha_2 x_2 < s_1 x_1\}.$$

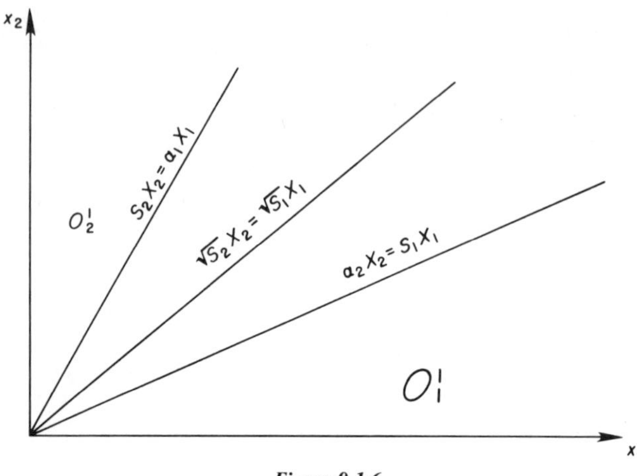

Figure 9.1.6

Furthermore, using the same reasoning that is employed in the proof of Theorem 9.1.1, it can be shown that if at the initial moment the first player chooses $\bar{\phi} = 1$, and the initial data satisfies

$$\alpha_2 x_2^0 - s_1 x_1^0 < -\varepsilon_0,$$

where $\varepsilon_0 > 0$, then

$$\dot{x}_2(t) = \alpha_2 x_2(t) - s_1 x_1(t) < -\varepsilon_0$$

for any $t > 0$ and any $\varepsilon_0 > 0$. That is, the function $x_2(t)$ is strictly monotone decreasing. Therefore, if model 1 applies the control $\bar{\phi} = 1$, that model can achieve in a finite time the result which amounts to $x_2(T) = 0$ and $x_1(T) > 0$, i.e., that model will win.

By the same token, given the above relationships among parameters it can be shown that the second model can win in the region

$$O_2^1 = \{(x_1, x_2): \alpha_1 x_1 > s_2 x_2\}$$

in a finite time.

The remaining part of the region of the game can also be explored using Theorem 9.1.1. In other words, the wedge which is sandwiched between the regions O_1^1 and O_2^1 can also be explored. The line

$$\alpha_2 x_2 = s_1 x_1$$

will be considered as the new terminal surface. However, applying this theorem will require a great many calculations. Therefore, based on Theorem 9.1.1 we will only explore the situation when the initial point lies on the line

$$\alpha_2 x_2(0) = s_1 x_1(0), \tag{9.1.6}$$

that is, on the boundary of set O_1^1. If the first player applies the control $\bar{\phi} = 0$ at time t_0, then the set

$$\{\dot{x}(t_0) : \dot{x}(t_0) = (\dot{x}_1(t_0), \dot{x}_2(t_0)) = (\alpha_1 x_1(0) - s_2 \psi x_2(0), \alpha_2(1 - \psi) x_2(0)) \\ \text{and} \quad 0 \leq \psi \leq 1\},$$

i.e., the set of possible vectors of velocity of the trajectory that starts from $x_0 = (x_1(0), x_2(0))$ and satisfies (9.1.6). This set is convex and its boundary points occur when $\psi = 0$ or $\psi = 1$, i.e., when model 2 chooses its extreme controls. If $\psi = 0$, then

$$\dot{x}(t_0) = (\dot{x}_1(t_0), \dot{x}_2(t_0)) = (\alpha_1 x_1(0), s_1 x_1(0)),$$

which, due to $\alpha_1 > \alpha_2$, yields

$$\alpha_2 \dot{x}_2(t_0) < s_1 \dot{x}_1(t_0),$$

i.e., the vector $\dot{x}(t_0)$ forms an acute angle with the line defined by (9.1.6). If model 2 applies $\bar{\psi} = 1$ at time t_0, then the set of possible vectors of velocities is defined by

$$\dot{x}_1(t_0) = \alpha_1 x_1(t_0) - s_2 x_2(t_0) > 0,$$

$$\dot{x}_2(t_0) = 0.$$

These vectors also form an acute angle with the boundary of O_1^1. Therefore, by choosing $\bar{\phi} = 0$, model 1 can force the trajectory to continue to proceed inside region O_1^1, which makes that model the victor. This situation is illustrated in Figure 9.1.7.

Since applying Theorem 9.1.1 in exploring the interior of the wedge formed by O_1^1 and O_2^1 requires a great many calculations, in particular, when calculating the angle of the cone that starts from a point in the interior of the wedge, the following theorem will be used.

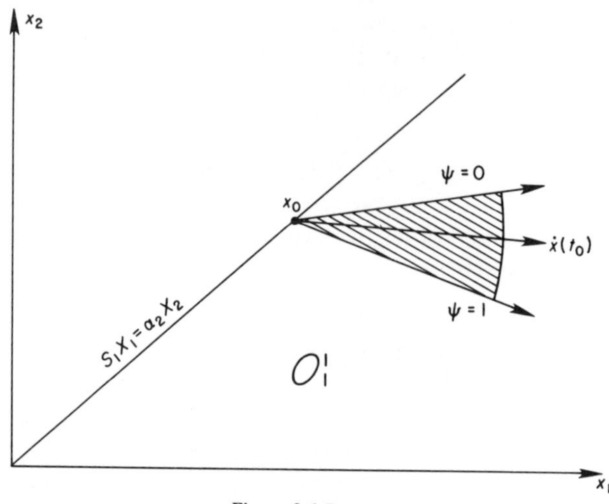

Figure 9.1.7

Theorem 9.1.2 Let the following considerations hold in region Q, which is contained in D.

(i) For every $x \in Q$ there are

(a) one and only one vector $s_1(x) \in \Omega_1$ and a number $t_1(x) \geq 0$ such that

$$x(t) = s_1(x) + \tau_1(x)v_1,$$

where v_1 is a normal to Ω_1 and

(b) one and only one vector $s_2(x) \in \Omega_2$ and a number $\tau_2(x)$ such that

$$x(t) = s_2(x) + \tau_2(x)v_2,$$

where v_2 is a normal to Ω_2 and where the functions $\tau_i(x)$ and $s_i(x)$, $i = 1, 2$, are differentiable; and

(ii) that

(a) $\min_\phi \max_\psi(v_1, f(x, \phi, \psi)) = (v_1, f(x, \bar{\phi}(x), \bar{\psi}(x))) \leq -\varepsilon < 0$ and
(b) $(v_2, f(x, \bar{\phi}(x), \psi(x))) \geq 0$ for all $\psi \in U_2$.

Then a trajectory that starts from $x_0 = (x_1^0, x_2^0) \in Q$ and that always stays inside Q under the control function $\bar{\phi}(x)$ will end in the set Ω_1.

Proof In region Q we have

$$x(t) = s_1(x) + \tau_1(x)v_1.$$

Differentiating this equation with respect to t yields

$$\frac{dx}{dt} = \frac{ds_1}{dt} + v_1 \frac{d\tau_1}{dt}.$$

Multiplying both sides by v_1 gives

$$\left(v_1 \frac{dx}{dt}\right) = \left(v_1 \frac{ds_1}{dt}\right) + \frac{d\tau_1}{dt}$$

since $(v_1 \cdot v_1) = 1$. But $(v_1\, ds_1/dt) = 0$ because ds_1/dt lies in the plane tangent to Ω_1, to which v_1 is normal. Then

$$\frac{d\tau_1}{dt} = \left(v_1 \frac{dx}{dt}\right).$$

However, under condition (iia) it can be seen that $d\tau_1/dt < -\varepsilon_1 < 0$. That is, $\tau_1(x)$ is a strictly monotone decreasing function with respect to time. It can be shown by employing similar reasoning that under conditions (i-b) and (ii-b) the function $\tau_2(x)$ is nondecreasing with respect to time, i.e., $d\tau_2/dt \geq 0$. Therefore, the trajectory $x(t)$ gets closer to the terminal set Ω_1, but it does not come any closer to the terminal set Ω_2. Specifically, the trajectory proceeds toward the set Ω_1 at a speed not less than ε, and at time $\Delta \leq \tau_1(x_0)/\varepsilon$ it reaches Ω_1. Q.E.D.

This theorem will be applied when the initial states of the game are located above the line defined by (9.1.6). In this case the terminal surface of the first player is defined by (9.1.6), $x_1 \geq 0$, and $x_2 \geq 0$. The terminal surface of model 2 is defined by the x_2 axis (i.e., $x_2 \geq 0$ and $x_1 = 0$). As a consequence, the normals v_1 and v_2 of Theorem 9.1.2 are defined as $v_1 = (-s_1, \alpha_2)$ and $v_2 = (1, 0)$. It should be obvious that condition (i) of Theorem 9.1.2 is satisfied. Therefore, condition (ii) should be verified. After making the necessary substitutions, (ii-a) becomes

$$\min_{\phi} \max_{\psi}(v_1, f(x, \phi, \psi)) = (v_1, f(x, \bar{\phi}, \bar{\psi})) = \alpha_2^2 x_2 - \alpha_1 s_1 x_1, \quad (9.1.7)$$

where $\bar{\phi} = 0$ and $\bar{\psi} = 0$. Condition (ii-b) becomes

$$(v_2, f(x, \bar{\phi}, \psi)) = \alpha_1 x_1 - s_2 \psi x_2 \geq \alpha_1 x_1 - s_2 x_2$$

since $\psi \in [0, 1]$.

Next, consider the region

$$O_1^2 = \{(x_1, x_2) : \alpha_2^2 x_2 - \alpha_1 s_1 x_1 < 0 \text{ and } \alpha_2 x_2 \geq s_1 x_1\}$$

and suppose the relations among the parameters are $\alpha_1 > \alpha_2$ and $\alpha_2^2 > s_1 s_2$. Then $\alpha_1 x_1 - s_2 x_2 > 0$. That is, $(v_2, f(x, \bar{\phi}, \psi)) > 0$ for all $\psi \in [0, 1]$ and condition (iib) is satisfied. Moreover, the region O_1^2 lies above the line defined by (9.1.6).

Now let us denote

$$q(t) = \alpha_2^2 x_2^2(t) - \alpha_1 s_1 x_1(t).$$

Then

$$\begin{aligned} \frac{dq(t)}{dt} &= \alpha_2^2 \dot{x}_2(t) - \alpha_1 s_1 \dot{x}_1(t) \\ &= (\alpha_2^3 - \alpha_1 s_1 s_2) x_2 (1 - \psi) + \alpha_1 s_1 (s_2 x_2 - \alpha_1 s_1) \end{aligned} \tag{9.1.8}$$

because $\bar{\phi} = 0$. Next it will be shown that $dq(t)/dt < 0$. First we consider the case where the relations between the parameters satisfy

$$\alpha_1 > \alpha_2 \qquad \text{and} \qquad \alpha_2^3 > \alpha_1 s_1 s_2.$$

Then the inequality

$$\frac{dq(t)}{dt} \leq \alpha_2^3 x_2 - \alpha_1^2 s_1 x_1 < 0$$

holds if the point (x_1, x_2) belongs to the region O_1^2 (see Figure 9.1.8).

Now consider the case when $\alpha_2^3 < \alpha_1 s_1 s_2$. Then

$$\frac{dq(t)}{dt} < \alpha_1 s_1 (s_2 x_2 - \alpha_1 x_1) < 0,$$

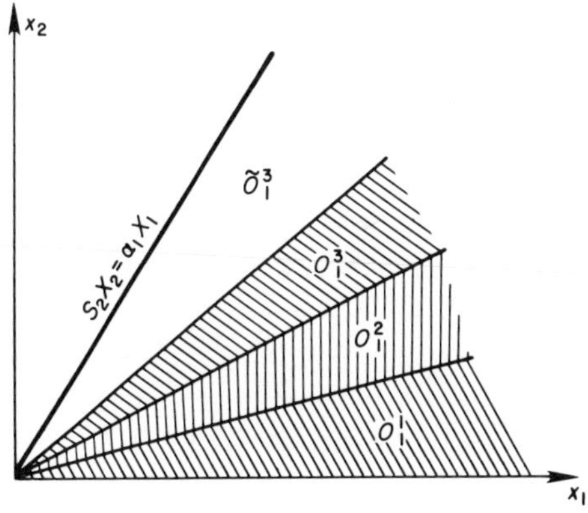

Figure 9.1.8

which is due to the inequality $(v_2, f(x, \bar{\phi}, \psi)) > 0$. Therefore, in region O_1^2, when $\bar{\phi} = 0$, the following statement is true. If at the initial moment t_0 the function

$$q(t_0) = \alpha_2^2 x_2^0 - \alpha_1 s_1 x_1^0 < -\varepsilon,$$

then $q(t)$ will only decrease (i.e., $dq/dt < 0$). Therefore, condition (ii-a) is satisfied and Theorem 9.1.2 applies. Then due to this theorem, model 1 is the winner if the initial state belongs to O_1^2 and that model's optimal strategy is $\bar{\phi} = 0$. In other words, model 1 wins the game in this region without firing a shot at its opponent. Model 1 considers the region O_1^2 as a stage for picking up steam and preparing for a full attack in a subsequent stage.

Note that in region O_1^2, model 2 is interested in maximizing $-dq/dt$ because its absolute value is equal to the "speed" at which the trajectory proceeds to the "terminal line" [defined by (9.1.6)] of model 1. Therefore, if $\alpha_2^3 > \alpha_1 s_1 s_2$, the optimal strategy (i.e., in the sense of maximizing time to delay loss) of model 2 is $\bar{\psi} = 0$ and if $\alpha_2^3 \leq \alpha_1 s_1 s_2$, that model's optimal strategy is $\bar{\psi} = 1$. That is, model 2 must launch a full attack against model 1 in order to inflict the heaviest damage and to make the first model susceptible to defeat in a new battle.

If $\alpha_2^3 < \alpha_1 s_1 s_2$, by making use of Theorem 9.1.2, and by employing the same reasoning as above, it can be shown that model 1 can win in the region

$$\tilde{O}_1^3 = \{(x_1, x_2) : \alpha_2^2 x_2 - \alpha_1 s_1 x_1 \geq 0 \text{ and } \alpha_1 x_1 > s_2 x_2\}$$

by choosing $\bar{\phi} = 0$. That is, model 1 can win in the wedge above region O_1^2 and below the line $s_2 x_2 = \alpha_1 x_1$. The optimal strategy (in the sense mentioned before) of model 2 is $\bar{\psi} = 1$.

If $\alpha_2^3 \geq \alpha_1 s_1 s_2$, model 1 can also win in the region

$$O_1^3 = \{(x_1, x_2): \alpha_2^3 x_2 < \alpha_1^2 s_1 x_1 \text{ and } \alpha_2^2 x_2 - \alpha_1 s_1 \geq 0\}$$

by choosing $\bar{\phi} = 0$.

Further analysis will depend on the sign between α_2^j and $\alpha^{j-2} s_1 s_2$, where $j = 4, 5, \ldots$. Then since $\alpha_1 > \alpha_2$, there exists $\bar{k}$ such that

$$\alpha_2^{\bar{k}} > \alpha_1^{\bar{k}-2} s_1 s_2 \qquad \text{and} \qquad \alpha^{\bar{k}+1} \leq \alpha_1^{\bar{k}-1} s_1 s_2.$$

By applying Theorem 9.1.2, it can be shown that below the line

$$\alpha_2^{\bar{k}} x_2 - \alpha_1^{\bar{k}-1} s_1 x_1 = 0.$$

Model 1 will win by choosing $\bar{\phi} = 0$ up to the line

$$\alpha_2 x_2 = s_1 x_1.$$

After this line, model 1 can win by choosing $\bar{\phi} = 1$. Correspondingly, the optimal strategy of model 2 is $\bar{\psi} = 0$.

Above the line

$$\alpha_2^{\bar{k}} x_2 - \alpha_1^{\bar{k}-1} s_1 x_1 = 0$$

in the region

$$\bar{O}_1^{\bar{k}} = \{(x_1, x_2): \alpha_2^{\bar{k}} x_2 \geq \alpha_1^{\bar{k}-1} s_1 x_1 \text{ and } \alpha_1 x_1 > s_2 x_2\}.$$

Model 1 can also win by choosing $\bar{\phi} = 0$; but in this case, the optimal strategy of model 2 is $\bar{\psi} = 1$.

Above the line $\alpha_1 x_1 > s_2 x_2$, model 1 loses and model 2 wins by applying the strategy $\bar{\psi} = 1$. The optimal strategy of model 1 is $\bar{\phi} = 1$. Therefore, both models launch a full attack in this region.

Finally, the line $\alpha_1 x_1 = s_2 x_2$ is a stationary barrier. If the initial state belongs to this line, then under strategies $\bar{\phi} = 0$ and $\bar{\psi} = 1$ the state will not change. In fact, if $\bar{\phi} = 0$ and $\bar{\psi} = 1$, then

$$\alpha_1 \dot{x}_1(t) - s_2 \dot{x}_2(t) = \alpha_1(\alpha_1 x_1(t) - s_2 x_2(t)).$$

Therefore, if

$$\alpha_1 x_1(0) - s_2 x_2(0) = 0,$$

then

$$\alpha_1 x_1(t) - s_2 x_2(t) = 0$$

for all $t \geq t_0$ and hence $\dot{x}_1(t) = \dot{x}_2(t) = 0$. If either model deviates from these strategies (i.e., $\bar{\phi} = 0$ and $\bar{\psi} = 1$) while its opponent sticks with its optimal strategy, that model will lose.

9.2 FRIEDMAN'S APPROACH

This approach as well as that of Krasovsky, which will be presented in Section 9.3, serve a purely theoretical purpose. They "enlarge" the range of differential games for which the existence of solutions can be proved. The theorem of existence of solutions, which is proved in Section 8.4 of Chapter 8, depends heavily on assumption (A1). This assumption postulates the existence of Bellman's function and the optimal behavioral strategies. Verifying this assumption is, however, very cumbersome. Therefore, it is more convenient to find conditions which can be verified to establish the existence of solutions. Verifying these conditions amount to checking the properties of the parameters defining the game (ϕ, f, U_1, U_2). It is worth mentioning that the procedure for finding solutions almost always (with the exception of Section 9.1) begins with attempts to solve Isaacs' system in regression form. In other words, it starts with checking the validity of assumption (A1). Any approaches that use the new conditions to verify the properties of the parameters of the game will face difficulties associated with behavioral strategies as discussed in Section 8.1. Thus the first task of those approaches is to change the notion of a strategy and a solution.

Avner Friedman circumvents these difficulties by introducing δ-approximated solutions and δ advantage of information (i.e., more up-to-date information) available for the players. It is assumed that the control sets of the game under discussion are constant (i.e., do not depend on the state of the game) and that the duration of the game is bounded (i.e., not more than $T < +\infty$). Moreover, let the interval $(t_0, T]$ be partitioned with points t_j uniformly. That is, $t_j = t_0 + j\delta$, where $j = 1, \ldots, n$, $\delta = (T - t_0)/n$ and $T = t_0 + n\delta$. Let the set of all measurable functions mapping the interval

$$I_j = \{t : t_{j-1} < t \leq t_j\}$$

into U_1 be denoted by Y_j, and the set of all measurable functions mapping I_j into U_2 be denoted by Z_j. Then Friedman's idea amounts to constructing a strategy for either of the players, based only on the information that player has regarding his/her choices and those of his/her opponent in the previous intervals. These intervals are each of length δ. That is, if until moment t_{j-1} both players have already chosen their strategies in the intervals $I_1, \ldots, I_{j-1}$, and these strategies belong to Y_i and Z_i, where $1 \leq i < j$, then every player must define his/her strategy as a function of time at all intervals $I_1, \ldots, I_{j-1}, I_j$. Each player makes use of his/her past behavior and that of his/her opponent (i.e. strategies chosen up to moment t_j) in choosing his/her future strategies. This method, therefore, defines the strategies as an approximation of behavioral strategies.

The assumptions that will be imposed on the parameters of the game give rise to a unique trajectory beginning from $x(t_0) = x_0$ and determined by the controls which are elements of the sets Y_i and Z_i, where $1 \leq i \leq j$. Then the state $x(t_{j-1})$, through which the system goes at moment t_{j-1}, can be calculated using the information about those controls. Thus choosing an element of the set Y_j or Z_j as a function of the already chosen elements Y_i and Z_i, where $1 \leq i \leq j$, makes the choice of strategies dependent on the current state with δ accuracy.

Next, Friedman considers a method of constructing strategies for the first player when that player has δ-advantage of information and when he/she does not. This is done by introducing the following scheme.

An *upper δ-strategy* Γ^δ for the first player is a sequence of n maps

$$\Gamma^\delta = (\Gamma^{\delta_1}, \ldots, \Gamma^{\delta_n}),$$

where $n = (T - t_0)/n$ and Γ^{δ_j}, $i \leq j \leq n$, maps

$$Z_1 \times Y_1 \times Z_2 \times Y_2 \times \cdots \times Z_{j-1} \times Y_{j-1} \times Z_j$$

into Y_j. That is, when the first player defines his/her component of the control function in the interval $(t_{j-1}, t_j]$, that player has information on the controls chosen by himself/herself and by his/her opponent up to moment t_{j-1} and that player also has additional information on the control of his/her opponent in the interval $(t_{j-1}, t_j]$. That is, the first player is ahead of his/her opponent in terms of information at one δ-step. At the initial moment t_0, for example, the first player knows the control of his/her opponent at the interval $(t_0, t_1] = (t_0, t_0 + \delta]$ before he/she makes a choice in that interval.

A *lower δ-strategy* Γ_δ for the first player is a sequence of n maps

$$\Gamma_\delta = (\Gamma_{\delta_1}, \ldots, \Gamma_{\delta_n}),$$

where $n = (T - t_0)/n$ and Γ_{δ_j}, $1 \leq j \leq n$, maps

$$Y_1 \times Z_1 \times Y_2 \times Z_2 \times \cdots \times Y_{j-1} \times Z_{j-1}$$

into Y_j. Knowing the controls of both players, $u(t)$ and $w(t)$, in the interval $(t_0, t_{j-1}]$, the first player must define his/her controls at the next step of length δ, i.e., at the interval $(t_{j-1}, t_j]$. At the initial moment t_0, that player has no information on his/her control or on that of his/her opponent in the interval

$$(t_0, t] = (t_0, t_0 + \delta].$$

Then, by definition, Γ_{δ_1} is a constant map, i.e., it defines the function $u(t)$ for $t \in (t_0, t_1]$, which is fixed a priori.

Similarly, an upper δ strategy for the second player is a vector

$$\Delta^\delta = (\Delta^{\delta_1}, \ldots, \Delta^{\delta_n}),$$

where $n = (T - t_0/n)$ and Δ^{δ_j} is a map from

$$Y_1 \times Z_1 \times Y_2 \times Z_2 \times \cdots \times Y_{j-1} \times Z_{j-1} \times Y_j$$

into Z_j. A lower δ-strategy Δ_δ of the second player is a vector

$$\Delta_\delta = (\Delta_{\delta_1}, \ldots, \Delta_{\delta_n}),$$

where Δ_{δ_j} is a map from

$$Z_1 \times Y_1 \times \cdots \times Z_{j-1} \times Y_{j-1}$$

into Z_j and where $n = (T - t_0)/\delta$.

Given any pair of strategies $(\Gamma^\delta, \Delta_\delta)$, it is possible to uniquely construct, step by step, pairs of control functions (u, w) with components (u_j, w_j) on $(t_{j-1}, t_j]$ by $u_j(t) = u(t)$, $w_j(t) = w(t)$, where $t \in (t_{j-1}, t_j]$, $j = 1, \ldots, n$ and u_j, w_j are defined by

$$\begin{aligned} w_j &= \Delta_{\delta_j}(w_1, u_1, w_2, u_2, \ldots, w_{j-1}, u_{j-1}), \\ u_j &= \Gamma^{\delta_j}(w_1, u_1, w_2, u_2, \ldots, w_{j-1}, u_{j-1}, w_j), \end{aligned} \tag{9.2.1}$$

where $j = 1, \ldots, n$. The control functions defined by (9.2.1) are called the *outcome* of the pair $(\Gamma^\delta, \Delta_\delta)$.

Two restrictions will be imposed on the function ϕ that define the kinematic equation in the game. These restrictions are as follows:

(F1) ϕ is continuous in all its arguments.

(F2) ϕ satisfies the generalized Lipschitz condition in x, i.e., there is an integrable function $k_0(t)$ such that

$$|\phi(t, x_1, u, w) - \phi(t, x_2, u, w)| \le k_0(t)|x_1 - x_2|,$$

where $\int_{t_0}^{\infty} k_0(t) < +\infty$. The game takes place in the region D, which is assumed to be compact. It is terminated when the trajectory starting from x_0 first reaches the boundary $\partial D = F$, which is usually called the terminal set.

(F3) Any trajectory that is subjected to the kinematic equation

$$\dot{x} = \phi(t, x, u, w)$$

and which starts from $x_0 = x(t_0) \in D$ must reach the terminal set by time T (e.g., as in a game of fixed duration).

In this approach, no convexation of ϕ is assumed. Let $u(t)$, $w(t)$ be two measurable functions that map $(t_0, T]$ into U_1 and U_2, respectively. Then as discussed in Section 7.2, Chapter 7, given assumptions (F1), (F2), and (F3), the kinematic equation defined above gives rise to a unique trajectory $x(t)$, which is a function that is absolutely continuous and satisfies

$$\dot{x} = \phi(t, x(t), u(t), w(t)) \quad \text{a.e.}$$

Then given any pair of strategies $(\Gamma^\delta, \Delta_\delta)$, the outcome of the control functions u, w can be defined by (9.2.1). The corresponding payoff to this pair can be written in the form

$$P(\Delta_\delta, \Gamma^\delta) = P(\Delta_{\delta_1}, \Gamma^{\delta_1}, \ldots, \Delta_{\delta_n}, \Gamma^{\delta_n}). \tag{9.2.2}$$

This scheme, in which the first player chooses an upper δ-strategy Γ^δ and the second player chooses a lower δ-strategy Δ_δ and then "play" according to (9.2.1), with the payoff of this "play" given by (9.2.2) is called an *upper δ-game* G^δ. Since the first player is the one making the last move Γ^{δ_n}, then that player should choose Γ^{δ_n} to make (9.2.2) be at maximum. In case the maximum does not exist, he/she should choose Γ^{δ_n} to make the payoff equal to

$$\sup_{\Gamma^{\delta_n}} P(\Delta_{\delta_1}, \Gamma^{\delta_1}, \ldots, \Delta_{\delta_{n-1}}, \Gamma^{\delta_{n-1}}, \Delta_{\delta_n}, \Gamma^{\delta_n}). \tag{9.2.3}$$

The second player should make his/her move in such a way as to make the payoff in (9.2.3) equal to

$$\inf_{\Delta_{\delta_n}} \sup_{\Gamma^{\delta_n}} P(\Delta_{\delta_1}, \Gamma^{\delta_1}, \ldots, \Delta_{\delta_{n-1}}, \Gamma^{\delta_{n-1}}, \Delta_{\delta_n}, \Gamma^{\delta_n}).$$

If these moves are extended step by step to intervals $I_{n-1}, \ldots, I_1$, then the resulting payoff should be defined by the number

$$V^\delta = \inf_{\Delta_{\delta_1}} \sup_{\Gamma^{\delta_1}} \cdots \inf_{\Delta_{\delta_n}} \sup_{\Gamma^{\delta_n}} P(\Delta_{\delta_1}, \Gamma^{\delta_1}, \ldots, \Delta_{\delta_n}, \Gamma^{\delta_n}). \tag{9.2.4}$$

The number V^δ is called the *upper δ-value* of the game G^δ.

Similarly, a *lower δ-game* G_δ and a *lower δ-value* V_δ can be defined. Here, the first player chooses a lower δ strategy and the second player chooses an upper δ-strategy Δ^δ. The outcome of the pair $(\Gamma_\delta, \Delta^\delta)$ can be defined by constructing control functions u and w with components u_j and w_j, respectively, by $u_j(t) = u(t)$ and $w_j(t) = w(t)$ for $t \in (t_{j-1}, t_j]$ such that

$$u_j = \Gamma_{\delta_j}(u_1, w_1, u_2, w_2, \ldots, u_{j-1}, w_{j-1}),$$

$$w_j = \Delta^{\delta_j}(u_1, w_1, u_2, w_2, \ldots, u_{j-1}, w_{j-1}).$$

The corresponding payoff is written as

$$P(\Gamma_\delta, \Delta^\delta) = P(\Gamma_{\delta_1}, \Delta^{\delta_1}, \ldots, \Gamma_{\delta_n}, \Delta^{\delta_n}).$$

Then V_δ, the lower δ-value of the game, can be defined by

$$V_\delta = \sup_{\Gamma_{\delta_1}} \inf_{\Delta^{\delta_1}} \cdots \sup_{\Gamma_{\delta_n}} \inf_{\Delta^{\delta_n}} P(\Gamma_{\delta_1}, \Delta^{\delta_1}, \ldots, \Gamma_{\delta_n}, \Delta^{\delta_n}).$$

Before introducing the main properties of upper and lower δ-values, it is assumed that

(F4) the functions f_1 and f_2, which define the payoff, are continuous.

Lemma 9.2.1 Let the assumptions (F1) and (F2) hold. Then

$$V^\delta = \inf_{\Delta_\delta} \sup_{\Gamma^\delta} P(\Delta_\delta, \Gamma^\delta) = \sup_{\Gamma^\delta} \inf_{\Delta_\delta} P(\Delta_\delta, \Gamma^\delta),$$

where

$$\inf_{\Delta_\delta} = \inf_{\Delta_{\delta_1}} \inf_{\Delta_{\delta_2}} \cdots \inf_{\Delta_{\delta_n}}$$

and

$$\sup_{\Gamma^\delta} = \sup_{\Gamma^{\delta_1}} \sup_{\Gamma^{\delta_2}} \cdots \sup_{\Gamma^{\delta_n}}.$$

[In other words, all infimum and supremum in (9.2.4) are permutable. Recall that usually

$$\inf_{x \in X} \sup_{y \in Y} F(x, y) \neq \sup_{y \in Y} \inf_{x \in X} F(x, y),$$

where F maps $X \times Y$ into R.]

Proof The proof will be made for $n = 2$, i.e., $\delta = (T - t_0)/2$. The generalization of this case for $n > 2$ is a tedious exercise. Let

$$B = \sup_{\Gamma^{\delta_1}} \sup_{\Gamma^{\delta_2}} \inf_{\Delta_{\delta_1}} \inf_{\Delta_{\delta_2}} P(\Gamma^{\delta_1}, \Delta_{\delta_1}, \Gamma^{\delta_2}, \Delta_{\delta_2}).$$

Then from properties of infinum and supremum, one will have

$$\inf_{\Delta_{\delta_1}} \inf_{\Delta_{\delta_2}} P(\Gamma^{\delta_1}, \Delta_{\delta_1}, \Gamma^{\delta_2}, \Delta_{\delta_2}) \le \inf_{\Delta_{\delta_1}} \sup_{\Gamma^{\delta_1}} \inf_{\Delta_{\delta_2}} \sup_{\Gamma^{\delta_2}} P(\Gamma^{\delta_1}, \Delta_{\delta_1}, \Gamma^{\delta_2}, \Delta_{\delta_2})$$

or, in compact form, $\inf_{\Delta_\delta} P(\Gamma^\delta, \Delta_\delta) \le V^\delta$ for all Γ^δ, which implies that $B \le V^\delta$.

Next it will be shown that $B \ge V^\delta$. As discussed before, the functions u_1, u_2, w_1, and w_2 are defined by (9.2.1) to be the outcome of the pair $(\Gamma^\delta, \Delta_\delta)$, and vice versa. If $u_j \in Y_j$ and $w_j \in Z_j$, where $i = 1.2$, then by the kinematic equation a unique trajectory of the system and the payoff $P(u_1, w_1, u_2, w_2)$ can be defined. Let ε be any positive number. Then given any functions u_1, w_1 and w_2 in the sets Y_1, Z_1, and Z_2, respectively, one can find a function $\tilde{u}_2 \in Y_2$ such that

$$\sup_{u_2 \in Y_2} P(u_1, w_1, u_2, w_2) \le P(u_1, w_1, \tilde{u}_2, w_2) + \varepsilon.$$

Then

$$\inf_{w_2 \in Z_2} \sup_{u_2 \in Y_2} P(u_1, w_1, u_2, w_2) \le \inf_{w_2 \in Z_2} P(u_1, w_1, \tilde{u}_2, w_2) + \varepsilon. \tag{9.2.5}$$

It is obvious that

$$\tilde{u}_2 = \tilde{u}_2(u_1, w_1, w_2).$$

Denoting this map $\tilde{\Gamma}^{\delta_2}$, (9.2.5) yields

$$\inf_{\Delta_{\delta_2}} \sup_{\Gamma^{\delta_2}} P(\Gamma^{\delta_1}, \Delta_{\delta_1}, \Gamma^{\delta_2}, \Delta_{\delta_2}) \le \inf_{\Delta_{\delta_2}} P(\Gamma^{\delta_1}, \Delta_{\delta_1}, \tilde{\Gamma}^{\delta_2}, \Delta_{\delta_2}) + \varepsilon, \tag{9.2.6}$$

where Γ^{δ_1} and Δ_{δ_1} are fixed maps. Moreover, let us write

$$\inf_{\Delta_{\delta_2}} P(\Gamma^{\delta_1}, \Delta_{\delta_1}, \tilde{\Gamma}^{\delta_2}, \Delta_{\delta_2}) = P_1(\Gamma^{\delta_1}, \Delta_{\delta_1}). \tag{9.2.7}$$

By the same token, one can define $\tilde{\Gamma}^{\delta_1}$ such that

$$\inf_{\Delta_{\delta_1}} \sup_{\Gamma^{\delta_1}} P_1(\Gamma^{\delta_1}, \Delta_{\delta_1}) \leq \inf_{\Delta_{\delta_1}} P_1(\tilde{\Gamma}^{\delta_1}, \Delta_{\delta_1}) + \varepsilon.$$

But, by definition of P_1,

$$\inf_{\Delta_{\delta_1}} P_1(\tilde{\Gamma}^{\delta_1}, \Delta_{\delta_1}) = \inf_{\Delta_{\delta_1}} \inf_{\Delta_{\delta_2}} P(\tilde{\Gamma}^{\delta_1}, \Delta_{\delta_1}, \tilde{\Gamma}^{\delta_2}, \Delta_{\delta_2}),$$

which together with (9.2.6) and (9.2.7) yields

$$\begin{aligned}&\inf_{\Delta_{\delta_1}} \sup_{\Gamma^{\delta_1}} \inf_{\Delta_{\delta_2}} \sup_{\Gamma^{\delta_2}} P(\Gamma^{\delta_1}, \Delta_{\delta_1}, \Gamma^{\delta_2}, \Delta_{\delta_2})\\ &\qquad \leq \inf_{\Delta_{\delta_1}} \inf_{\Delta_{\delta_2}} P(\tilde{\Gamma}^{\delta_1}, \Delta_{\delta_1}, \tilde{\Gamma}^{\delta_2}, \Delta_{\delta_2}) + 2\varepsilon\end{aligned}$$

or, in compact form, $V^\delta \leq \inf_{\Delta_\delta} P(\tilde{\Gamma}^\delta, \Delta_\delta) + 2\varepsilon$, where $\tilde{\Gamma}^\delta = (\tilde{\Gamma}^{\delta_1}, \tilde{\Gamma}^{\delta_2})$ and and $\Delta_\delta = (\Delta_{\delta_1}, \Delta_{\delta_2})$. Note that this inequality can be expressed in the form

$$V^\delta \leq \sup_{\Gamma^\delta} \inf_{\Delta_\delta} P(\Gamma^\delta, \Delta_\delta).$$

That is, $V^\delta \leq B + \varepsilon$. Since $\varepsilon > 0$ is arbitrary, then

$$V^\delta = B.$$

Analogously, it can be shown that

$$V^\delta = \inf_{\Delta_\delta} \sup_{\Gamma^\delta} P(\Gamma^\delta, \Delta_\delta). \quad \text{Q.E.D.}$$

Similarly, it can be proved that

$$V_\delta = \inf_{\Delta^\delta} \sup_{\Gamma_\delta} \mathrm{P}(\Gamma_\delta, \Delta^\delta) = \sup_{\Gamma_\delta} \inf_{\Delta^\delta} P(\Gamma_\delta, \Delta^\delta).$$

Lemma 9.2.2 Under conditions of Lemma 9.2.1, it is true that $V^\delta \geq V_\delta$.

Proof This lemma will also be proved for $n = 2$. Given any pair of strategies $(\Gamma^\delta, \Delta_\delta)$, then by successive applications of maps $\Delta_{\delta_1}, \Gamma^{\delta_1}, \Delta_{\delta_2}$, and Γ^{δ_2} to sets Z_1, $Z_1 \times Y_1$, $Z_1 \times Y_1 \times Z_2$, and $Z_1 \times Y_1 \times Z_2 \times Y_2$, one can define by (9.2.1) the functions u_1, w_1, u_2, w_2 in the sets Y_1, Z_1, Y_2, Z_2. That is, if the first player makes the last choice in the interval $[\frac{1}{2}(T - t_0) + t_0, T]$, then that player knows not only his/her control function u_1, but also all the control functions of the second player, i.e., w_1 and w_2. Let us assume first that the first player, who is a maximizer, has a δ-advantage over the second player. Then the first player will choose his/her last move from Y_2 such that

$$\begin{aligned} V^\delta &= \inf_{\Delta_{\delta_1}} \sup_{\Gamma^{\delta_1}} \inf_{\Delta_{\delta_2}} \sup_{\Gamma^{\delta_2}} P(\Delta_{\delta_1}, \Gamma^{\delta_1}, \Delta_{\delta_2}, \Gamma^{\delta_2}) \\ &= \inf_{\Delta_{\delta_1}} \sup_{\Gamma^{\delta_1}} \inf_{\Delta_{\delta_2}} \sup_{u_2 \in Y_2} P(\Delta_{\delta_1}, \Gamma^{\delta_1}, \Delta_{\delta_2}, u_2). \end{aligned}$$

Next it is the second player's turn to make a move. Since that player is a minimizer, then he/she will make his/her last choice w_2 from the set Z_2 such that

$$V^\delta = \inf_{\Delta_{\delta_1}} \sup_{\Gamma^{\delta_1}} \inf_{w_2 \in Z_2} \sup_{u_2 \in Y_2} P(\Delta_{\delta_1}, \Gamma^{\delta_1}, w_2, u_2).$$

Continuing this process yields that

$$V^\delta = \inf_{w_1 \in Z_1} \sup_{u_1 \in Y_1} \inf_{w_2 \in Z_2} \sup_{u_2 \in Y_2} P(w_1, u_1, w_2, u_2).$$

Analogously, if the second player has a δ advantage, then

$$\begin{aligned} V_\delta &= \sup_{\Gamma_{\delta_1}} \inf_{\Delta^{\delta_1}} \sup_{\Gamma_{\delta_2}} \inf_{\Delta^{\delta_2}} P(\Delta^{\delta_1}, \Gamma_{\delta_1}, \Delta^{\delta_2}, \Gamma_{\delta_2}) \\ &= \sup_{\Gamma_{\delta_1}} \inf_{\Delta^{\delta_1}} \sup_{\Gamma^{\delta_2}} \inf_{w_2 \in Z_2} P(\Delta^{\delta_1}, \Gamma_{\delta_1}, w_2, \Gamma^{\delta_2}) \\ &= \sup_{y_1 \in Y_1} \inf_{w_1 \in Z_1} \sup_{u_2 \in Y_2} \inf_{w_2 \in Z_2} P(w_1, u_1, w_2, u_2). \end{aligned}$$

Then by Lemma 1.3.1 of Chapter 1, $V_\delta \leq V^\delta$. Q.E.D.

Nowhere above was use made of the uniformity of the partition of the interval $[t_0, T]$ at which the game evolves. In other words, the interval $[t_0, T]$ can be arbitrarily partitioned by the points t_j, and Lemmas 9.2.1 and 9.2.2 will still hold. If $[t_0, T]$ is arbitrarily partitioned, then

$$\delta = \max[t_{j+1} - t_j],$$

which is called the *mesh of the partition.* Let us assume that there are two partitions of the interval $[t_0, T]$. These partitions are denoted by the points

$\{t_j\}_{j=1}^n$ and $\{t'_j\}_{j=1}^m$ and have meshes δ and δ', respectively. The partition $\{t'_j\}_{j=1}^m$ is said to be *finer* than the partition $\{t_j\}_{j=1}^n$ if

$$\{t_j\}_{j=1}^n \subset \{t'_j\}_{j=1}^m.$$

In other words, there are fewer points in the partition $\{t_j\}_{j=1}^n$ than in the partition $\{t'_j\}_{j=1}^m$. Therefore, $m > n$ and $\delta' \leq \delta$. These definitions lay the groundwork for the next lemma.

Lemma 9.2.3 Let $\{t_j\}_{j=0}^n$ and $\{t'_j\}_{j=0}^m$ be any two partitions of the interval $[t_0, T]$ with meshes δ and δ', respectively. Let the former partition be finer than the latter. If the conditions of Lemma 9.2.1 hold, then $V^\delta \geq V^{\delta'}$ and $V_\delta \leq V_{\delta'}$.

Proof Again, the lemma will be proved for case $n = 2$, when the first partition has only one point t_1 in the interval $[t_0, T]$ and the second partition has an extra point in the subinterval $[t_0, t_1]$. Then $m = 3$ and $t'_0 = t_0$, $t'_2 = t_1$, and $t'_3 = t_2 = T$, in addition to $t'_1 \in [t_0, t_1]$. Then in the upper δ-game G^δ, the second player has an information advantage in the case of the second partition as compared with the first partition of the same game. Specifically, when G^δ reaches time $t'_2 = t_1$, the second player in the case of the second partition knows the control of the first player in the interval $[t_0, t'_1]$, but in the case of the first partition, the second player, by the definition of G^δ, does not know any controls chosen by the first player in that interval. Therefore, the second player can decrease his/her loss or can descrease the payoff of the first player. At the same time, the first player has a disadvantage because he/she has to make his/her first choice on the interval $[t_0, t'_1)$ knowing only the control function of his/her opponent in this interval. Then when that player reaches the point $t'_2 = t_1$, he/she cannot improve his/her control chosen on the interval $[t_0, t'_1]$. Then due to these considerations, $V^\delta \geq V^{\delta'}$. This reasoning can be employed step by step for any m and n.

By the same token, it can be shown that $V_\delta \leq V_{\delta'}$. Q.E.D.

Now, let us consider the sequences of the partitions that become finer as their meshes decrease. Then, due to Lemmas 9.2.2 and 9.2.3, if $\delta_n \to 0$, the sequence V^{δ_n} is monotone decreasing and bounded from below, and the sequence V_{δ_n} is monotone increasing and bounded from above. Moreover, the limits of both sequences exist, and $\lim_{\delta_n \to 0} V^{\delta_n}$ will be denoted by V^+ and $\lim_{\delta_n \to 0} V_{\delta_n}$, will be denoted by V_-.

It can be shown that the values V^+ and V_- do not depend on the choice of a specific sequence of partitions. The value V^+ is the *upper value* of the game and V_- is the *lower value* of the game.

To understand the meaning of the values V^+ and V_-, we turn back to Lemma 9.2.1. Given the partition $\{t_j\}_{j=1}^n$ with the mesh δ, then due to Lemma 9.2.1 one will obtain

$$\begin{aligned} V^\delta &= \inf_{\Delta_{\delta_1}} \sup_{\Gamma^{\delta_1}} \cdots \inf_{\Delta_{\delta_n}} \sup_{\Gamma^{\delta_n}} P(\Gamma^{\delta_1}, \Delta_{\delta_1}, \ldots, \Gamma^{\delta_n}, \Delta_{\delta_n}) \\ &= \inf_{\Delta_{\delta_1}} \cdots \inf_{\Delta_{\delta_n}} \sup_{\Gamma^{\delta_1}} \cdots \sup_{\Gamma^{\delta_n}} P(\Gamma^{\delta_1}, \Delta_{\delta_1}, \ldots, \Gamma^{\delta_n}, \Delta_{\delta_n}) \\ &= \inf_{\Delta_\delta} \sup_{\Gamma^\delta} P(\Gamma^\delta, \Delta_\delta), \end{aligned} \tag{9.2.8}$$

where Γ^δ and Δ_δ are the upper and lower δ-strategies of the first and second players with components Γ^{δ_i} and Δ_{δ_i}, $i = 1, \ldots, n$, respectively. Then due to (9.2.8) it can be said that for any $\varepsilon > 0$, there exists a lower δ- strategy, $\Delta_\delta(\varepsilon)$, of the second player such that the inequality

$$P(\Gamma^\delta, \Delta_\delta(\varepsilon)) < V^\delta + \varepsilon \tag{9.2.9}$$

holds, independently of any choice of the first player. In other words, as explained in Section 1.3 of Chapter 1, it can be said that V^δ is the ensurance level which the second player can guarantee for himself/herself with ε-accuracy if the partition is fixed and even if that player has δ-disadvantage in getting information about the development of the game. In a sequence of partitions such that $\delta_n \to 0$, the corresponding sequence of strategies $\Delta_{\delta_n}(\varepsilon)$ more closely approximates the ensurance behavioral strategy, at least in terms of information (because a real behavioral strategy which makes it possible to solve the equations of the game may not exist at all). Therefore, due to these considerations, if $\delta_n \to 0$ and

$$P(\Gamma_{\delta_n}, \Delta_{\delta_n}(\varepsilon)) < V^{\delta_n} + \varepsilon, \tag{9.2.10}$$

then the sequence $\{\Delta_{\delta_n}(\varepsilon)\}$ will be called the *quasibehavioral ε-ensurance strategy* of the second player. Note that due to Lemma 9.2.3, $V^{\delta_n} \to V^+$ as $\delta_n \to 0$, and thus V^{δ_n} in (9.2.10) can be replaced by V^+.

Analogously, for any $\varepsilon > 0$ and any δ, there exists a vector of strategies $\Gamma_\delta(\varepsilon)$ of the first player such that

$$P(\Gamma_\delta(\varepsilon), \Delta^\delta) > V_\delta - \varepsilon$$

given any upper δ strategies of the second player. That is, $\Gamma_\delta(\varepsilon)$ is the ε-ensurance strategy of the first player, which guarantees him/her the ensurance level V_δ with ε-accuracy, even under δ disadvantage in obtaining information about the development of the game. Therefore, if $\delta_n \to 0$, the sequence $\{\Gamma_{\delta_n}(\varepsilon)\}$ is called the quasibehavioral ε-ensurance strategy of the first player. Then similar to (9.2.9), one will have

$$P(\Gamma_{\delta_n}(\varepsilon), \Delta^{\delta_n}) > V_- - \varepsilon. \tag{9.2.11}$$

If $V_+ = V_- = V$, then V is the value of the game and it can be said that the game has the value V. The sequences $\{\Gamma_{\delta_n}(\varepsilon)\}$ and $\{\Delta_{\delta_n}(\varepsilon)\}$ are called the *quasibehavioral ε-saddle point strategies* of the first and second players, respectively.

To conclude this section, a theorem of existence of strategies, in the sense defined above, will be proved. The conditions for existience of the value of the game include, in addition to (R1), (R2), and (R3) of Section 8.1, a condition on the separability of controls u, w in the function ϕ, which define the kinematic equations, and in the function f_2, which defines the payoff. That is,

$$\phi(t, x, u, w) = \phi^1(t, x, u) + \phi^2(t, x, w),$$

$$f_2(x, u, w) = f_2^1(x, w) + f_2^2(x, w).$$

This condition will be denoted by (R5). Note that assumption (A2) of Section 8.3 holds under condition (R5).

Theorem 9.2.1 Let the game Γ satisfy conditions (R1), (R2), and (R5). Then Γ has a value.

Proof By following reasoning familiar to that used in defining an ensurance strategy for every player, with a given partition, another kind of strategy can be defined. If V^δ is the upper value of the game with a given partition, then based on Lemma 9.2.1 a strategy $\bar{\Gamma}^\delta(\varepsilon)$ can be defined for any $\varepsilon > 0$ such that

$$-\varepsilon + V^\delta \le P(\Delta_\delta, \bar{\Gamma}^\delta(\varepsilon)) \tag{9.2.12}$$

for any Δ_δ. In other words, $\bar{\Gamma}^\delta(\varepsilon)$ could be an ensurance strategy of the first player, which guarantees him/her the payoff V^δ with ε-accuracy. However, $\bar{\Gamma}^\delta(\varepsilon)$ is not a "real" ensurance strategy because it is assumed in constructing it that the first player has a δ-advantage in getting information. In contrast, this assumption is not included in constructing the ensurance strategy $\Gamma^\delta(\varepsilon)$.

Similarly, if V^δ is the upper value of the game with the given partition then by Lemma 9.2.1, there exists a strategy $\bar{\Delta}^\delta(\varepsilon)$ such that for any $\varepsilon > 0$,

$$V_\delta + \varepsilon \geq P(\Gamma_\delta, \bar{\Delta}^\delta(\varepsilon)) \tag{9.2.13}$$

for any Γ_δ. This strategy is also not a "real" ensurance strategy for the second player.

The proof will be completed by showing that with a special choice of strategies, Δ_δ and Γ^δ, which satisfy (9.2.13) and for any $\varepsilon > 0$, the inequality

$$V^\delta - V_\delta < 3\varepsilon \tag{9.2.14}$$

holds. Then due to Lemma 9.2.2, we know that $V^\delta \geq V_\delta$, which together with (9.2.14) shows that $V_\delta \to V^\delta$ as $\delta \to 0$. In the proof it is assumed that the interval $[t_0, T]$ is uniformly partitioned, since the objective is to show that $V^+ = V_-$.

Let us start from Eq. (9.2.12) and then construct, step by step, the controls of both players. At the interval $I_1 = [t_0, t_1]$ it is assumed that $\bar{w}_1(t)$ is an arbitrary function from Z_1 and

$$\bar{u}_1(\cdot) = \bar{\Gamma}^{\delta_1}(\varepsilon)(\bar{w}_1(\cdot)) \in Y_1,$$

where $t \in I_1$. At the next interval,

$$\bar{w}_2(\cdot) = \bar{\Delta}^{\delta_1}(\varepsilon)(\bar{u}_1(\cdot), \bar{w}_1(\cdot)),$$

where $\bar{\Delta}^{\delta_1}(\varepsilon)$ is the first component of $\bar{\Delta}^\delta(\varepsilon)$, which is defined in (9.2.13), and

$$\bar{u}_2 = \bar{\Gamma}^{\delta_2}(\varepsilon)(\bar{w}_1(\cdot), \bar{u}_1(\cdot), \bar{w}_2(\cdot)).$$

This process will continue until point T. Then by (9.2.12)

$$-\varepsilon + V^\delta \leq P(\bar{u}_1(\cdot), \bar{w}_1(\cdot), \ldots, \bar{u}_n(\cdot), \bar{w}_n(\cdot)). \tag{9.2.15}$$

Note that by the definition of an upper δ-strategy of the second player, one can write the strategies

$$\bar{w}_2(\cdot) = \bar{\Delta}^{\delta_1}(\varepsilon)(\bar{u}_1(\cdot)),$$

$$\bar{w}_3(\cdot) = \bar{\Delta}^{\delta_2}(\varepsilon)(\bar{u}_1(\cdot), \bar{w}_1(\cdot), \bar{u}_2(\cdot)),$$

and so on.

Next, another pair of strategies for the players will be constructed. The strategies $\bar{u}_j(\cdot)$, $j = 1, \dots, n$ will be considered strategies of the first player. The strategies of the second player will be defined as

$$\bar{\bar{w}}_1(\cdot) = \bar{\Delta}^{\delta_1}(\varepsilon)(\bar{u}_1(\cdot)),$$

$$\bar{\bar{w}}_2(\cdot) = \bar{\Delta}^{\delta_2}(\varepsilon)(\bar{u}_1(\cdot), \bar{\bar{w}}_1(\cdot), \bar{u}_2(\cdot),$$

and so on. Then (9.2.13) can be written as

$$V_\delta + \varepsilon \geq P(\bar{u}_1(\cdot), \bar{\bar{w}}_1(\cdot), \bar{u}_2(\cdot), \bar{\bar{w}}_2(\cdot), \dots, \bar{u}_n(\cdot), \bar{\bar{w}}_2(\cdot)). \tag{9.2.16}$$

It can be seen from this construction of strategies that strategies $\bar{\bar{w}}_j(\cdot)$, $j = 1, \dots, n$, are connected with strategies $\bar{w}_j(\cdot)$ by the formula

$$\bar{\bar{w}}_j(\cdot) = \bar{w}_j(t + \delta),$$

where $t \in I_j$ and $j = 1, \dots, n$.

Next, a lemma will be proved from which it follows that

$$\max_{t \in [t_0, T]} |\bar{\bar{x}}(t) - \bar{x}(t)| < c_1(\delta) \tag{9.2.17}$$

and

$$\left| \int_{t_0}^{T} f_2(\bar{\bar{x}}(t), \bar{u}(t), \bar{\bar{w}}(t))\, dt - \int_{t_0}^{T} f_2(\bar{x}(t), \bar{u}(t), \bar{w}(t))\, dt \right| \leq c_2(\delta)$$

such that $c_1(\delta) \to 0$ and $c_2(\delta) \to 0$ if $\delta \to 0$, where $\bar{\bar{x}}(t)$ is the trajectory determined by the controls $(\bar{u}, \bar{\bar{w}})$, and $\bar{x}(t)$, is the trajectory determined by the controls $(\bar{u}, \bar{w})$, and these trajectories start from the same initial point, i.e., $\bar{\bar{x}}(t_0) = \bar{x}(t_0) = x_0$.

Then it follows from (9.2.17) that there exists $\delta(\varepsilon)$ such that for any $\delta < \delta(\varepsilon)$ the inequality

$$|P(\bar{u}_1, \bar{\bar{w}}_1, \bar{u}_2, \bar{\bar{w}}_2, \dots, \bar{u}_n, \bar{\bar{w}}_n) - P(\bar{u}_1, \bar{w}_1, \dots, \bar{u}_n, \bar{w}_n)| < \varepsilon$$

holds. This inequality implies (9.2.14). Q.E.D.

Lemma 9.2.4 Let the game Γ satisfy conditions (R1), (R2), and (R5) and let $(\bar{u}, \bar{\bar{w}})$ and $(\bar{u}, \bar{w})$ be any two pairs of control functions such that

$$\bar{\bar{w}}(t) = \bar{w}(t + \delta) \qquad \text{for} \quad t \in [t_0, T]$$

and $\bar{w}(t)$ for $t \in [0, \delta]$ is an element of Z_1. Then the relations defined by (9.2.17) hold.

Proof Let us define $|\bar{\bar{x}}(t) - \bar{x}(t)|$ by $a_\delta(t)$. Then by condition (R1) it follows that

$$|\phi(\bar{x}, \bar{u}, \bar{w}) - \phi(\bar{\bar{x}}, \bar{u}, \bar{w})| \leq k a_\delta(t).$$

But due to condition (R5), we will have

$$\begin{aligned} a_\delta(t) &= \left| \int_{t_0}^{t} [\phi(\bar{x}(\tau), \bar{u}(\tau), \bar{w}(\tau)) - \phi(\bar{\bar{x}}(\tau), \bar{u}(\tau), \bar{\bar{w}}(\tau))]\, d\tau \right| \\ &\leq \left| \int_{t_0}^{t} [\phi^1(\bar{x}(\tau), \bar{u}(\tau)) - \phi^1(\bar{\bar{x}}(\tau), \bar{u}(\tau)]\, d\tau \right| \\ &\quad + \left| \int_{t_0}^{t} [\phi^2(\bar{\bar{x}}(\tau), \bar{w}(\tau)) - \phi^2(\bar{\bar{x}}(\tau), \bar{\bar{w}}(\tau))]\, d\tau \right| \\ &\leq k \int_{t_0}^{t} a_\delta(\tau)\, d\tau + \left| \int_{t_0}^{t} [\phi^2(\bar{\bar{x}}(\tau), \bar{w}(\tau)) - \phi^2(\bar{\bar{x}}(\tau), \bar{\bar{w}}(\tau)]\, d\tau \right|. \end{aligned} \tag{9.2.18}$$

Note that the term

$$\int_{t_0}^{t} [\phi^2(\bar{\bar{x}}(\tau), \bar{w}(\tau)) - \phi^2(\bar{\bar{x}}(\tau), \bar{\bar{w}}(\tau))]\, d\tau$$

can be written as

$$\begin{aligned} &\int_{t_0}^{t_0+\delta} \phi^2(\bar{\bar{x}}(\tau), \bar{w}(\tau))\, d\tau + \int_{t_0+\delta}^{t} \phi^2(\bar{\bar{x}}(\tau), \bar{w}(\tau))\, d\tau \\ &\quad - \int_{t_0}^{t-\delta} \phi^2(\bar{\bar{x}}(\tau), \bar{\bar{w}}(\tau))\, d\tau - \int_{t-\delta}^{t} \phi^2(\bar{\bar{x}}(\tau), \bar{w}(\tau))\, d\tau. \end{aligned} \tag{9.2.19}$$

The terms $\int_{t_0}^{t_0+\delta} \phi^2(\bar{\bar{x}}(\tau), \bar{w}(\tau))\, d\tau$ and $\int_{t-\delta}^{t} \phi^2(\bar{\bar{x}}(\tau), \bar{\bar{w}}(\tau))\, d\tau$ will go to zero if $\delta \to 0$. This is so because all functions are restricted to the compact region D, which contains all trajectories of the system of differential equations. Substituting $\tau = t + \delta$ in the integral,

$$\int_{t_0+\delta}^{t} \phi^2(\bar{\bar{x}}(\tau), \bar{w}(\tau))\, d\tau.$$

Then

$$\int_{t_0+\delta}^{t} \phi^2(\bar{\bar{x}}(\tau), \bar{w}(\tau))\, d\tau - \int_{t_0}^{t-\delta} \phi^2(\bar{\bar{x}}(\tau), \bar{\bar{w}}(\tau))\, d\tau$$

becomes

$$\int_{t_0}^{t-\delta} \phi^2(x(\tau - \delta), \bar{\bar{w}}(\tau))\, d\tau - \int_{t_0}^{t-\delta} \phi^2(x(\tau), \bar{\bar{w}}(\tau))\, d\tau,$$

where $\bar{\bar{w}} = \bar{w}(t + \delta)$. Since the region D is compact, then

$$|x(\tau) - x(\tau - \delta)| < c\delta,$$

where c is a positive number. This, together with condition (R1), implies that

$$\left| \int_{t_0}^{t-\delta} \phi^2(x(\tau - \delta), \bar{\bar{w}}(\tau))\, d\tau - \int_{t_0}^{t-\delta} \phi^2(x(\tau), \bar{\bar{w}}(\tau))\, d\tau \right| < \gamma(\delta),$$

where $\gamma(\delta) \to 0$ if $\delta \to 0$. Then from (9.2.18) it follows that

$$a_\delta(t) \leq k \int_{t_0}^{t} a_\delta(\tau)\, d\tau + \gamma(\delta) + 2c\delta, \tag{9.2.20}$$

where $2c\delta$ is the difference between the first and last terms of (9.2.19). Then from (9.2.20) it follows that

$$\max_{\tau \in [t_0, t]} a_\delta(t) \to 0 \qquad \text{if} \quad \delta \to 0, \tag{9.2.21}$$

which proves the first relation in (9.2.17). The proof of the second relation in (9.2.17) follows from (9.2.20) and (R5), employing the same reasoning used in establishing the first relation of (9.2.17). Q.E.D.

Friedman also discusses the condition under which the ensurance strategies described above define behavioral strategies. The computation of these strategies, however, is based on Isaacs' approach.

9.3 KRASOVSKY'S APPROACH

This approach is, to some extent, a generalization of two approaches: the geometrical approach of Section 9.1 and Friedman's approximation approach described in the preceding section.

First, Nikolai Krasovsky notes that if a solution of the system of differential equations in (7.1.3) is defined as a general solution, then the existence of solutions for some differential games cannot be proved. The reason for the nonexistence of this kind of solution is that the set of general solutions that starts from a given initial state with a given control function is very broad. Therefore, Krasovsky attempts to narrow this set by introducing the concept of "movement," an idea arising from the nature of calculating trajectories using a first-order approximation. Movements are the solutions of the games described by this approach. The jet of these movements contains all the classical solutions defined in Section 7.2 and is a subset of the jet which contains all general solutions.

Let the differential game Γ be defined by the kinematic equation

$$\dot{x} = \phi(x, u, w), \qquad x(t_0) = x_0,$$

where $u \in U_1$ and $w \in U_2$. (This is a case in which the control sets do not depend on the state of the game.) Moreover, let $w(t)$ be a program strategy of the second player that is not known to the first player, where $t \in [t_0, T]$ and T is the maximum duration of the game. Let us also assume that the function $w(t)$ is Lebesque integrable on $[t_0, T]$ and $u(x, t)$ is a control function or a strategy of the first player. If $\{t_i\}_{i=1}^n$, where $t_n = T$, is a partition of the interval $[t_0, T]$ with a mesh δ, then *Euler's linear curve* which corresponds to the controls $u(x, t)$ and $w(t)$ is a curve $x_\delta(t)$ that satisfies the system

$$\dot{x}_\delta(t) = \phi(x_\delta(t), u(x(t_i), t_i), w(t)), \qquad x(t_0) = x_0 \quad \text{a.e.},$$

where $t \in [t_i, t_{i+1}]$, $i = 1, \ldots, n$. Then due to an analogy of Theorem 7.2.1 with the given restrictions on the function ϕ and on the sets U_1 and U_2, which are assumed to be compact, Euler's linear curve always exists for the given partition $\{t_i\}_{i=1}^n$. By reasoning similar to that used in proving the existence of a solution for a system of differential equations (Coddington and Levinson, 1955), it is possible to prove that the set of all Euler's linear curves for the given control functions $u(x, t)$ and $w(t)$ and for the given initial state x_0 is a compact set in the space $C[t_0, T]$, the space of all continuous functions on $[t_0, T]$ with norm

$$\|x\| = \max_{t \in [t, T]} |x(t)|.$$

Therefore, if $\delta_n \to 0$, there exists at least one sequence from these Euler's linear curves that will converge to a continuous function. This function is called a *movement* starting from the initial state x_0 and determined by the control functions $u(x, t)$ and $w(t)$. It can be seen from this definition of movements that no restriction is imposed on the strategy of the first player. It approximates, to some extent, the control function $u(x, t)$ with the help of a sequence of partitions, as in Friedman's approach. Therefore, a movement is a continuous function which, in general, does not satisfy

$$\dot{x} = \phi(x(t), u(x(t), t), w(t)), \qquad x(t_0) = x_0. \tag{9.3.1}$$

But if there is a continuous function $x(t)$ that satisfies (9.3.1) a.e., then $x(t)$ is a movement. On the other hand, if the jet of all general solutions of (9.3.1) that start from $x(t_0)$ is denoted by

$$X(x_0, u(x, t), w(t)),$$

and if the jet of all movements which are defined by the same differential equation as described above and that start from the same initial point is denoted by

$$X_0(x_0, u(x, t), w(t)),$$

then

$$X_0(x_0, u(x, t), w(t)) \subset X(x, u(x, t), w(t)).$$

Introduction of the concept of movement will serve a similar purpose to that served by the introduction of general solutions to prove the existence of solutions when the right-hand side of the system of differential equations is discontinuous, which is equivalent to switching and reswitching of controls by the players.

Although Krasovsky's approach allows us to cope with most of the problems encountered in proving the existence of solutions of differential games, in particular the case where the control sets depend on the state of the game, we shall consider only the case which is applicable to the economic models described before.

Let x_0 belong to D, the region of the game, which in general is assumed to be a closed set of R^n. Let F, the terminal set of the first player, also be a closed set in R^n. The set $X(t_0, x_0, U_1)$ will denote the set of all movements starting at t_0, when the strategy of the second player is an arbitrary program strategy $w(t)$ such that $w(t) \in U_2$ for $t \geq t_0$. Then the problem for the first player of reaching the terminal surface in the fixed time $[t_0, T]$ is as follows:

Problem I Find a behavioral strategy $\bar{u}(x, t)$, which is a function from $R^n \times [t_0, T]$ into U_1 and which is integrable in both x and t, such that for any movement

$$x(t) = x(t_0, x_0, t, \bar{u}(x, t)) \in X_0(t_0, x_0, U_1)$$

it follows that

$$\begin{aligned} x(t) &\in D \quad \text{for} \quad t_0 \leq t \leq \tau \leq T_0, \\ x(\tau) &\in F \quad \text{for} \quad \tau \leq T_0. \end{aligned} \tag{9.3.2}$$

In other words, the first player can keep the trajectory in the region of the game and can reach the terminal set before or at the terminal time T_0, independent of the program strategy of the second player. The time τ, in general, depends on the program strategy of the second player.

In the case of the game between two one-commodity models, the region D is the positive orthant of R^2 and F, the terminal set of the first player, is

$$F = \{(x_1, x_2) : x_2 = 0 \text{ and } x_1 \geq 0\},$$

as illustrated in Figure 9.3.1. The problem of the first player is to force the trajectory to terminate in the set F before the time T_0 is exhausted. Since problem I amounts to finding a strategy that makes the first player win the game, then a draw, which is denoted by (0, 0), is impossible. Therefore it is assumed that $(0, 0) \in F$, and since $(0, 0) \in F$, this makes the first player the victor even if he/she can reach the origin before time t_0 is exausted.

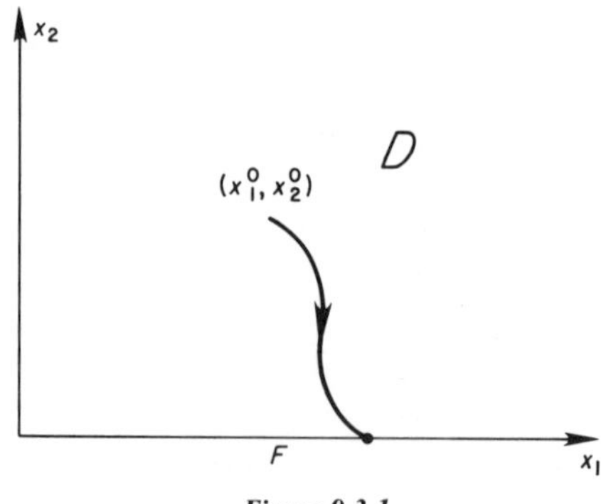

Figure 9.3.1

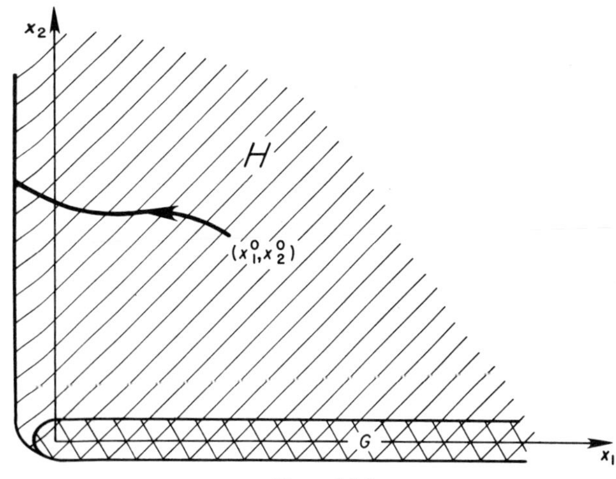

Figure 9.3.2

and another open set H that covers the positive orthant. Then the problem of the second player is to find a strategy which gives him/her the options before or at T_0 not to be in set G while being in set H, or to leave the set H without being in G. The last option means that the second player can definately reach the set

$$\{(x_1, x_2) : x_1 = 0 \text{ and } x_2 > 0\},$$

which makes him/her the victor. This situation is shown in Figure 9.3.2.

Generally speaking, problems I and II seem not to be antagonistic problems. However, as will be seen later, for any $x_0 \in D$, there exists either a strategy $\bar{u}(x, t)$, which solves problem I, or a strategy $\bar{w}(x, t)$, which solves problem II. To solve those problems Krasovsky has developed a geometric approach which he called a "bridge." The set $W_u \in R^n$ is called a *bridge* for the first player if

(1) $x_0 \in W_u$,
(2) $W_u \subset D$, and
(3) there exists a behavioral strategy $\bar{u}(x, t)$ of the first player such that for any $x^* \in W_u$, there is $t^* \in [t_0, T]$ ($t^* = t_0$ if $x^* = x_0$) such that any movement

$$x(t) = x(t^*, x^*, t, \bar{u}(x, t)) \in X_0(t^*, x^*, \bar{u}(x, t)),$$

starting from x^* at the moment t^* reaches the terminal set F at a moment $\tau \leq T$. That is, the strategy $\bar{u}(x, t)$ allows the first player, independent of the

It may seem that this approach is not general enough since the first playe competes with his/her opponent who uses only a program strategy $w(t)$. Th is not the case because no specific program strategy [i.e., $w(t)$] is identified f the second player. Formally, given any behavioral strategy $w(x, t)$ of t second player, the jet of all movements

$$X_0(t_0, x_0, \bar{u}(x, t), w(x, t))$$

starting from x_0 at the moment t_0 under the controls $\bar{u}(x, t)$ and $w(x$ satisfies

$$X_0(t_0, x_0, \bar{u}(x, t), w(x, t)) \subset X_0(t_0, x_0, \bar{u}(x, t)).$$

That is, if the first player's strategy $\bar{u}(x, t)$ is effective against any prog strategy of the second player, then it is effective against any behav strategy of the second player.

The problem of the second player is somewhat different.

Problem II Let H and G be any open sets containing the sets D a respectively. Then the problem is to find a behavioral strategy $\bar{w}(x, t)$ that among all the movements $X_0(t_0, x_0, \bar{w}(x, t))$ there does not e movement

$$x(t) = x(t_0\ x_0, t, \bar{w}(x, t)) \in X_0(t_0, x_0, \bar{w}(x, t))$$

such that

$$x(t) \in H \supset D \qquad \text{for} \quad t \in [t_0, \tau]$$

and

$$x(\tau) \in G \supset F \qquad \text{for} \quad \tau \leq T_0.$$

Here $X_0(t_0, x_0, \bar{w}(x, t))$ is the set of all movements that can exist if the of the first player is $\bar{u}(t)$ (i.e., a fixed program strategy), and the strate second player is $\bar{w}(x, t)$ (i.e., a behavioral strategy). In other words, th player has to exclude the movements that always belong to sor neighborhood of the region of the game and that reach the tern before or at T_0. That is, the second player tries to avoid the set $G \supset$ the period $[t_0\ T_0]$.

Applying problem II to the war between two one-commodity r can be said that there is an open set G that covers the x_1 axis define

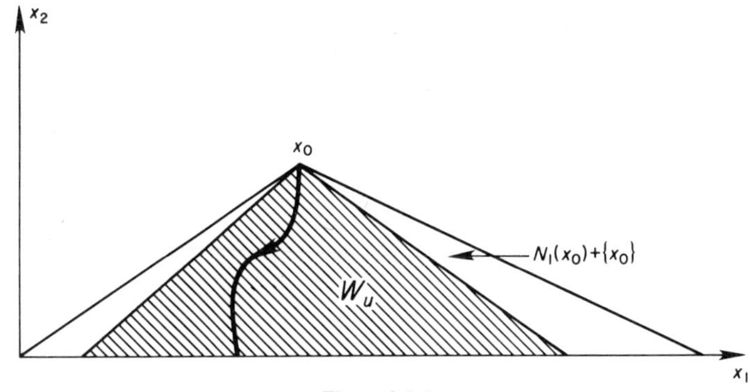

Figure 9.3.3

strategy of the second player, to reach the terminal set before or at the exhaustion time T, beginning from any initial state in the bridge.

In the case of war between two one-commodity models, the bridge has approximately the shape depicted in Figure 9.3.3. This figure is based on Theorem 9.1.1 of Section 9.1, which implies that the first player always has a strategy which allows him/her to keep the trajectory, independent of the actions of the second player, in the set $N_1(x_0) + \{x_0\}$, where $N_1(x_0)$ is the first player's cone of desired directions.

Similarly, the set $W_w \in R^n$ is called a bridge for the second player if

(1) $x_0 \in W_w$ and $W_w \subset H \supset D$,
(2) $W_w \cap G = \varnothing$, where G is an open neighborhood of the set F, and
(3) there exists a strategy $\bar{w}(x, t)$ such that for any x^*, there exists $t^* \in [t_0, \tau]$ ($t^* = t_0$ if $x^* = x_0$) such that for which any movement

$$x(t) = x(t^*, x^*, t, \bar{w}(x, t)),$$

$$x(t) = x(t^*, x^*, t, \bar{w}(x, t)) \in X_0(t^*, x^*, \bar{w}(x, t)),$$

starting from x^* at the moment t^* stays in the set W_w up to the moment T or leaves the open set $H \supset D$ at a moment $\tau \leq T_0$, and $x(t) \in W_w$ for $t \in [t^*, \tau]$.

In other words, the second player can keep the movement from reaching the terminal set F up to the terminal time or until it leaves the region D before the time is exhausted (i.e., detouring the set $G \supset F$).

In the case of the war between two one-commodity models, the graph for this definition is shown in Figure 9.3.4.

In addition to the definition of the bridge, Krasovsky introduces the concept of stability of the bridge from the point of view of every player. The

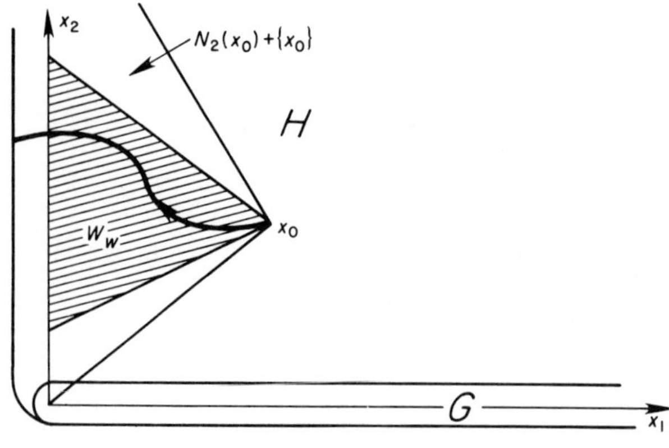

Figure 9.3.4

set $W \subset D$ is called *u-stable* (i.e., stable for the first player) if for any $x_* \in W$, $t_* \geq t_0$ and $t_* < t^* \leq T_0$, and for any fixed control $w^* \in U_2$ of the second player there exists a solution $x(t)$ in the jet that starts from x_* at the moment t_* and satisfies

$$\dot{x} \in F_u(t, x(t), w^*) \tag{9.3.3}$$

such that $x(t^*) \in W$ or $x(\tau) \in F$ for some $\tau \in [t_*, t^*]$ where

$$F_u(t, x(t), w^*) = \mathrm{CO}\{z : z = \phi(x, u, w^*) \text{ and } u \in U_1\}.$$

That is, in a stable set, the first player can choose a strategy that successfully [in the sense of forcing the movement $x(t)$ to return to the set W after a short time if it leaves that set or to go to the terminal set F] competes with any constant strategy of the second player. Then it follows directly from the definition of a bridge for the first player that this bridge has to be a u-stable set. In fact, in the opposite case in which the bridge is not stable, the second player can leave the bridge by choosing the appropriate constant strategy.

The set $W \subset D$ is called w-stable (i.e., stable for the second player) if for any $x_* \in W$, $t_* \geq t_0$, $t_* < t^* \leq T_0$, and for any fixed control $u^* \in U_1$ of the first player there exists a solution $x(t)$ in the jet that starts from x_* at the moment t_* and satisfies

$$\dot{x} \in F_w(t, x(t), u^*)$$

such that $x(t^*) \in W$ or $x(\tau) \notin H$ for some $\tau \in [t_*, t^*]$, where H is an open set that contains D and where

$$F_w(t, x(t), u^*) = \mathrm{CO}\{z : z = \phi(x, u^*, w) \text{ and } w \in U_2\}$$

and $u^* \in U_2$. In other words, in the w-stable set, the second player can choose a strategy that successfully (in the sense of forcing the movement to return to W or to leave some open neighborhood of D) competes with any constant strategy of the first player. It also follows from the definition of a bridge that any bridge of the second player must be a w-stable set.

Since the sets U_1 and U_2 are compact and the function $\phi(x, t, u, w)$ is continuous, the closure of any u- or w-stable set is also u or w stable.

If additional conditions are imposed on the equations that define the game, then a saddle point for this game can be defined. Let $l \in R^n$ be an arbitrary vector and let the equation

$$\min_{u \in U_1} \max_{w \in U_2} l \cdot \phi(x, u, w) = \max_{w \in U_2} \min_{u \in U_1} l \cdot \phi(x, u, w) \tag{9.3.4}$$

hold. Then the control $u^* \in U_1$ that satisfies

$$\max_{w \in U_2} l \cdot \phi(x, u^*, w) = \min_{u \in U_1} \max_{w \in U_2} l \cdot \phi(x, u, w)$$

is called a minimax control. The control $w^* \in U_2$, which satisfies

$$\min_{u \in U_1} l \cdot \phi(x, u, w^*) = \max_{w \in U_2} \min_{u \in U_1} l \cdot \phi(x, u, w),$$

is called a *maximin* control. Then it follows from (9.3.4) that if u^* and w^* are minimax and maximin, respectively, they constitute a saddle point. That is,

$$l \cdot \phi(x, u, w^*) \leq l \cdot \phi(x, u^*, w^*) \leq l \cdot \phi(x, u, w^*) \tag{9.3.5}$$

for any $u \in U_1$ and $w \in U_2$.

The meanings of the maximin and minimax may be expressed as follows. Suppose the vector $l \in R^n$ defines a direction $l/\|l\|$. If the first player is interested in choosing a control that minimizes the angle between l and the trajectory for a rather small lapse of time, and if the second player is interested in maximizing the same angle, then the strategies u^* and w^* are their optimal strategies. If the second player chooses a strategy that is different from w^*, then the first player can only decrease the angle. Figure 9.3.5 shows the following: the optimal trajectory, determined by the optimal strategies u^* and w^*; a first-order approximation of the optimal trajectory when u^* and w^* are chosen; a first-order approximation of the optimal trajectory when u^* is chosen by the first player and an arbitrary strategy w is chosen by the second player. Then the angle defined by the line l and the approximated optimal trajectories decreases if the second player chooses a strategy different from w^*, while the first player keeps choosing u^*.

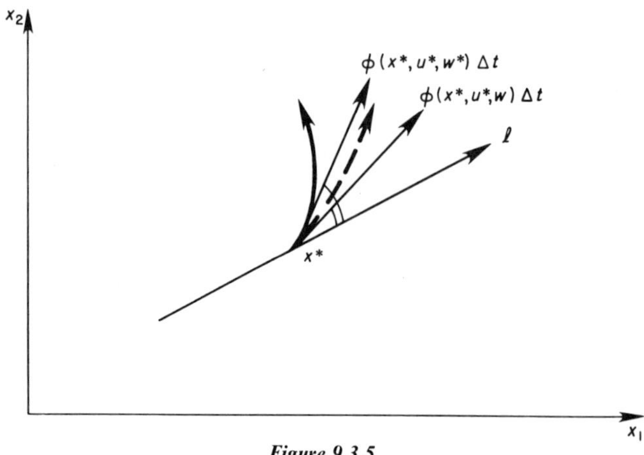

Figure 9.3.5

Condition (9.3.4) holds for any function ϕ which is separable in controls, e.g.,

$$\phi(x, u, w) = \phi^1(x, u) + \phi^2(x, u).$$

This property of function ϕ is always assumed in Isaacs' and Friedman's approaches. However, (9.3.4) can also hold under less restrictive conditions, when ϕ is a vector-valued function. Specifically, if for any $l \in R^n$ it follows that

$$l \cdot \phi(x, u, w) = \phi^1(l, x, u) + \phi^2(l, x, w), \tag{9.3.6}$$

then (9.3.6) holds, as in the case of war between two Leontief models, for example.

Based on the definition of a minimax strategy, an extremum strategy[1] with respect to a given u-stable set will be defined. Let W be a u-stable set and $x_* \in D$. Moreover, let $w_* \in W$ be the vector closest to x_* in the Euclidean metric space. Then $u_l(x_*)$ will be chosen as a minimax control for the vector $l = x_* - w_*$, i.e., a control that establishes the equation

$$\max_{w \in U_2} (x_* - w_*) \cdot \phi(x^*, u_l(x_*), w) = \min_{u \in U_1} \max_{w \in U_2} (x_* - w_*) \cdot \phi(x^*, u_l(x_*), w). \tag{9.3.7}$$

The control $u_l(x_*)$ is called an *extremum* strategy of the first player. Note that when $x_* \in W$, any element of U_1 can be chosen as an extremum strategy

[1] This terminology is a transliteration of "ekstremalnaya strategya" in Russian.

of the first player because in this case w_*, which is the closest vector to x_* in the set W, coincides with x_*.

It follows from the definition of extremum strategies that for any states that do not belong to a u-stable set W, these strategies will "pull" any trajectory inside the set W. Therefore, if the trajectory is already in W, the extremum strategy does not force that trajectory to leave that set. The worst that can happen is that this strategy will allow the trajectory to move indefinitely on the surface of set W. Also, if W is the bridge of the first player, then to some extent the direction

$$\frac{x^* - w^*}{\|x^* - w^*\|}$$

is a desired direction for the first player to move and the extremum strategy $u_l(x_*)$ determines a movement in a desired direction.

Analogously, if W is a stable set for the second player, then the extremum strategy $w_l(x_*)$ of that player for $x_* \in D$ is defined as the maximin strategy for the direction

$$\frac{w_* - x_*}{\|w_* - x_*\|},$$

where $w_* \in W$ is the vector closest to x_* in the set W.

The following theorem characterizes an extremum strategy of the first player.

Theorem 9.3.1 Let W be a closed u-stable set, let $u_l(x)$ be an extremum strategy of the first player with respect to the set W, and let $x_0 \in W$. Then for any movement

$$x(t) = x(t_0, x_0, t, u_l(x))$$

it follows that $x(t) \in W$ up to moment τ at which $x(\tau) \in F$. If there does not exist $\tau > t_0$ such that $x(\tau) \in F$, then $x \in W$ and this movement will continue forever.

The proof of this theorem is based on two lemmas.

Lemma 9.3.1 Let x_1^* and x_2^* belong to the compact set G that contains the region D such that any movement of the system $\dot{x} = \phi(x, u, w)$, which starts from x_1^* or x_2^* at the moment t_*, stays in G for any $t \in [t_*, t_* + T]$ when T is a constant. Let u^* and w^* be extremum strategies of the first and second players with respect to the directions $x_1^* - x_2^* = l_*$ in the state x_1^* and x_2^*, respectively. That is,

$$\begin{aligned}\max_{w\in U_2} l_* \cdot \phi(x_1^*, u^*, w) &= \min_{u\in U_1}\max_{w\in U_2} l_* \cdot \phi(x_1^*, u, w),\\ \min_{u\in U_1} l_* \cdot \phi(x_2^*, u, w^*) &= \max_{w\in U_2}\min_{u\in U_1} l_* \cdot \phi(x_2^*, u, w).\end{aligned} \tag{9.3.8}$$

If $x_1(t)$ is a movement that is defined by the differential equations

$$\dot{x}_1(t) = \phi(x_1(t), u^*, w(t)), \qquad x_1(t_*) = x_1^*, \tag{9.3.9}$$

where $w(t)$ is a program strategy of the second player and $x_2(t)$ is a general solution of

$$\dot{x}_2(t) \in F_u(x_2(t), w^*), \qquad x_2(t_*) = x_2^*, \tag{9.3.10}$$

where

$$F_u(x(t), w^*) = \mathrm{CO}\{z : z = \phi(x, u, w^*) \text{ and } u \in U_1\},$$

then

$$(d(t_* + \delta))^2 \le (d(t_*))^2(1 + \beta\delta) + c\delta^2, \tag{9.3.11}$$

where $d(t) = \|x_1(t) - x_2(t)\|$, $\delta \in [0, T]$, and β and c are positive constants.

This lemma evaluates the distance between two trajectories that start from the points x_1^* and x_2^*. In order to reach point x_2^* from x_1^*, the first player uses the extremum strategy u^*, which minimizes the angle between the direction l_* and that player's movement, as shown in Figure 9.3.6. The second player intends to reach x_1^* from x_2^* by choosing the extremum strategy w^* that also minimizes the angle between that player's movement and l_*.

Proof Let γ denote the maximum of $\|\phi(x, u, w)\|$ when $x \in G$, and let λ be the Lipschitz constant for the function ϕ. Then the trajectories $x_1(t)$ and $x_2(t)$ defined by (9.3.9) and (9.3.10) satisfy the relations

$$\begin{aligned}&\|x_1(t) - x_1\| \le \gamma(t - t_*),\\ &\|x_2(t) - x_2^*\| \le \gamma(t - t_*),\\ &\|\dot{x}_1(t)\| \le \gamma \qquad \text{and} \qquad \|\dot{x}_2(t)\| \le \gamma.\end{aligned} \tag{9.3.12}$$

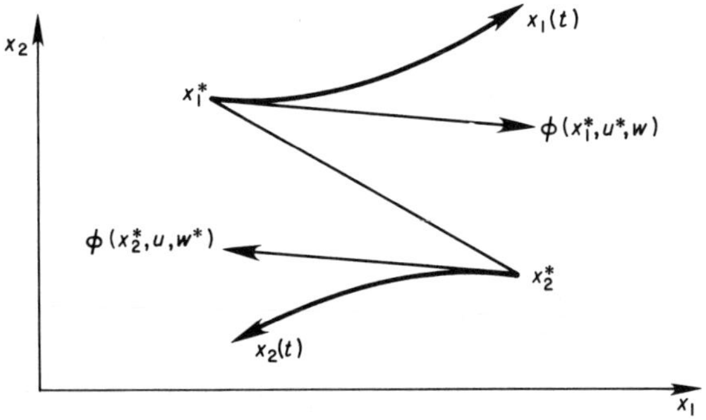

Figure 9.3.6

Since $d^2(t) = ((x_1(t) - x_2(t))(x_1(t) - x_2(t))$, then

$$\begin{aligned}\frac{d}{dt} d^2(t) &= 2(x_1(t) - x_2(t))(\dot{x}_1(t) - \dot{x}_2(t)) \\ &= 2(x_1^* - x_2^*)(\dot{x}_1(t) - \dot{x}_2(t)) \\ &\quad + ((x_1(t) - x_1^*) - (x_2(t) - x_2^*))(\dot{x}_1(t) - \dot{x}_2(t)) \\ &\leq 2l_* \cdot (\dot{x}_1(t) - \dot{x}_2(t)) + 8\gamma(t - t_*). \end{aligned} \tag{9.3.13}$$

Let us consider the term $2l_* \cdot (\dot{x}_1(t) - \dot{x}_2(t))$ in (9.3.13). By (9.3.10),

$$\dot{x}_2(t) \in F_u(t, x_2(t), w^*) = \text{CO}\{\phi : \phi(x_2(t), u, w^*) \text{ and } u \in U_1\}.$$

Then by Carathéodory's theorem (Carathéodory, 1967), there exist $(n + 1)$ points in the set U_1, namely u_i and $i = 1, \ldots, n + 1$, such that

$$\dot{x}_2(t) = \sum_{i=1}^{n+1} \alpha_i(t)\phi(x_2(t), u_i, w^*),$$

where $\alpha_i(t) \geq 0$ and $\sum_{i=1}^{n+1} \alpha_i(t) = 1$. Then this formula can be written as

$$\begin{aligned}\dot{x}_2(t) &= \sum_{i=1}^{n+1} \alpha_i(t)\phi(x_i^*, u, w^*) \\ &\quad + \sum_{i=1}^{n+1} \alpha_i(t)(\phi(x_2(t), u_i, w^*) - \phi(x_1^*, u_i, w^*)).\end{aligned}$$

But

$$\|\phi(x_2(t), u_i, w^*) - \phi(x_1^*(t), u_i, w^*\| \leq \lambda\|x_1^*(t) - x_2(t)\|,$$

where λ is the Lipschitz constant of ϕ. Then by (9.3.12),

$$\|x_1^*(t) - x_2(t)\| \leq \|x_1^*(t) - x_2^*(t)\| + \gamma(t - t_*)$$

or

$$\dot{x}_2(t) = \sum_{i=1}^{n+1} \alpha_i(t)\phi(x_1^*(t), u_i, w^*) + \Delta\phi_2(t),$$

where $\|\Delta\phi_2(t)\| \leq \lambda\|l_*\| + \lambda\gamma(t - t_*)$. By the same token, it can be shown that

$$\dot{x}_1(t) = \phi(x_1^*(t), u^*, w(t)) + \Delta\phi_1(t),$$

where $\|\Delta\phi_1(t)\| \leq \lambda\|l_*\| + \lambda\gamma(t - t_*)$. So the term $l_*(\dot{x}_1(t) - \dot{x}_2(t))$ has an upper value such that

$$\begin{aligned} l_*^{\cdot}(\dot{x}_1(t) - \dot{x}_2(t)) \leq l_*^{\cdot}(&\phi(x_1^*(t), u^*, w(t)) \\ &- \sum_{i=1}^{n+1} \alpha_i(t)\phi(x_1^*(t), u_i, w^*)) \\ &+ \lambda\|l_*\|^2 + 2\lambda\gamma(t - t_*). \end{aligned} \tag{9.3.14}$$

Since u^* and w^* are the extremum strategies of the first and second players, then

$$l_*^{\cdot}\,\phi(x_1^*(t), u^*, w(t)) \leq l_*^{\cdot}\,\phi(x_1^*, u_i, w^*).$$

Multiplying both sides of this inequality by $\alpha_i(t)$ and summing over $i = 1, \ldots, n$ yields

$$l_*^{\cdot}\,\phi(x_1^*(t), u^*, w(t)) - l_* \sum_{i=1}^{n} \alpha_i(t)\phi(x_1^*(t), u_i, w^*) \leq 0. \tag{9.3.15}$$

Substituting (9.3.15) in (9.3.14) and then (9.3.14) in (9.3.13) gives

$$\frac{d}{dt}\, d^2(t) \leq 2\lambda\|l_*\|^2 + 2c(t - t_*).$$

Hence, integrating this inequality with respect to t and making use of $\|l_*\|^2 = d^2(t_*)$ and $\beta = 2\lambda$ gives (9.3.12) as required. Q.E.D.

Lemma 9.3.2 Let W be a closed u-stable set, $u_l(x)$ be an extremum strategy with respect to W, and $w(t)$ be a program strategy of the second player. Moreover, let us assume that $x(t)$, which is a movement defined by

$$\dot{x}(t) = \phi(x(t), u_l(x), w(t)), \qquad x(t_0) = x_0 \in W,$$

leaves W at the moment t_* and that $x_{\delta_k}(t)$, which is a sequence of Euler's linear curves, converges to $x(t)$ as $k \to \infty$. Then for $t \in [t_0, t_* + \tau^*]$ the function

$$\varepsilon_k(t) = d(x_{\delta_k}(t), W)$$

is lower semicontinuous and continuous from the right, where τ^* is the moment at which any movement which starts from $x(t_*)$ at time t_* cannot reach F. Furthermore, the relation

$$\varepsilon_k^2(t) \leq [\varepsilon_k(t_0) + (1 + (t - t_0))\phi_k] \exp[\beta(t - t_0)] \tag{9.3.16}$$

holds, where ϕ_k is a positive constant such that $\phi_k \to 0$ if $k \to +\infty$, and β is the positive constant from (9.3.11).

Proof First it will be proved that $\varepsilon_k(t)$ is lower semicontinuous. Let t_i converge to $\bar{t} \in [t_0, t_* + \tau^*]$ and $\varepsilon_k(t_i)$ converge to the limit ε_* as $i \to \infty$. If v_i is the closest vector to $x_{\delta_k}(t_i)$ in W, then

$$\varepsilon_k(t_i) = \|x_{\delta_k}(\cdot) - v_i\|.$$

Without loss of generality, it can be assumed that $v_i \to \bar{v}$. Since W is a closed set, then $\bar{v} \in W$, which implies that

$$\varepsilon_k(t_i) = \|x_{\delta_k}(t_i) - v_i\| \to \|x_{\delta_k}(\bar{t}) - \bar{v}\| = \varepsilon_* \geq \varepsilon_k(\bar{t}), \tag{9.3.17}$$

where $\varepsilon_* \geq \varepsilon_k(\bar{t})$, due to the definition of $\varepsilon_k(t)$. This proves the lower semicontinuity of $\varepsilon_k(t)$.

Now let $t_i \to \bar{t}$, where $t_i > \bar{t}$, and

$$\varepsilon_k(\bar{t}) = \|x_{\delta_k}(\bar{t}) - v_*\|,$$

where v_* is the closest vector to $x_\delta(\bar{t})$ in W. Consider the fixed strategy $w^* \in U_2$. Since the set W is u stable, then among the movements that start from the point $v_* \in W$ at moment $\bar{t}$, there exists a movement $\tilde{x}(t)$ that at the moment $t_i > \bar{t}$ goes back to the set W, i.e., $\tilde{x}(t_i) = v_i \in W$. Since $t_i \to \bar{t}$, then $v_i \to v_*$, and consequently

$$\varepsilon_k(t_i) \le \|x_{\delta_k}(t_i) - v_i\| \le \|x_{\delta_k}(\bar{t}) - v_*\| + \|x_{\delta_k}(\bar{t}) - x_{\delta_k}(t_i)\| + \|v_i - v_*\|.$$

Taking the limit of these inequalities, when $t_i \to \bar{t}$, yields

$$\varepsilon_* \le \|x_{\delta_k}(\bar{t}) - v_*\| = \varepsilon_k(\bar{t}), \tag{9.3.18}$$

where ε_* is the limit to which the sequence $\varepsilon_k(t_i)$ converges as $i \to \infty$. Hence, (9.3.18) together with (9.3.17) gives that

$$\varepsilon_k(\bar{t}) = \varepsilon_* = \lim_{t_i \to \bar{t}+} \varepsilon_k(t_i),$$

which proves that $\varepsilon_k(t)$ is continuous from the right.

Finally, we shall prove (9.3.16). Suppose that (9.3.16) is not true. In this equation, $\phi_k = c\delta_k$, where c is defined as in (9.3.11) and t_i^k, $i = 1, \ldots, n$ are the points of a partition with mesh δ_k. The partition defines the Euler's linear curve $x_{\delta_k}(t)$. Let $\bar{t}$ be the lower bound of all the moments t at which (9.3.16) is violated. Since $\varepsilon_k(t)$ is lower semicontinuous and continuous from the right, then at moment $\bar{t}$ it follows that

$$\varepsilon_k(\bar{t}) = \psi_k(\bar{t}),$$

where

$$\psi_k(t) = [\varepsilon_k(t_0) + (1 + (t - t_0)\phi_k] \exp[\beta(t - t_0)]. \tag{9.3.19}$$

Let the point $\bar{t} \in [t_i^k, t_{k+1}^k]$. Then by the definition of point $\bar{t}$ one will have

$$\varepsilon_k^2(t_i^k) \le \psi_k(t_i^k), \qquad \varepsilon_k^2(\hat{t}) > \psi_k(\hat{t}) \tag{9.3.20}$$

where the point $\hat{t} > \bar{t}$. Making use of (9.3.20), (9.3.19) yields

$$\varepsilon_k^2(t_i^k) \le [\varepsilon_k^2(t_0) + (1 + (t_i^k - t_0))\phi_k] \exp[\beta(t_i - t_0)],$$

and consequently

$$\begin{aligned}\exp[\beta(\hat{t} - t_i^k)\varepsilon_k^2(t_i^k)] &\le [\varepsilon_k^2(t_0) + (1 + (t_i^k - t_0))\phi_k] \exp[\beta(\hat{t} - t_0)] \\ &= \psi_k(\hat{t}) - [(\hat{t} - t_i^k)\phi_k] \exp[\beta(\hat{t} - t_0)],\end{aligned}$$

which due to (9.3.20) gives

$$\begin{aligned}\varepsilon_k^2(\hat{t}) &> \varepsilon_k^2(t_i^k)\exp[\beta(\hat{t} - t_i^k)] + [(\hat{t} - t_i^k)\phi_k]\exp[\beta(\hat{t} - t_0)] \\ &> \varepsilon_k^2(t_i^k)(1 + \beta(\hat{t} - t_i^k)) + (\hat{t} - t_i^k)\phi_k \end{aligned} \tag{9.3.21}$$

since $e^{\beta x} > 1 + \beta x$ and $e^{\beta x} > 1$ for $x > 0$. Next it will be shown that (9.3.21) gives rise to a contradiction. Let $\bar{v}_k$ be the vector in W closest to the point $x_{\delta_k}(t_i^k)$. Then by the definition of an extremum strategy, $u_l(x_{\delta_k}(t_i^k))$ is a minimax strategy for thc direction $(x_{\delta_k}(t_i^k) - \bar{v}_k)$. Moreover, by the definition of $\varepsilon_k(t)$ one will have

$$\varepsilon_k(t_i^k) = \|x_{\delta_k}(t_i^k) - \bar{w}_k\|.$$

If w^* is a maximin strategy of the second player for the state $x_{\delta_k}(t_i^k)$ and with respect to the direction $(x_{\delta_k}(t_i^k) - \bar{v}_k)$ and if

$$X(t_i^k, t, \bar{v}_k, w^*)$$

is the jet of all movements that start from the point $\bar{v}_k$ at moment t_i^k under strategy w^*, which satisfies (9.3.10), then all conditions of Lemma 9.3.1 hold. In these conditions $x_1^* = x_{\delta_k}(t_i^k)$ and $x_2^* = \bar{v}_k$. Since W is u stable, then there exists a trajectory

$$\bar{x}(t) \in X(t_i^k, t, \bar{v}_k, w^*)$$

in the jet $X(t_i^k, t, \bar{v}_k, w^*)$ such that $\bar{x}(\hat{t}) \in W$ because $\bar{t} > t_i^k$. Applying Lemma 9.3.1 to this trajectory and setting

$$d(t) = \|x_{\delta_k}(t) - \bar{x}(t)\|$$

and making use of the property that $d(\bar{t}) \geq \varepsilon_k(\bar{t})$, which holds since $\bar{v}(t) \in W$ and $\varepsilon(\bar{t})$ is the minimum distance between x_{δ_k} and W, yields

$$\varepsilon_k(\bar{t}) \leq d(\bar{t}) \leq \varepsilon^2(t_i^k)(1 + \beta(\bar{t} - t_i^k)) + c(t_i^k - \bar{t})^2.$$

Substituting the relation $\phi_k = c_{\delta_k}$ and using the property of $\bar{t} \in [t_i^k, t_{i+1}^k]$ in the above inequality gives a contradiction to (9.3.21), which proves the lemma. Q.E.D.

Proof of Theorem 9.3.1 Assume that the theorem is not true. That is, there exists a movement $\hat{x}(t)$ in the jet $X(t_0, x_0, t, u_l)$, which leaves the set W at some moment. Let t_* be the upper bound of all moments for which

$\hat{x}(t) \in W$. Then since W is closed, $\hat{x}(t_*) \in W$ and $x(t_*) \notin F$. Furthermore, since F is also closed and compact, it can be assumed that there is a closed ball with $\hat{x}(t_*)$ as its center, such that any movement that starts from $\hat{x}(t_*)$ cannot leave this ball, for all $t \in [t_*, t_* + T]$, given any controls chosen by the players. This ball does not intersect with F. It will represent set G described in Lemma 9.3.1. Then if $x_{\delta_k}(t)$ is a sequence of Euler's linear curves that converges to $\hat{x}(t)$, then all conditions of Lemma 9.3.2 and, consequently, (9.3.16) hold. If $k \to \infty$, then since $x_{\delta_k}(t) \to \hat{x}(t)$, $\varepsilon_k(t_0) = 0$ [because $\hat{x}(t_0) \in W$] and $\phi_k \to 0$, one will have $\varepsilon_k(t) \to 0$ for any $t \in [t_*, T]$. Finally, since W is closed, then $\hat{x}(t) \in W$ for $t \in [t_*, T]$, which contradicts the definition of t_*. Q.E.D.

Theorem 9.3.2 Let W be a closed w-stable set, let $w_l(t)$ be an extremum strategy of the second player with respect to W, and let $x_0 \in W$. Then for any movement $x(t) = x(t_0, x_0, t, w_l(x))$ it is true that $x(t) \in W$ up to the moment τ, at which $x(\tau) \notin H$, where H is an open set containing D. If there is no τ such that $x(\tau) \notin H$, then $x \in W$ indefinitely (i.e., forever).

This theorem can be proved using reasoning similar to that employed in proving Theorem 9.3.1.

As explained before, if the first player has a bridge, then that bridge is u stable. Therefore, we shall try to make that bridge as large as possible. Let set Y stand for the set of all initial states for which problem II, which amounts to finding a strategy that enables the second player to avoid an open neighborhood G of F for any initial state $x_* \in Y$, up to a fixed time T is assumed to have a solution, where $x_* = x(t_*)$ and $t_0 \le t_* \le T$. In other words, given any initial state $x_* \in Y$, there exists a strategy $\bar{w}(x)$ for the second player such that any movement of the jet

$$X(t_*, x_*, t, \bar{w}(x)),$$

while being in $H \supset D$, does not go inside G until time t is exhausted or leaves H before T.

Next it will be shown that Y is an open set. If $x_* \in Y$, then it will be shown that there exists $\delta > 0$, such that for any $\hat{x}$ for which $\|x_* - \hat{x}\| < \delta$, the strategy $\bar{w}(x)$ will make any movement of the jet

$$X(t_*, \hat{x}, t, \bar{w}(x))$$

avoid an open set G_1 that contains F, and which its closure is contained in G. Moreover, these movements will go inside some set H_1, which contains D, and which its closure is a subset of H, or leaves H before T. In fact, if it is not true that there will be a sequence $\hat{x}_k \to x_*$ such that among the movements of the jet

$$X(t_*, \hat{x}_k, t, \overline{w}(x))$$

there exists a movement $\hat{x}_k(t)$ such that $\hat{x}_k(t_*) = \hat{x}_k, \hat{x}_k(t) \in H_1$, and $\hat{x}_k(t_k) \in G_1$ for some $t_k \in [t_*, T]$. Since the set that contains all the movements is compact in space $C[t_0, T]$, it can be assumed that the sequence $\hat{x}_k(t)$ uniformly converges to a movement $\bar{x}(t)$ from the jet

$$X(t_*, x_*, t, \overline{w}(t)).$$

Moreover, it can also be assumed that $t_k \to \tau \in [t_0, T]$. But then this movement at time t will belong to $\overline{H}_1$ [i.e., $x(t) \in H$] and at time τ will belong to G_1 [i.e., $\bar{x}(\tau) \in \overline{G}_1$, where $t_* \leq \tau_1 \leq T$], which contradicts the hypothesis of avoiding the set G.

Let set W^T be the complement of set Y. Then W^T is closed and any bridge of the first player that gets him/her to the terminal set F before or at time T can only be located in set W^T. If the bridge is not located in W^T, then there exists an initial state that belongs to this bridge and to set Y. This is impossible because it is assumed that if the initial state belongs to Y, then problem II has a solution.

Theorem 9.3.3 The set W^T is the maximum[2] u-stable bridge (i.e., W_u^T), which is closed and is contained in D.

Proof The maximality and closedness of W^T is discussed in the paragraph preceding the theorem. Therefore, we shall only show that W^T is a u-stable set. Suppose it is not. There exists $t_* \in [t_0, T]$, $x_* \in W_u^T$, $w_* \in U_2$, and $t^* \in [t_*, T]$ such that at time t, all movements

$$X(t_*, x_*, t, w_*)$$

leave the set W_u^T and will belong to set Y. Then the second player can find a strategy that helps him/her to avoid the set F until time T is reached or to leave an open neighborhood of D before time T is reached. Because of the definition of Y, it can be concluded that $x_* \in Y$, which contradicts the initial assumption that

$$(Y \cap W^T) = \varnothing. \quad \text{Q.E.D.}$$

[2] This terminology is a transliteration of "maximalnii most" in Russian. It means maximum in the sense of the largest bridge.

By the same token, the maximum w-stable bridge W_w^T of the second player can be formed such that for any $x_* \in W_w^T$ there is a time $t_* \in [t_0, T]$ and an extremum strategy $w_l(x)$ that helps that player avoid being in the open set G, which contains F. Indeed, similar to the definition of Y, let set Y' represent the set of all states x^* for which there is a time t_* and for which there is a strategy of the first player which forces the movements, while being in the set $\bar{H}_1 \supset D$, to be in a closed set $G_1 \supset F$. (Note that G_1 and H_1 are open sets such that $G \supset G_1 \supset F$ and $H \supset H_1 \supset D$ and $\bar{H}_1$ is the closure of H_1.) As before, it can be shown that Y_1 is an open set and its complement is the desired w-stable closed bridge W_w^T. Let F be an open ε-neighborhood that contains the set F, i.e.,

$$F_\varepsilon = \bigcup_{x_0 \in F} S(x_0, \varepsilon),$$

where $S(x_0, \varepsilon)$ is an open sphere with center x_0 and radius ε. Let D_ε be an ε-neighborhood of set D. Then based on the definition of the maximum stable bridge, it is easy to prove the theorem of alternatives for movements.

Theorem 9.3.4 For any initial data, t_0, x_0 and T, there exists either

(i) a strategy $u(x)$ for the first player that provides for all movements of the jet

$$X(t_0, x_0, t, u_l(x))$$

to go to the terminal set F, before or at time T, or

(ii) there is $\varepsilon > 0$ and a strategy $w_l(x)$ for the second player that forces all the movements of the jet

$$X(t_0, x_0, t, w_l(x))$$

to avoid going into set F_ε before or at time T while being in D, or to leave the set D_ε, before or at T, where F_ε and D_ε are ε-open neighborhoods of the sets F and D, respectively.

Note that the strategies $u_l(x)$ and $w_l(x)$ are extremum strategies of the first and second players, with respect to the maximum stable bridges W_u^T and W_w^T, respectively.

In conclusion, this approach provides tools for exploring the possibility of solving specific differential games. Unfortunately, these tools are not useful for finding optimal strategies even for simple differential games. This drawback is due to the difficulty of constructing the stable bridges W_u^T and W_w^T.

Bibliography

Bellman, R. E. *Dynamic Programming*. Princeton, New Jersey: Princeton Univ. Press, 1957.

Berge, C. *Theorie Gênêrale des Jeuv a'n Personnes*. Paris: Gauthier-Villars, 1957.

Berkovitz, L. D. Necessary conditions for optimal strategies in a class of differential games and control problems. *SIAM J. Control* **5**, 1–24 (1967).

Blackwell, D. H., and Girshick, M. A. *Theory of Games and Statistical Decisions*. New York: Wiley, 1954 and 1956.

Bliss, G. A. *Lectures on the Calculus of Variations*. Chicago: Univ. of Chicago Press, 1946.

Carathéodory, C. *Calculus of Variations and Partial Differential Equations of the First Order*, Volumes I and II. San Francisco, California: Holden-Day, 1965 and 1967.

Coddington, E. A., and Levinson, N. *Theory of ordinary differential equations*, New York: McGraw-Hill, 1955.

Doob, J. L. *Stochastic processes*. New York: Wiley (Interscience), 1953.

Filippov, A. F. On certain questions in the theory of optimal control, *SIAM J. Control* **1**, 76–84 (1962).

Fleming, W. H. The convergence problem for differential games. *J. Math. Anal. Appl.* **3**, 102–116 (1961).

Friedman, A. *Differential games*. New York: Wiley (Interscience), 1971.

Gale, D. *The Theory of Linear Economic Models*. New York: McGraw-Hill, 1960.

Germeir, S. V. *Games with Nonantagonistic Objects*. Moscow: Nauka, 1976 (in Russian).

Hadley, G. *Linear-programming*. Reading, Massachusettes: Addison-Wesley, 1962.

Halmos, P. R. *Measure Theory*. New York: Springer-Verlag, 1974.

Hartman, P. *Ordinary Differential Equations*. New York: Wiley, 1964.

Hildenbrand, W. *Core and Equilibrium of a Large Economy*. Princeton, New Jersey: Princeton Univ. Press, 1974.

Hirsch, W. H., and Smale, S. *Differential Equations, Dynamic Systems, and Linear Algebra*. New York: Academic Press, 1974.

Isaacs, R. *Differential Games*. New York: Wiley, 1965.

Krasovsky, N. N. *Game Problems in Meeting Movements*. Moscow: Nauka, 1970 (in Russian).

Krasovsky, N. N. and Subbotin, A. I. *Differential Positional Games*. Moscow: Nauka, 1974 (in Russian).

Krass, I. *Mathematical Models of Economic Dynamics*. Moscow: Sovetskoe Radio, 1975 (in Russian).

Krass, I. On the value of information for games: Interrelationship of economic models. *Proceedings of the Eighth Prague Conference of Information Theory, Statistical Decisions and Random Processes*. Prague, Czechoslovakia: Academic Press, 1978.

Krass, I. and Muksinov, A. Some methods of exploration of qualitative games with many terminal surfaces. *Upravliaemii Systemi* (Controlled Systems) **7** (1972) (in Russian), pp. 10–26.

Krass, I., and Volokitin, E. One method of exploration of a qualitative differential game. *Upravliaemii Systemi* (Controlled Systems) **6**, 3–16 (1970) (in Russian).

Kuratowski, K. *Topology*. New York: Academic Press, 1966.

Luce, R. D. and Raiffa, H. *Games and Decisions*. New York: Wiley, 1957.

Makarov, V. L., and Rubinov, A. M. *Mathematical Theory of Economic Dynamics and Equilibrium* (M. El-Hodiri, trans.). New York: Springer-Verlag, 1977.

McKinsey, J. C. *Introduction to the Theory of Games*. New York: McGraw-Hill, 1952.

Morishima, M. *Equilibrium, Stability and Growth, a Multi-Sectoral Analysis*. London and New York: Oxford Univ. Press, 1964.

Nash, J. Non-cooperative games. *Ann. of Math.* **54**, 286–295 (1951).

Nikaido, H. *Convex Structures and Economic Theory*. New York: Academic Press, 1966.

Osipov, Iu. S. To theory of differential games. *Prikladnaia Matematica i Mehanika*, **35NI** (1971), (in Russian).

Owen, G. *Game Theory*. Philadelphia, Pennsylvannia: Saunders, 1968.

Parthasarathy, T. and Raghaven, T.. E. S., *Some Topics in Two-Person Games*. New York: American Elsev., 1971.

Poletaev, I. A. Application of models of production. In *Exploration in Cybernetics* (A. A. Liapunov, ed.). Moscow, Sovetskoe Radid, 1970 (in Russian).

Pontryagin, L. S., Boltyanskii, V. G., Gamrelidze, R. V., and Mischenko, E. F. [*The Mathematical Theory of Optimal Processes*] (K. Trirogoff, trans.) New York: Wiley (Interscience), 1962.

Pshenichnyi, B. N. *Necessary Conditions for an Extremum*. New York: Marcel Dekker, 1971.

Rockafellar, R. *Convex Analysis*. Princeton, New Jersey: Princeton University Press, 1970.

Rudin, W. *Functional Analysis*. New York: McGraw-Hill, 1973.

Rudin, W. *Principles of Mathematical Analysis*. New York: McGraw-Hill, 1953.

Schwartz, L. *Analyse Mathematique* I. Paris: Herman, 1967 (in French).

Spivak, M. *Calculus on Manifolds: A Modern Approach to Classical Theorems of Advanced Calculus*. New York: Benjamin, 1965.

Taylor, A. E. *General Theory of Functions and Integration*. New York: Ginn (Blaisdell), 1965.

Vatel, I. On mathematical models of incentives in economics. In *Planning and Control in Economic Systems with Objectiveness* (Planirovanie i upravlenie Ekonomicheskimy Tselenapravlennimy Sistemami) (E. L. Berlignd, ed.). Novesibirsk: Nauka, 1975 (in Russian).

Vatel, I. and Eresko, F. *Mathematics of Conflicts and Relationships*. Moscow: Znanie, 1973 (in Russian).

Vatel, I. A., Eresko, F. I., Kononenko, A. F. *Games with Given Sequence of Moves and Hierarchy in Economics*. Irkutsk, USSR: Siberian Energy Institute Press, 1974 (in Russian).

Volokitin, E. P. *Games with Some Terminal Surfaces*, Ph.D. Dissertation, Novosibirsk State University, Novosibirsk, 1975 (in Russian).

Von Neumann, J., and Morgenstern, O. *Theory of Games and Economic Behavior*. Princeton, New Jersey: Princeton Univ. Press, 1944.

Vorob'ev, N. N. Modern situations in game theory. *Uspehi Matematicheskih Nauk* (Proceedings of Mathematical Science) **25**(3), 81–140 (1970) (in Russian).

Vorob'ev, N. N. *Game Theory: Lectures for Economists and Systems.* New York: Springer-Verlag, 1977.

Yosida, K. *Functional Analysis.* New York: Springer-Verlag, 1968.

Zauberman, A. *Differential Games and Other Game-Theoretic Topics in Soviet Literature.* New York: New York Univ. Press, 1975.

Index

K

L

M

N

P

Q

R

S

T

ECONOMIC THEORY, ECONOMETRICS, AND MATHEMATICAL ECONOMICS

Consulting Editor: Karl Shell

UNIVERSITY OF PENNSYLVANIA
PHILADELPHIA, PENNSYLVANIA

Franklin M. Fisher and Karl Shell. **The Economic Theory of Price Indices:** ***Two Essays on the Effects of Taste, Quality, and Technological Change***

Luis Eugenio Di Marco (Ed.). **International Economics and Development:** ***Essays in Honor of Raúl Presbisch***

Erwin Klein. **Mathematical Methods in Theoretical Economics:** ***Topological and Vector Space Foundations of Equilibrium Analysis***

Paul Zarembka (Ed.). **Frontiers in Econometrics**

George Horwich and Paul A. Samuelson (Eds.). **Trade, Stability, and Macroeconomics:** ***Essays in Honor of Lloyd A. Metzler***

W. T. Ziemba and R. G. Vickson (Eds.). **Stochastic Optimization Models in Finance**

Steven A. Y. Lin (Ed.). **Theory and Measurement of Economic Externalities**

David Cass and Karl Shell (Eds.). **The Hamiltonian Approach to Dynamic Economics**

R. Shone. **Microeconomics:** ***A Modern Treatment***

C. W. J. Granger and Paul Newbold. **Forecasting Economic Time Series**

Michael Szenberg, John W. Lombardi, and Eric Y. Lee. **Welfare Effects of Trade Restrictions:** ***A Case Study of the U.S. Footwear Industry***

Haim Levy and Marshall Sarnat (Eds.). **Financial Decision Making under Uncertainty**

Yasuo Murata. **Mathematics for Stability and Optimization of Economic Systems**

Alan S. Blinder and Philip Friedman (Eds.). **Natural Resources, Uncertainty, and General Equilibrium Systems:** ***Essays in Memory of Rafael Lusky***

Jerry S. Kelly. **Arrow Impossibility Theorems**

Peter Diamond and Michael Rothschild (Eds.). **Uncertainty in Economics:** ***Readings and Exercises***

Fritz Machlup. **Methodology of Economics and Other Social Sciences**

Robert H. Frank and Richard T. Freeman. **Distributional Consequences of Direct Foreign Investment**

Elhanan Helpman and Assaf Razin. **A Theory of International Trade under Uncertainty**

Edmund S. Phelps. **Studies in Macroeconomic Theory, Volume 1:** ***Employment and Inflation.*** **Volume 2:** ***Redistribution and Growth.***

Marc Nerlove, David M. Grether, and José L. Carvalho. **Analysis of Economic Time Series:** ***A Synthesis***

Thomas J. Sargent. **Macroeconomic Theory**

Jerry Green and José Alexander Scheinkman (Eds.). **General Equilibrium, Growth and Trade:** ***Essays in Honor of Lionel McKenzie***

Michael J. Boskin (Ed.). **Economics and Human Welfare:** ***Essays in Honor of Tibor Scitovsky***

Carlos Daganzo. **Multinomial Probit:** ***The Theory and Its Application to Demand Forecasting***

L. R. Klein, M. Nerlove, and S. C. Tsiang (Eds.). **Quantitative Economics and Development:** ***Essays in Memory of Ta-Chung Liu***

Giorgio P. Szegö. **Portfolio Theory:** ***With Application to Bank Asset Management***

M June Flanders and Assaf Razin (Eds.) **Development in an Inflationary World**

Thomas G. Cowing and Rodney E. Stevenson (Eds.). **Productivity Measurement in Regulated Industries**

Robert J. Barro (Ed.). **Money, Expectations, and Business Cycles:** ***Essays in Macroeconomics***

Ryuzo Sato. **Theory of Technical Change and Economic Invariance:** ***Application of Lie Groups***

Iosif A. Krass and Shawkat M. Hammoudeh. **The Theory of Positional Games:** ***With Applications in Economics***

In preparation

Giorgio P. Szegö (Ed.). **New Quantitative Techniques for Economic Analysis**